How to RESTORE Your MUSCLECAR

Greg Donahue and Paul Zazarine

Motorbooks International
Publishers & Wholesalers ®

First published in 1990 by Motorbooks International Publishers & Wholesalers, P O Box 2, 729 Prospect Avenue, Osceola, WI 54020 USA

Motorbooks International books are also available at discounts in bulk quantity for industrial or sales-promotional use. For details write to Special Sales Manager at the Publisher's address

Library of Congress Cataloging-in-Publication Data
Zazarine, Paul.
    How to restore your musclecar / Paul Zazarine, Greg Donahue.
    p.   cm.
    Includes index.
    ISBN 0-87938-432-8
    1. Muscle cars—Conservation and restoration.
I. Donahue, Greg.
II. Title.
TL152.2.Z388   1990   90-49034
629.28′722—dc20

On the front cover: Three of the greatest American musclecars, all restored by Greg Donahue and owned by John Scanelli of Norfolk, Virginia: 1969 Chevrolet Yenko Camaro, 1969½ Dodge Charger 500 and 1969 Ford Talladega. *Paul Zazarine*

Printed and bound in the United States of America

Contents

Acknowledgments

Putting a book like this together requires the help of many friends, and this is our opportunity to thank them. Most of the work was performed by Teddy Kempgens, who would patiently stop his work so pictures could be taken. Thanks also to master paint and body man Don Witherspoon, one of the best panel beaters around. Special thanks to Dobbs Publications, publishers of *Musclecar Review*, for permitting us the use of archive pictures used in this book. Thanks also to Harvey Hester for his masterful photo development and Motorbooks editor Michael Dregni for his infinite patience and understanding.

When we first considered the idea of writing this book, it was the encouragement and support of our wives, Karyl Donahue and Nancy Zazarine, that convinced us we should do it. Their help, patience and love are the reasons the dream became reality. This book is dedicated to them, and to the memory of James P. Donahue, Jr.

Greg Donahue
Paul Zazarine
Florida, 1990

Introduction

It's happening with more frequency every day. Baby Boomers are returning to the high-powered Chevys, GS Stage 1s, GTOs, 442s, Fords, SC/Ramblers and Mopars of their youth. Today, we call cars like these *musclecars*. These street warriors recall a time when gasoline was cheap and high performance meant big displacement V-8 engines and virtually everyone was ready for a stoplight drag. Back in those heady days before the insurance surcharges of the late sixties, anyone from bag boys to bank presidents could afford an SS396, Mach One Mustang or a Hemi Road Runner.

Now, twenty years later, those bag boys are executives, and those great musclecars they jacked up twenty years ago are now collectibles. To recapture the halcyon time of their youth, they're snapping up musclecars like never before. But instead of modifying them as they did twenty years ago, there's a desire to return the cars to original condition. In other words, they're *restoring* them.

Before we go any further, we need to clearly define what the word "restore" means. In the musclecar hobby, it may be the most fractured word used. We've seen "restored" musclecars that were adorned with aftermarket valve covers, braided lines, modular wheels and other modifications. That's not a restored car. And unfortunately, there's too many car magazines that use the word "restored" when they shouldn't.

If you want a unique car, a car that makes a personal statement, then by all means modify it to your own satisfaction, but don't call it restored. Also, before you get started on that tired warrior out in the garage awaiting rebirth, now is the time to make some concrete decisions on how the car will be presented. Do you want to show the car? If so, do you want to compete in the stock classes? If you do, then plan on performing a restoration dedicated to correctness.

In the late seventies and early eighties when musclecar restorations first began, it was very popular to add factory options. Today, if you want an AM/FM radio for your car, make sure it's the correct unit. An aftermarket radio may be easier to find and install, but don't get hot when show judges deduct points for it at a show. Playing the game to win dictates you follow the rules.

Want to alter the car? Remember that a combination of minor modifications can place you in a class dominated by blowers and trick paint jobs. The few times you've chromed under the hood and the aftermarket wheels aren't going to be enough to keep you from being buried by wildly modified cars shown in the same class.

If restoration is the route you choose, remember that to restore a car is to return it to its original factory condition—warts and all. That means if assembly line workers put things together a little sloppy, then so should you. Remember that these workers were putting in their eight hours screwing cars together in the mind-numbing environment of mass production. They weren't hand crafting show cars. Paint runs and overspray, slag on the frame, poor fitting panels and other imperfections are representative of how the cars were built. It's tempting to over-restore a musclecar by correcting these faults. Remember that bare metal parts should look bare, chalk marks are essential and stencils and other codes should be duplicated when the car goes back together.

Now consider the economics of restoring a musclecar. From an investment standpoint, you'll be much better off than modifying. Modified cars rarely recoup even the cost of construction. Your chances of finding a buyer who appreciates with his checkbook all the work and money you've invested are slim. A restored musclecar, on the other hand, will be much easier to sell, and a buyer will get out his wallet much more willingly if he sees he's buying a car that's all there and has been done correctly.

That's what this book is all about. We're going to show you how to restore your musclecar.

In many places, we'll advise you to refer to your factory literature for assembly, torque or alignment information. This book doesn't replace the information found in the factory service manuals. Instead, it supplements the factory books, and tells you what the factory doesn't. Along the way, we're going to suggest that some tasks be farmed out, such as seat reupholstery. And if you can't perform all the jobs illustrated herein, at least you'll understand how the process works, enabling you to have a clearer understanding of what the restoration or machine shop is telling you when you farm the work out.

Whether you perform all the work yourself or just drop in an engine built at the machine shop, trim out a body repaired and painted by a professional and install an interior done by an upholstery shop, there's a tremendous satisfaction gained from working with your hands and bringing back to life a car that once ruled the boulevards of America. Big-block musclecars mark a long-gone era in American automotive history, and restoring one yourself may be the most enjoyable task you'll ever accomplish.

1

Getting Started: How to Choose Your Musclecar

Before you buy the first musclecar that strikes your fancy, do some research. P. T. Barnum's observation about a fool and his money soon parting ways holds true in the musclecar hobby. Horror stories abound about uninformed buyers paying large sums for bogus cars. With the kind of prices some of the most desirable musclecars are commanding, enter the unscrupulous seller who won't hesitate to take advantage of your lack of knowledge to sell you a Hemi 'Cuda that may have started life as a 318 Barracuda or a 351 Torino that's been transformed into a 429 Super Cobra Jet. The parts and information are available for the dishonest to construct a silk purse from a sow's ear.

Fortunately, the information to protect yourself by learning how to decode a car's true identity is also available. If you don't have any idea how to read date codes, trim tags, data plates and casting codes, you stand a good chance of getting fleeced. Too many times novices have bought cars first and then learned how to read codes. Only then do they discover how badly they've been burned.

How do you keep from getting taken? Today there are numerous sources you can refer to for information. Your first decision, however, is what kind of musclecar you wish to buy. Most of us are drawn to one particular make or model. If you find yourself wanting a 1970 Stage 1 Buick Gran Sport, or a 1966 Tri-Power GTO or 1969 Charger 500, learn as much as you can about the car before you go shopping for one. It sounds like simple advice, doesn't it? But you'd be surprised just how many new hobbyists buy the first car they see without doing any research. One memorable example is the doctor who went to a large collector car auction looking for a convertible—any convertible. He fell in love with a red 1965 GTO convertible and let himself get caught up in a bidding war (possibly by a shill in the audience). He purchased the GTO for $25,000 and proudly brought it home. His first outing at a Pontiac show fetched him not a trophy but some very bad news: The engine was not a correct 389, but a late model 400. The heads were not correct, nor were the Tri-Power (off of a 1966), the paint or the Rally II wheels. Running the VIN number through Pontiac (when the service for pre-1969 models was still available) revealed the worst news of all. The car had started life as a 326 powered LeMans convertible. He had bought a bogus car.

For example, you decide a Charger 500 is what you want. Begin your search by assembling and absorbing as much information as you can. There are a variety of magazines on the newsstands such as *Musclecar Review* (P.O. Box 7157, Lakeland, FL 33807) that provide information on determining authenticity. *Hemmings Motor News* (P.O. Box 100, Bennington, VT 05201) is a 700 page monthly compilation of hobby cars, parts, literature and services that is absolutely indispensable for the musclecar enthusiast. In *Hemmings* you'll find books available listing all the numerical data needed to decipher the VIN, date and casting codes that unlock a particular car's history.

Car clubs are the backbone of the hobby, and there are plenty of clubs that cater to virtually every make and model of muscle. Not only do these clubs provide knowledgeable technical advisors, they also have local chapters that you can join and get some one-on-one expertise about the car you want. Most newcomers to the musclecar hobby join a club after they've purchased their car, and that's the wrong way to go. It's like buying a set of encyclopedias and then learning how to read. Join a club before you buy the car. Buy the research books and learn all you can before you buy the car. Don't do it after the fact.

Consider our hypothetical Charger 500. You've searched out and joined a national Mopar club and gotten involved with the local chapter. There may be plenty of good cars available within the club, and since everyone knows one another, your chances of getting ripped off are reduced significantly. And if you do track down that Charger 500, take a knowledgeable club member with you to help scrutinize the car. His or her knowledge and your deciphering of coded information could save you thousands of dollars if the car isn't correct.

For many enthusiasts, the search for the perfect musclecar is nearly as much fun as the restoration itself. Making sure you get the right car in the right condition could make that first restoration a fulfillment of your dream. The wrong car could turn your dream into a nightmare.

1. Musclecar shows are popular all across the country. This is where your car could be—on display for fellow hobbyists to admire your work. And if you win a trophy, it's one of the most satisfying things you can receive. For many musclecar enthusiasts, this is heaven.

2. It's called the paper chase. There are virtually hundreds of books, brochures, newsletters, magazines and manuals available for musclecar reading and research. Once you know the kind of musclecar you want, begin your research and learn as much as you can before making the purchase.

3. Factory brochures are a great way to start your research. These are available at most swap meets or in the "Books and Literature" section of *Hemmings Motor News*. The Classic Motorbooks (P.O. Box 1, Osceola, WI 54020) catalog is also brimming with books about musclecars. You'll learn option availability, color choices, correct interior upholstery and other pertinent information. One caution: Manufacturers always update their brochures, and some of the information or pictures may not represent actual production, so consider this information a good base to begin learning about the musclecar you've targeted for purchase.

4. Here's an essential part of your restoration library, the factory service manuals, assembly manuals and parts books. Dealer sales albums are also beneficial for their interior samples, allowing you to compare reproduction pieces to the originals. The factory service manuals will outline the proper procedures for disassembly, repair and reassembly of mechanical components. The General Motors Fisher Body manual was used for body and soft trim repair. These books are often found at swap meets or in *Hemmings*.

5. Almost every make and model of musclecar has a supporting car club. These national clubs have members who share your enthusiasm for a particular marque. Their experience and knowledge are there to be shared. Many clubs also have technical advisors who volunteer their time to assist club members. All clubs put out a newsletter that features stories, histories, restoration tips and a classified section for buying and selling cars and parts.

Understanding VIN and data plates

Each automobile built for sale to the public is required to have a VIN (Vehicle Identification Number) stamped on a metal plate and affixed to the car body. The VIN contains coded information detailing make, model, year, assembly plant, sequence number, and in some cases, engine application and other information.

1. VIN plates were located on the left-hand door pillar post until 1968, when Federal law required the plate to be located on the top of the instrument panel, visible through the windshield. On most cars, the plate is located on the left-hand side; however, on some cars, like this 1968 Mustang, the plate is on the right-hand side.

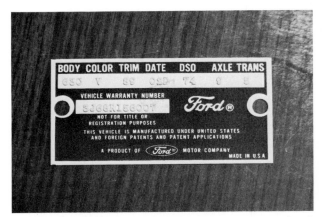

2. Chrysler products provide indepth information broken down with the VIN. For example, decoding this plate indicates it's from a 1971 Barracuda two-door hardtop equipped with a 318 ci engine. An unwitting victim could purchase this car, dressed out as a 383, 440 or even a Hemi, unless he knew how to decode this plate. There are a variety of books that explain how to decode the VIN available from Classic Motorbooks or through the various Mopar clubs.

3. The VIN plate (also referred to as a warranty plate) for early Fords provides information usually found on data plates. This VIN number indicates it is a 1963 Galaxie XL fastback. The "R" is the identifier for the dual-quad 427 high-performance engine. The XL was built at the Los Angeles assembly plant and was the 56,007 unit off the line. The numbers above the VIN describe the Galaxie's color, equipment and build date. This car is a two-door fastback, painted Chestnut with Chestnut crushed vinyl interior, built the second day of April and shipped to the Seattle district. Since this was a dual-quad 427, it also received a high-performance drivetrain, as indicated by the code 9 axle (4.11:1 rear) and code 5 transmission (four-speed manual). Understanding how the codes break down can prevent you from buying a faked car. For example, suppose an unscrupulous seller wants to pawn off a plain 500 as an XL by installing the high-line XL interior with its bucket seats and console. The numbers in the VIN will give him away. And even if he did change the data plate, the numbers on the counterfeit data plate wouldn't agree with the numbers found on the cowl plate and the hidden plate under the left-hand fender.

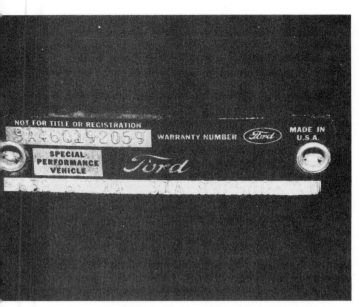

4. This Ford VIN plate was affixed to a 1969 Talladega. Converting a plain-Jane Torino into a Talladega would be profitable for the musclecar counterfeiter, but if you can read the codes you can possibly identify a bogus car. This plate reads as follows: 63, Fairlane 500 Sports Roof hardtop; B, Royal Maroon exterior color; 1A, Black cloth and vinyl interior; 31A, January 31 build date; DSO 892500, Talladega equipment; U, Cruise-O-Matic transmission. Breaking down the VIN in the upper left-hand corner of the plate: 9, 1969 model year: A, Atlanta assembly plant; 46, Fairlane 500 Sports Roof; Q, 428 four-barrel engine; 192059, the 92,059 unit built at Atlanta during the 1969 model year.

5. Knowing how to read a VIN could land you a lucky find, like this 1969 Firebird hardtop. The sequence number (100001) indicates it was the first 1969 Firebird built at the Van Nuys, California, assembly plant.

6. The VIN plate was located on the door pillar prior to 1968. The coded information remains the same for some manufacturers. And, once again, knowing how to decipher a plate can save you thousands of dollars. Imagine looking at a 1966 Hemi Satellite that's for sale. It looks like a Hemi car, right? But read the plate. This particular 1966 Plymouth is a Satellite alright, but it was built with an "E" code engine—a 318!

7. The VIN plate from this early Mopar is coded differently from later years, but there is still enough information to identify the model and engine. The plate reads: 7, Dodge Dart six-cylinder engine; 4, GT model; 4, 1964; 6, Newark, Delaware, assembly plant; 180747, the 80,747 unit built at the Newark plant during the 1964 model year.

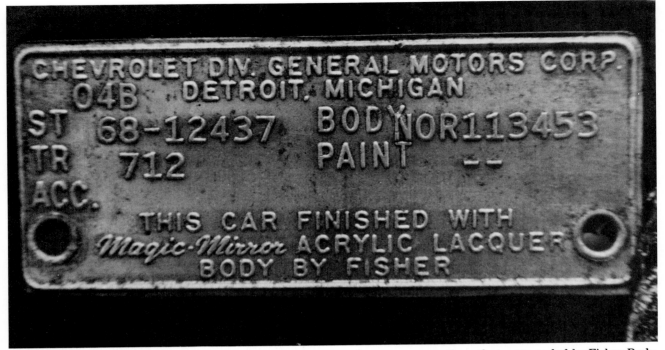

8. While the Ford VIN plates carry the information regarding color and trim, GM and Chrysler use a separate plate located in the engine compartment area (AMC mounted the plate on the door). In all cases, the data plate supplies information on exterior color, interior color, body sequence (not the same as the VIN), date built and other information pertinent to that particular car. Specific information about decoding data plates is usually found in the manufacturer's service and parts manuals. The "04B" in the upper left-hand corner represents the date the car was assembled. To decode this three-character code, reading from left to right, the first two digits indicate the month of the year (here, "04" indicates April). The third character represents the week of the month the car is assembled (in this case, "B" indicates the second week).

The "ST" indicates style; in this case, "68-12437" breaks down as follows: 68, 1968; 1, Chevrolet; 24, Camaro; 37, hardtop body. "TR" indicates trim (interior color): in this case, 712 is a black interior. "ACC" stands for accessory options that were coded by Fisher Body. Breaking accessory codes has been nearly impossible for GM restorers; only the Camaro codes are known by the United States Camaro Club. The use of the ACC codes has also raised some questions for 1964–65 GTO owners. Many 1964–65 GTOs have a code that begins with a "5" and may or may not have one or more letters following. This is not empirical, however; some legitimate GTOs did not receive this coding.

The "BODY" stamping indicates the asembly plant and unit sequence. In this example, "NOR" stands for the Norwood, Ohio, assembly plant; this particular Camaro was the 113,453 unit built at Norwood during the 1968 model year. The "PAINT" stamp would normally be followed by letter codes. This particular Camaro, however, is stamped "- -", which indicates the car was ordered as a stripe delete. In some cases, cars with special or non-recommended colors received the codes "SP," "SPEC," "XX" or "00" in place of the usual paint code.

9. After 1967, some GM plates (primarily on A-bodies such as Chevelle, Tempest, Cutlass and Skylark) were moved to the left-hand upper cowl, such as this 1968 GTO hardtop (code "37"), assembled the fourth week of June 1968 (06D), painted black with black vinyl top and equipped with a black interior.

10. Chrysler data plates are located on the left-hand inner fender and are extremely detailed, listing all options included in the car. A heavily optioned or special model Chrysler product may have more than one plate. While Ford, GM and AMC chose to rivet data plates to the car, Chrysler data plates are retained by Phillips-head screws. This has led to data plates being switched to build a more desirable—although counterfeit—car.

11. Here's the genuine article for Mopar fans, the Hemi fender plate attached to the data plate. Models like this Hemi-equipped 'Cuda had the upper portion of the front wheel opening rolled (or radiused) to clear the larger front tires.

12. These two examples of earlier Mopar data plates are placed in the same location as the later models; however, the information is coded differently. The plate with the number series at the upper left was used until the 1965 model year. The plate with the alphabet across the top was used only from 1966 through 1968. Because of the number of option codes, models and years, a source book that provides decoding information on Mopars is essential.

13. American Motors products used this style data plate listing body sequence number, model, trim and paint codes for identification purposes. On some AMC models, the plate was mounted on the door.

14. Checking numbers extends to body panels as well. This 1964 Falcon Sprint has the VIN stamped at the top left-hand inner fender where it meets the outer fender.

15. This Galaxie has a plate with the VIN stamped in it attached to the left-hand cowl. This plate would ordinarily be obscured by the fender.

16. This is the VIN plate, also attached to the cowl and is visible on the passenger side of the cowl, above the heater box. It is located on Ford products built before the 1968 model year.

17. Additional plates were sometimes added to specialty-built cars, such as this Yenko Camaro. Yenko Chevrolet in Canonsburg, Pennsylvania, built big-block Camaros equipped at the dealership with 427 engines. Each car received a sequentially numbered plate installed on the door pillar post by Yenko.

18. After 1970, car makers placed a decal on the end of the door indicating date of manufacture and VIN.

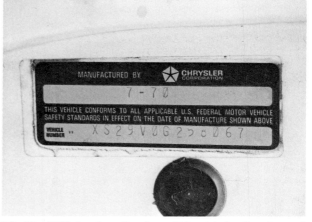

19. The VIN decal on the door did not take the place of the metal VIN plate on the upper cowl beneath the windshield. This particular decal was on the door of a 1970 Charger equipped with the 440 Six-Pack engine.

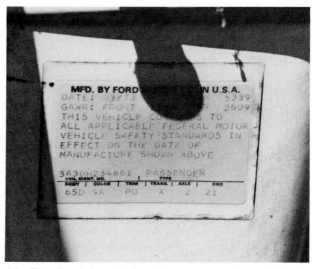

20. This Ford decal lists all the data for the vehicle, in this case, a 1973 Gran Torino.

Understanding casting and date codes

It's like the classic line, "the check's in the mail." "All the numbers match" is one of the most overused and misunderstood terms in the car hobby. It's mouthed by novices and con men alike, it appears in ads and on "for sale" signs. Just what does "all the numbers match" mean and what numbers is everyone referring to?

The term "numbers" refers to codes utilized throughout the vehicle that indicate component usage or date of manufacture. For example, assume a 1968 Camaro is built the third week of October 1967. The engine components such as the heads, block, water pump, and intake and exhaust manifolds should have foundry casting dates anywhere from one to six weeks prior to the car's assembly date.

The engine components aren't the only parts that are dated. The transmission—whether automatic or manual gearbox—will be dated (the automatic will have additional coded information located on a plate attached to the case). The third member will also have a casting date, along with a code to indicate gear ratio.

Parts that attach to the engine and the chassis are also dated, as is the chassis itself. GM cars using full frames, for example, will carry a stamped code on the front rail indicating manufacturer (A.O. Smith, Parish Pressed Steel and so on) and the date of manufacture. Components such as alternators, steering boxes, carburetors and radiators are also date stamped.

Body parts are also stamped. For example, some Chrysler products carry the VIN stamped into radiator core supports, firewalls and fenders. In the trunk gutter area on many GM cars is a coded stamping that designates quarter panel usage. For example, a 1966 GTO hardtop may have a 242Z17 stamp (242 indicates GTO series), while a LeMans will read 237Z17 (237 indicates LeMans series). You could determine if a quarter panel has been replaced if the codes on the left-hand and right-hand quarters don't match. And if they are mismatched, you don't have to be a rocket scientist to determine that major body work has been performed and the wrong quarter was hung. That could cost you big time on resale if an educated buyer detects what you missed.

Know your block

All *original* engines, regardless of manufacturer, have a code stamped into the block, usually on a machined pad, that indicates the engine's application. Note the emphasis on the word original. Most musclecars were driven hard in their early years of service, and many an over-enthusiastic driver missed a shift and grenaded a block, spun a rod or did other mortal damage to the engine. If the car was still under warranty, the dealer would sometimes install a "service replacement" engine. The replacement engine could either be coded by the factory as a replacement, or have no code at all.

Many a musclecar also received an underhood transplant. A 1965 GTO may have had its 389 yanked and a 421 or 455 dropped in. A 350 SS Camaro could have become a 396 (the sneaky owner may have left the 350 emblems on to rouse unwitting Mustang owners).

No matter what the circumstances, it was commonplace to change engines back in the good old days. That practice makes your job as a restorer even harder. Knowing where to look for engine codes, intake casting numbers, head cast numbers and other dated information on the engine will help you spot incorrect engines and components. The factory service and parts manuals are invaluable sources for this information. Remember never to enter a battle of the wits unarmed, and never buy a musclecar without knowing the numbers and where they're located.

1. Chrysler foundry dates are the easiest to decipher. This casting date, found on a 1970 Mopar Six-Pack intake manifold, reads 11 18 69, indicating it was cast November 18, 1969.

2. This casting information, taken from the side of a Dodge 440 block, indicates the block was cast May 6, 1969.

13

1. This casting information is found on a 1966 Pontiac Tri-Power intake manifold. The numbers C246 indicate the intake was cast March 24, 1966. The number 9782898 is the Pontiac part number. Not all casting numbers correlate to the part number assigned to the component.

3. The numbers in this Chevy 427 head read A 9 8, which deciphers to January 9, 1968. Also notice the head is specified for high performance. The clock to the left of the "HI-PERF" casting indicates the head was cast at 11 AM.

2. Date codes were cast with the part to identify the day and time the part was manufactured. If the shift working that particular time and day had a run of defective parts, those parts could then be identified by the coded information and pulled from inventory. The date cast in this Ford water pump indicates it was manufactured December 18, 1962. The two dots indicate it was made during the night shift. One or no dots would indicate the part was made during the day shift.

4. This Ford intake manifold was cast on June 29, 1968 (8F29). The circle of numbers is the clock indicating when the part was cast on June 29. The single dot above the screw indicates day shift, and the numbers 1 3 5 7 9 are hours of the day. In this case, the part was cast at approximately 7:30 AM. The slot in the center of the clock was used by the foundry worker to insert a tool to turn the clock as the work day progressed.

5. The concept of matching numbers also includes this Ford steering box, which reads January 28, 1964 (4A28).

6. On this Chrysler four-speed transmission, detailed information is stamped into a machined pad. The VIN number is clearly visible, along with the transmission serial number and the Julian date the transmission was manufactured. Julian dates are determined by counting the day number (in this case, 0042) and checking that day against the calendar (February 11).

7. Information is not always stamped into the part. This 1968 Mustang Top Loader four-speed has information on a tag riveted to the case.

8. Another coding source, especially on drivetrain components, is stenciled on, like this Ford four-speed gearbox. Color paint dabs are also common to identify components.

9. This transmission has two important codes on it. The last half of the VIN is stamped to the machined pad near the tailshaft housing. The tag bolted to the case is coded "B-W" (for Borg Warner). The "AS7" identifies the transmission series and the "T10S" shows it is a Super T10.

15

10. Not all Warner boxes use tags for identification. This T-10 is date coded October 27, 1972, and was used for certain GM applications.

11. Date codes are also stamped into body parts, especially on Ford products. This stamp "2 24 3C" indicates the sheetmetal was stamped on February 24, 1963 (the "C" stands for third shift). The stamps can be found on doors, hood, fenders, decks and rockers. They will not be dated the same, however, if the build date on the data plate reads January and some of the body panels are stamped with dates after January, the panels have been changed.

12. The frame on this early production 1966 GTO was manufactured by Parish Pressed Steel on August 13, 1965. To verify this is the original frame for the October-built GTO, a check of the top rear left-hand frame rail will determine if the serial number stamped there matches the VIN of the car.

13. Starters are also date coded, like this Delco unit removed from a 1966 Nova Super Sport with the L79 327 ci 350 hp engine.

14. Even windshield wiper motor cases can be coded, like this 1966 GM unit. While the GM codes are difficult to crack, the "66" is perfectly understandable. Before refinishing the case, you should mark the code down, measure the size and style of the characters and restencil the case after it's refinished. Most Ford and Chrysler dates would be easier to determine. Assuming a case was stenciled on April 4, 1966, the Chrysler code would read "4466," while the Ford code would be "APR 4 66."

15. Axles are also coded for gear ratio identification. On most GM cars, the code is stamped on the axle tube. Ford and Mopar generally stencil the code onto the differential housing or use a tag attached to the right axle tube or cover.

16. Carburetors are usually tagged on some GM, Ford, Chrysler and AMC cars. The tag may not indicate date of manufacture; however, it will code out for application. Knowing these codes (usually found in the factory service or parts books) will help you determine if the correct carburetor is on the engine.

17. This Carter carburetor model 4640 was used on a Chrysler product. The SA suffix indicates application.

18. Casting and date codes are also used on distributors. The GM unit on the left has the information stamped into the base. Some distributors also have coded information on a red band around the shaft. The Mopar unit in the center has a tag attached to the distributor body. The Ford distributor on the right has the application and date code information stamped into the housing.

19. GM steering boxes have a Julian date stamped into a machined pad on the side cover. This box is dated "094 8," which translates to April 4, 1968.

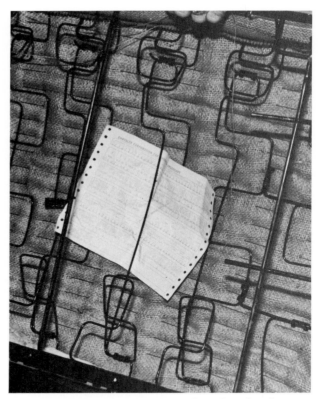

20. This Mopar steering box uses both a Julian date (stamped into the boss at top) and a date code (4229, April 22, 1969). The clock at lower right indicates the case was cast just past 6 AM (note the single dot just above the 12 o'clock mark indicating day shift. Two dots would designate night shift). Also notice the paint dab.

The build sheet for a musclecar found under the rear seat cushion.

21. Even window glass has date codes stenciled on. The Mopar stencil also has a PPG logo on it. Don't expect the factory to install window glass perfectly; the glass on this 1970 Hemi 'Cuda was all original and yet the date code

stencils were reversed on the right quarter window and the left door glass! GM usually used a PPG logo. Fords generally used a "FoMoCo" logo.

18

The Chrysler Certicard found in a holder riveted to the inner fender under the hood.

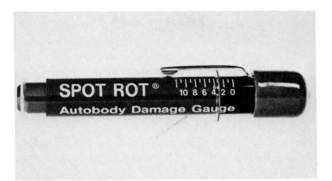

The Spot Rot gauge detects rust damage and repainted areas.

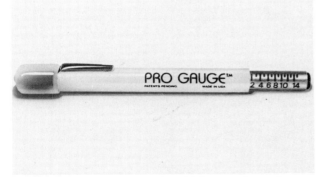

The Pro Gauge measures the thickness of non-ferrous materials, ideal for gauging how much Bondo or paint is on a car.

Documentation

You've done your research, memorized VIN codes, learned to decipher date built codes, casting numbers and foundry date codes. Knowing these numbers will arm you with the information and confidence to seek out the musclecar of your dreams (assuming that you find the right car, the numbers seem to check out, and you're relatively positive the car is legitimate). There's only one other burden of proof left to wash away any doubts and secure your purchase, and that's documentation.

Nothing is as critical as documentation. Nothing. The smart musclecar buyer will walk away from a loaded, desirable car like a Hemi 'Cuda or a Ram Air IV Judge if there isn't a shred of evidence to prove that the car is legitimate. Documentation can take the form of bills of sale, affidavits from previous owners, dealer invoices and so forth.

There is also the broadcast (or "build") sheet. This sheet contains a series of letters and codes that were used by the factory to instruct the assembly line personnel what options and special parts were to be installed. For example, a 442 would receive special springs, shocks, trim and other components for that option. It would also indicate the engine, transmission, rear axle ratio and other information. It is literally the fingerprint of an automobile. If you can find the build sheet, you can prove the car's authenticity.

Build sheets can be found in a variety of locations. Check under the rear seat cushion, under the front seat, under the carpet, stuffed above the glovebox or under the dash. GM cars also have a copy of the sheet sandwiched between the trunk pan and the top of the gas tank. These are usually pretty weathered and may crumble when the tank is dropped and the sheet is removed.

There's another bonafide piece of documentation that will at least verify the engine option, and that's a metal or plastic card about the size of a credit card. This card, known as a "Protecto-Plate or "Certicard" was either attached to the owner's warranty book or, in the case of Chrysler products, secured in a holder riveted to the inner fender under the hood. Many GM warranty books also had the last six digits of the VIN stamped on the cover.

Without a broadcast sheet or warranty card, there is little else to verify the authenticity of the car. At the time this book was published, the only manufacturer that offers a VIN documentation service is Pontiac Motor Division. Unfortunately, they can only research billing information for Pontiac models built after 1969.

Look for the best but expect the worst

Physical inspection of a potential purchase requires not only knowing the numbers and seeking documentation. There's also some common logic involved. When scrutinizing the car, look under the hood and examine not only the engine but the overall engine compartment. Inspect the harness and look for splices and burnt wires. Check for signs of modifications to the body like cut inner fenders (for header clearance) or holes where an oil or transmission cooler was installed (racing or trailer pulling).

Pull off the air cleaner and inspect the carburetor, intake, heads, exhaust manifolds and block for damage or fluid leakage. Pull the crankcase dipstick and inspect the oil. Place some of the oil from the dipstick between your thumb and forefinger and rub it, feeling for small particles of metal. If the car was equipped with an emission system, are all the components intact?

Start the motor and allow it to warm up to operating temperature. A cold engine can mask a lot of ills. Listen for internal component noise like lifter tick or rod knock as you increase the rpm. Now turn off the engine and check for oil leakage at the gaskets and under the car at the oil pan. Check the front and rear seals for oil leakage. Remove the radiator cap and check the fluid for rust scales. Even if you're going to rebuild the engine completely, checking its running condition before purchasing the car could save you money by not having to replace the crankshaft, connecting rods or other major internal components.

Manual transmission-equipped cars should be checked for leakage around the case and tailshaft. Have the shifter arms been modified or tampered with? If the car is equipped with automatic transmission, pull the dipstick and smell the fluid. If it smells burnt, a major rebuild could be in the cards. A puddle of transmission fluid on the pavement under the car or a coating of oil or fluid on the underside (where it's been flung up during operation) indicates leakage.

Crawl underneath the car and inspect the undercarriage, frame or sub-frame. If the frame's severely rusted (surface rust is acceptable, rotted-out metal is not), start looking for another car unless you're prepared to replace it, and that means your frame numbers won't match the body. Take a look at the control arms, rear suspension and leakage around the differential. Look carefully for signs of mounting holes for traction bars. What shape is the exhaust system in? Patched holes in the mufflers, coat hangers holding pipes in place and coffee cans wrapped around rotted-out pipes tell you more than the car has a lousy exhaust system; it's a tip-off to how poorly the car has been maintained overall.

Now sit in the driver's seat and inspect the interior. Are the seats broken down and the upholstery torn? Are all the gauges, radio and control panels intact? Is the dash pad cracked or damaged? Look at the headliner for stains (indicates water leakage), rips and tears. Check the package shelf for stains and the installation of monster speakers. Roll the windows up and down and look for holes in the door and quarter trim panels where aftermarket speakers may have been mounted. Open and close the doors. If they don't swing smoothly on the hinges and latch and unlatch easily, they may just be misadjusted, or the body may be sagging so badly they can't operate properly. Inspect the front and rear carpets. Wear and tear is to be expected, but mildew, water stains and shrinkage are signals that the windshield leaks. Read the odometer. A low odometer reading and a worn-out set of pedal pads should tell you a registered 21,000 miles may actually be 121,000 miles.

Look under the dash and inspect the harness. Bare leads, amateur wiring and melted wires are evidence that bad things have happened under there. Look carefully at the harness plugs, especially at the ignition and headlamp switches. Check the operation of the head and taillamps, turn signals, radio, horn, air conditioning (if so equipped) and other accessories.

Take a test drive, making sure the brakes can stop the car first before you venture too far. Listen carefully to the drivetrain. Note the operation of the automatic transmission and how it shifts. A worn-out transmission won't shift cleanly and will slip in all rpm ranges. Also put the selector in reverse. There have been occasions when reverse wasn't checked and the car was purchased only to discover later there was no reverse gear!

If the car is equipped with a manual transmission, go through the gears and listen carefully. There should be no grinding or syncro problems, and the clutch should engage crisply with no slippage. As you drive, note if the car tends to wander to the inside of a curve, indicating a worn front suspension. Is there any vibration in the steering, especially over road irregularities?

When taking the car over dips and bumps in the road, does it bottom out or the exhaust bang against the floorpan? That's an indication the springs and shocks are history. A clunking or groaning noise when taking a turn means problems in the differential, a broken rear spring or spring shackle.

After the test drive, shut off the motor, wait about thirty seconds and then restart it. If it starts, try it again. By doing this, you're checking the valvetrain and pistons. If the car won't restart, the rings are worn and have expanded or the timing is so advanced or retarded it won't start.

Granted, the car you purchase is going to be restored, and many of the ills outlined here are commonplace with cars that are twenty years or older. And although you'll be repairing or replacing most of the components, make sure the car is as pristine and undamaged as possible. The less you have to repair or replace means the less money you'll spend during the course of the restoration.

Buying a basketcase because it's cheaper isn't always a bargain.

Looking for the best body

There are two rules you need to memorize before searching for your restoration project. Rule number one states: American musclecars (with the exception of the Corvette) were made of steel. Rule number two is: Steel rusts. Put the two together and you can understand how important it is to thoroughly inspect a potential purchase for rust—hidden or otherwise.

If rust wasn't enough to contend with, there is also Bondo, the shade-tree mechanic's best friend. Some wire screen and gobs of plastic filler sanded and painted can hide major body cancer. Your job is to know where to look for it and know how to detect it if it's there.

Until recently, the only tools the average restorer had to work with were his eyes, sensitive fingers to tactily feel any waves or surface irregularities and a small magnet to search for the dreaded plastic filler. Two affordable products have been introduced that replace eyes, fingers and pocket magnets in the search for rust: Spot Rot and Pro Gauge.

The Spot Rot performs as its name implies. It detects rust damage and repainted areas. The magnet end of the gauge is placed on the car body and the other end is pulled off to give a reading. The lower the reading, the worse the condition of the paint and the metal underneath. For about $15.00, it's an excellent investment to identify a car with major body damage. The Pro Gauge is a calibrated magnetic gauge that measures the thickness of non-ferrous materials (like paint) to 0.001 (one thousandth) of an inch. Professional paint gauges cost upwards of $200. The Pro Gauge retails for about $35. Spot Rot and Pro Gauge are available from Pro Motorcar Products (713 US Hwy. 19 North, Clearwater, FL 34625).

Remember that rust may be obvious or it may be hidden. Regardless of where it's located, extensive rust will cost you extra money during the course of a restoration. Patch panels or whole quarters, fenders, hoods, door skins, trunk and floorpans may have to be replaced, and the cost of removing old rotted metal and installing replacements will be substantial. The wise restorer will direct his search toward cars with little or no rot. Just be sure the body that looks good *is* good.

1. The cracked paint reveals the plastic filler beneath on the rear deck and quarter of a Camaro. The thick paint indicates major body work was performed, and it wasn't done very well. There's trouble aplenty here and a quarter panel and deck lid will be required to repair the damage done.

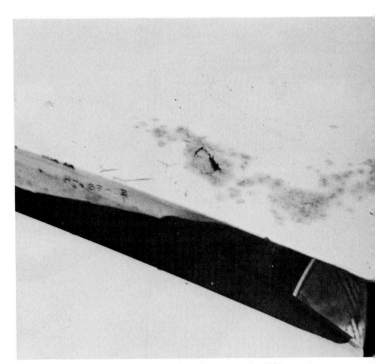

2. Some manufacturers were just better at building cars that resisted rust than others. The hood on this Charger is rotting out. The blemishes to the right of the damage are from the metal rusting out beneath the paint during the initial stages. The open hole to the left is the final result. If the metal is only blemished, it can possibly be saved by etching with acid to halt the rust and then repairing the surface. Once it's rotted through, however, the hood will have to be replaced.

3. Vinyl roofs add to the looks of a musclecar. They also add to the rust problem. Water seeps beneath the fabric and attacks the metal. You can't see it happening, but over the years the metal is deteriorating beneath the vinyl top. Eventually, the only thing holding it all together is the fabric because the metal is gone, as evidenced by the cracking and rust along the solder seam joining the top and the C-pillar.

4. While we're on the subject of vinyl tops and rust, one of the worst areas is around the rear window moldings. If the top is intact, you can't see the damage. You'll have to tap it and feel for soft or crumbling metal.

5. This is one of the most common rust-out areas, the deck and rear window glass. Water would pool and eventually work its way through the paint and into the metal. If there's no obvious rust, look carefully for plastic filler here.

6. Crawl into the trunk with a flashlight, lay on your back and have a look around, because there could be damage in places you never thought of. The water that pooled at the deck and back window glass and rusted the outer metal also attacked the inner metal as well. This is the underside of the rear deck at the back glass. The metal is gone and the water that would leak into the trunk began destroying the trunk pan as well.

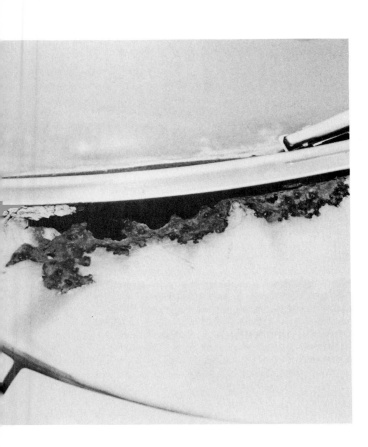

8. The bottom of this door panel demonstrates what northern winters can do to sheetmetal. Like the tip of an iceberg, what is visible on this door doesn't really tell just how badly the door and rockers are rusted. Leaves and debris can also clog door drain holes, speeding up the rust process. This can also happen to the front fenders, especially behind the wheel opening.

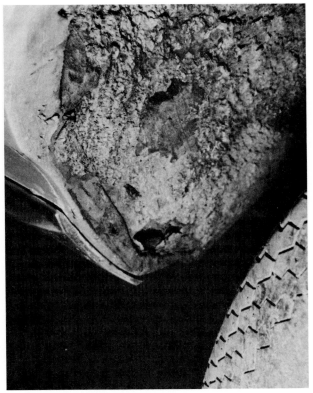

7. Old Man Rust also got to the windshield and cowl of this car. A lot of expensive body work will be needed to repair this damage. Not only is the cowl destroyed, but the metal under the windshield is also gone. Water has probably leaked down to the carpet and begun rusting out the floorpan as well. Peeling back the carpet will reveal the extent of the damage.

9. Most cars suffer rust-out in the bottom of the quarter panels and trunk. This car had a leaking rear window, allowing water to stand in the cavity at the bottom of the quarter where the trunk pan ends. This damage will have to be cut out and new metal installed.

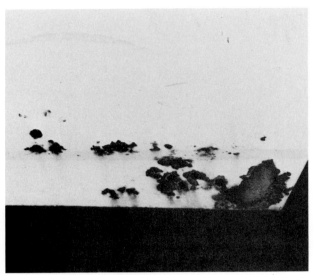

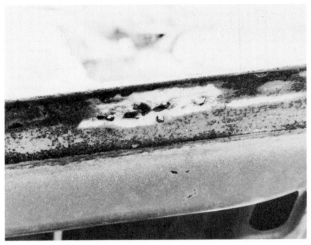

10. Road salt also inflicts heavy damage to cars. The salt was flung up by the rear wheels and never washed off. Over the years, the salt invaded the metal, causing rot and damage. A new patch panel may be adequate unless the damage is so extensive a quarter panel is required.

12. The deck lid can also be rusted out. Damage can range from bubbling paint to gaping holes. This deck lid will have to be replaced. While you're at it, look at the underside of the deck lid and compare the paint color to the exterior. Scrape away a little paint near the edge of the jacking decal. If different colors are present, you are assured the car was repainted.

11. Few cars escape some type of rust at the trunk pan. If the trunk mat is still there, peel it back. If there is just surface rust, it can be easily repaired. Substantial rot or flaked metal will have to be cut away and a reproduction pan installed. Also look carefully at the wheelhouse and trunk pan welds for separation and rust.

13. The top rear of the quarter panel where it meets the deck lid is another common rust area. Remember that surface rust can indicate substantial underlying destruction. Repairing this will cost money.

15. Don't overlook stickers and decals under the hood and in the trunk. Emission decals on the core support will tell you what engine was in the car. This Shaker decal under the hood is original. Notice that it wasn't positioned perfectly straight at the factory. Unfortunately, most show judges would deduct points if you duplicated exactly how it was originally installed.

14. No, it's not body damage, but it is found treasure. All these nuts and bolts were removed from the car and thrown in the trunk. Some of them are junk, but many are the original fasteners and are necessary for a correct restoration. That carburetor body may just be the original and have the correct dates stamped in it.

2

Tools, Equipment and Your Workspace

Before you begin to disassemble your musclecar, you need the proper equipment and environment—and that includes more than just having a set of tools and a place to work. Your work area should be clean, well ventilated and well lit. Working in the dark or holding a trouble light in one hand and a wrench in the other isn't the way to restore a musclecar. Install enough fluorescent lights in the ceiling to adequately light all areas of the garage. Light is a basic requirement in an organized and well-equipped garage.

A little warmth during cold winter nights is not a luxury—it's a necessity. If your garage is wood framed, install adequate insulation in the walls and roof to keep it warmer in the winter and cooler in the summer. And, since light-colored walls reflect light and will brighten up the working environment, put up plasterboard or gypsum and paint it white. If the rafters are exposed, finish the ceilng. Build shelves for parts and equipment storage. Kitchen cabinets are great in a garage. They're high enough on the wall to be out of your way and provide plenty of storage. Make sure there are electrical outlets in convenient locations so you're not tripping over extension cords. You'll also need a 220 volt outlet for your air compressor.

Construct at least one sturdy workbench out of ¾ in. plywood. Make sure it's well braced so you can throw a transmission on it without the bench collapsing. A shelf underneath the bench surface is handy for storing equipment and shop towels. If you don't want to build a workbench yourself, many hardware stores sell workbenches that can be easily assembled.

By putting together the proper working environment, you'll be able to work more efficiently and the time necessary for the restoration will be reduced significantly. Not everyone can build a dream garage and equip it with every tool available; however, a little planning and construction work before you tear the car down will facilitate the restoration. Sure, some people have restored cars in a dark, dirt-floor one-car garage, but by having a well-lit, warm garage that includes adequate work and storage space with all your tools and equipment close to hand, the restoration process will go easier and quicker.

All of the tools shown in this chapter are used sometime during the course of a restoration and are necessary if you're doing all of the work yourself. If you plan on farming out segments of the work, obviously you're not going to need as many tools. Logic dictates that a complete set of handtools is a must, as is a compressor and air tools. The remainder of the specialized tools and equipment are needed to do the job properly. Since safety should be your prime consideration, remember that using the wrong tool for the job can result in an accident and personal injury.

Many of the tools and equipment shown here are also available from tool rental companies for nominal fees. It makes sense, for example, to rent an engine hoist since you'll only be using it twice—once to remove the engine and transmission and once to reinstall them.

1. You'll need a set of ¼, ⅜ and ½ in. hand ratchets, breaker bars and extensions of both the straight and wobble type. Avoid discount tools. Purchase Craftsman, Snap-on or other quality tools that have lifetime warranties. You'll need lots of sockets in ¼ in. shallow and deep wells for small parts. Generally ⅜ in. shallow-well and deep-well sockets are used most of the time. The ½ in. shallow-, deep-well and impact sockets are necessary for big jobs. Occasionally you're going to run into a situation where you'll need some heavy hardware like this ¾ in. ratchet and socket set. These are great for upper shafts and Mopar upper ball joints when used with the Mopar ball joint socket.

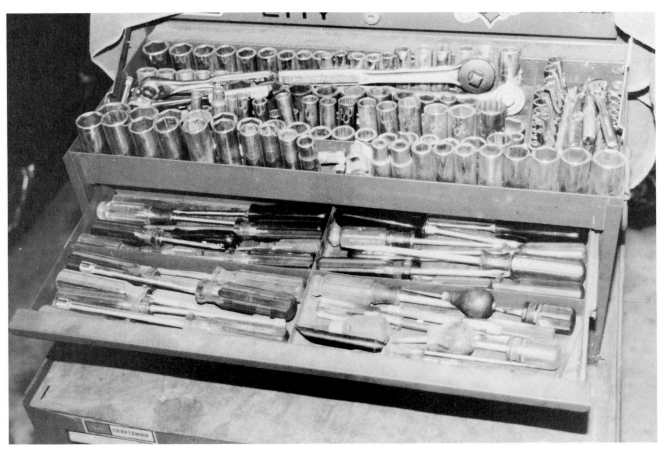

2. Your toolbox should be well stocked with a variety of flat- and Phillips-head screwdrivers and a full assortment of nut drivers.

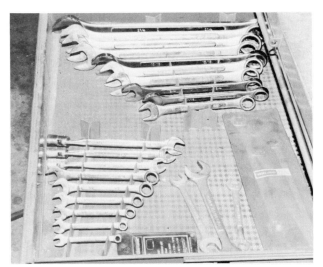

3. Have a complete set of combination wrenches ranging in size from $3/16$ to $1\frac{1}{4}$ in. You'll encounter situations where you'll need more than one wrench of the same size, so double up on the most common sizes used from $3/8$ to $5/8$ in. Also note the holders that keep the wrenches neatly stored in the tool drawer.

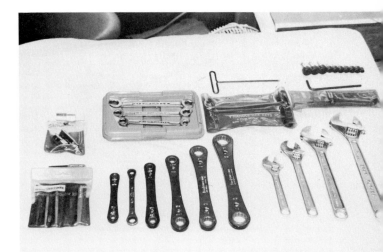

4. Line wrenches are a necessity for removing and installing brake and fuel lines without damaging brass fittings. You'll need a set sized from $3/8$ to $11/16$ in. Box wrenches (also known as ratchet wrenches) from $1/4$ to $7/8$ in. are handy in tight spaces. Have a full set of Allen wrenches, wiper bezel sockets, crescent, star or Torx wrenches.

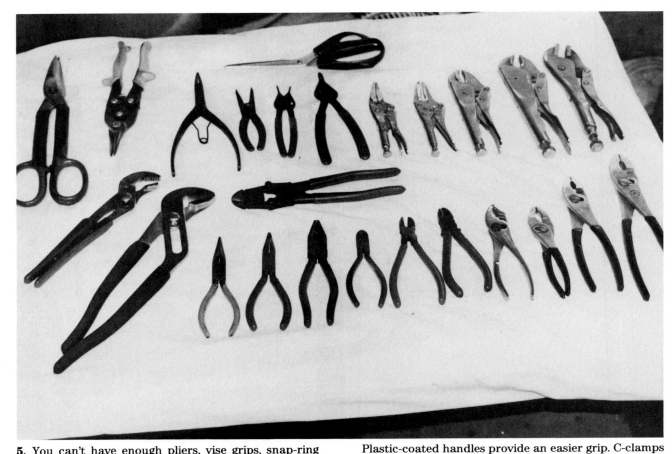

5. You can't have enough pliers, vise grips, snap-ring pliers, line cutters, adjustable pliers, tin snips and shears. Plastic-coated handles provide an easier grip. C-clamps will also come in handy.

6. You need a variety of hammers, including ballpeen hammers, brass hammer, rubber hammer, soft-blow hammer and trim hammer. Brass drifts, chisels, punches and drifts are also a necessity.

7. No home or garage should be without a fire extinguisher rated for class A-, B- and C-type fires. Install a dispenser with hand cleaner. You'll use it quite frequently. A washtub with spigot is handy for scrubbing parts with soap and water and general cleanup.

8. An electric welder or a Mig welder is indispensable. Remember to always use a welding hood and gloves. Gas welding equipment has gotten many a restorer out of a jam, whether it's to heat up a bent control arm so it can be straightened or to repair cracked manifolds. A soldering gun kit will also be necessary.

9. A tachometer, dwell meter, voltmeter and ignition analyzer are useful once the car is completed and you need to set timing and dwell. You don't need a fancy unit like this, however. Sears sells excellent engine analyzers for less than $100. Equipment like a vacuum gauge, timing light, radiator pressure checker, compression gauge, external starter switch, radiator cap remover and leakdown gauge are essential not for just your restoration but to maintain your other vehicles.

10. A drill press is not an essential piece of equipment, however it will be useful. Three- or five-speed units are available from many discount houses for under $150.

11. It may seem like a large investment, but a glass-bead blaster will pay for itself during the course of your restoration. Nearly all of the parts you'll be reusing must be refinished, and bead blasting is the easiest and fastest method for removing paint, rust and grime. You don't need as large a unit as pictured here: smaller, even tabletop size, units are available. A variety of different blast units are advertised in *Hemmings Motor News*.

12. There's a lot of difference between a bead blaster and a sandblaster. You need both. The bead blaster uses a fine glass bead to remove surface material without changing the texture of the component. A sandblaster also removes surface debris, however it works best on harder-alloy metals like frames, control arms and exhaust manifolds. Two types of sandblasters are available: pressure and gravity-fed. The pressure-type blaster is preferred because it works faster. If you are using a low-horsepower compressor (4 horsepower or less), purchase a low-pressure sandblaster to work with your compressor. Also make sure you have a good hood, gloves and extra face shield.

13. You need at least six jackstands and a floorjack. Under no circumstances should you purchase inexpensive jackstands and floorjacks. Laying under a car supported by cheap jackstands is an invitation to serious personal injury and possibly death. If the price of a new, top-quality floorjack is beyond your budget, consider a rebuilt floorjack. They're equal in quality to new ones and cost about $200.

14. Don't scrimp on a quality engine stand. A rebuilt engine isn't cheap and doesn't bounce well, so don't bolt it to a flimsy stand that could fail. Also equip your workbench with a 6 or 10 in. heavy-duty vise that's securely anchored for use with smaller components.

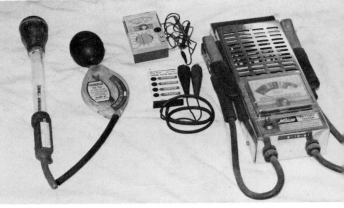

15. A battery tester, hydrometer, generator and alternator analyzer, battery gravity tester and ohmmeter will be useful not only for your project car but for maintaining all your vehicles.

16. For painting the body and components, you should have four spray guns—a large general-purpose gun, touch-up, quart-sized sprayer and a body schutz or underkote gun.

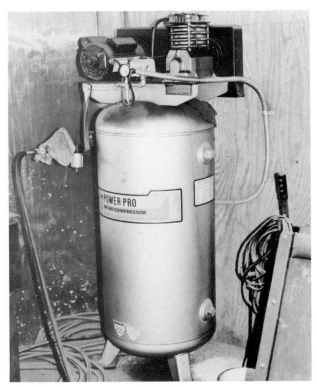

17. Your air compressor should be at least 3 horsepower and will require a 220 volt power supply. A water separator and pressure regulator are essential when using a sandblaster or for painting. Notice the rag on the separator: it's there to keep the gauge face clean of paint. If you're using a smaller compressor that must run constantly, wet a rag with cool water and wrap it around the hose at the separator. It cools the hot air as it leaves the compressor instead of going through the hose laying on the concrete floor, which causes the hot air to pick up moisture. This keeps water out of your spray gun, air tool or sand blaster.

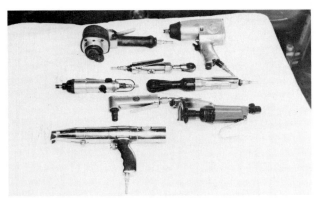

18. Air tools will save hours in disassembly and reassembly. Also shown is a hacksaw, muffler cutter, disc grinder, screwdriver, ¼ and ⅜ in. air ratchets, ½ in. air impact and DA sander. Remember to oil your air tools every time you use them.

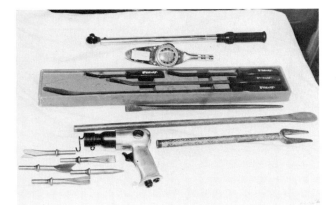

19. Have a few pry bars and ball joint forks on hand. Torque wrenches in pounds and inches are essentials. An air hammer is great for body work and removing bushings.

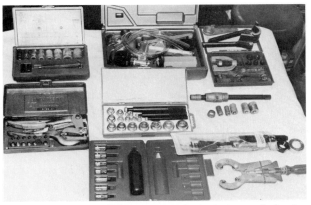

20. Impact driver, Whitney punch, gasket punch, brake bleeder, vacuum tester, flaring tool and tubing bender, tubing cutter, exhaust pipe cutter, clutch alignment tool, bearing and bushing installer, and harmonic balancer installer will all be needed at least once during the work.

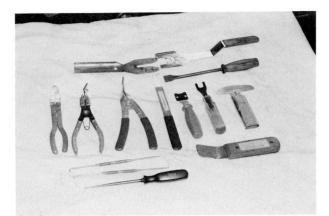

21. Picks and awls should be part of your tool set. Specialized tools like a doorhandle remover, headliner tucking tool, windshield and backglass molding clip installer, and wiper arm remover aren't expensive and facilitate reassembly.

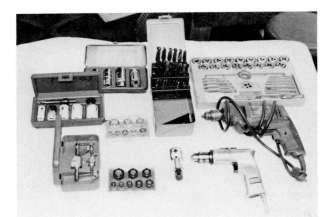

22. Thread cleaners, hole saws, stud remover, drill bits, taps and dies, electric and air drills, and bolt and nut cutter will all be used.

23. This puller assortment can handle any job. You can get by with a set of steering wheel, pulley and balancer pullers.

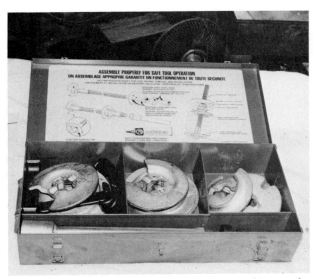

24. A coil spring removal and installation kit can be rented. Never attempt to remove or install coil springs without a spring compressor or kit. You'll also need a complete set of brake removal and installation tools, including a seal remover and emergency brake cable spring compressor.

25. A grinder is another must-have tool. Whether it's a large unit like this one mounted on a pedestal or a smaller unit bolted to your workbench, a grinder-polisher is indispensable. Also purchase a top-quality wire wheel, grinding wheel and a ScotchBrite wheel.

26. A parts washer will save a tremendous amount of time as you disassemble grease- and grime-caked components. Wooden-handled wirebrushes remove the caked-on dirt and rust. It beats scrubbing parts with Gunk in the driveway. Mineral spirits works well as a solvent. You can make a parts washer out of a 35 or 50 gallon drum cut in half length-wise and mounted on a wooden sawhorse base.

28. A 12 ton press is ideal for pressing in control arm bushings and rear axle bushings. Unless you're going to restore more than one car per year, it's not an essential piece of equipment. Your local machine shop can provide this service.

27. A wet-n-dry shop vacuum is necessary not only for shop cleanup but for vacuuming sand, dust, leaves and other debris in the car. It's also handy for removing water from shampooed carpets.

29. If you really want to impress your friends and make your restoration project easy, this body jig is the ticket. You can rotate the body or frame on the jig, which beats laying on the floor while you scrape undercoating. You'll also find it great for painting. Body jigs can be found in the Tools and Equipment section of *Hemmings Motor News*. Otherwise, a floor creeper will keep your back off of the cold concrete floor and out of the grease and dust.

3

Disassembly

Before beginning the disassembly process, remove the battery from the car and drain all fluids from the radiator, engine block, transmission and rear end.

Stock up with plenty of plastic bags, boxes, labels and marking pens to label and store all components and attaching hardware as they are removed from the vehicle. Make copious notes and take photographs before disassembly: this will help you put everything back together in the correct position.

Seat removal

2. The rear seatback is retained by either bolts or hooks. Most GM cars use a set of tabs that must be bent first before the seat can be removed. On Ford products, you must remove the rear seatback-to-floorpan retaining bolts. Lift the rear seat cushion up to unhook the clips at the top of the seatback and then pull the seat cushion out.

1. To remove the rear seat, begin by removing the rear-quarter trim panel armrests. On most cars, the seat cushion is retained by two hooks. Pushing down and forward on the front of the seat cushion will release it from the hooks. You may now remove the bottom rear seat cushion.

3. Removing the front seats is simple. On bucket-seat models, there are four bolts retaining each seattrack to the floorpan. On some models, the bolts are accessed from the bottom, underneath the car; other types are accessed from the top. Bench-seat cars also have four bolts retaining the seattrack assemblies to the floorpan.

Door and quarter trim panel removal

1. Depending on the make and year of your car, you may have to remove the upper garnish moldings on the quarter trim panel and the doors. These are retained by Phillips-head screws.

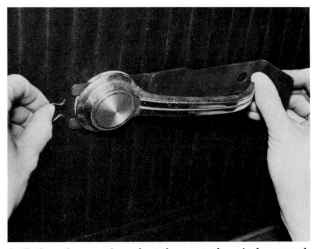

2. Before the panel can be taken out, the window crank must be removed. The crank is removed by one of two methods. Mopar cranks are removed by using an Allen wrench on a retaining bolt through the center of the crank. Most Fords and GM models have a clip that retains the crank on the regulator shaft, as shown here. To remove these cranks, a special tool is required that slips behind the crank seal and pushes the clip off the crank, releasing it from the regulator. Also remove the windlace trim that covers the edge of the quarter trim panel. The windlace snaps into place and requires no tools to remove.

3. Examine the panel for any other screws that may be holding it in place and remove them. The door panel is retained to the body by a series of clips attached to the panel. Carefully use a panel removal tool to gently pry the clips from the body. Be extremely careful here, as the panel's cardboard backing is sometimes weakened by water damage and can easily tear. The panel removal tool applies even pressure around the clip and the cardboard backing, reducing the possibility of damage to the panel.

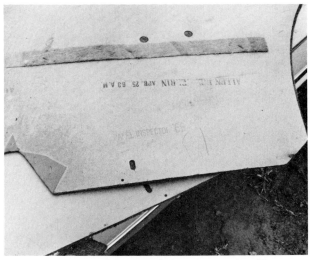

4. Even the rear of the panels has date codes. The most discerning of judges will never see these, but they are there.

7. Remove the lower-door-panel retaining channel if so equipped.

5. Carefully remove the plastic watershields that line the inside of the panels. The watershields are held in place by glue or adhesive caulking. You will either reuse them or use them as patterns to make new ones.

Headliner and trim removal

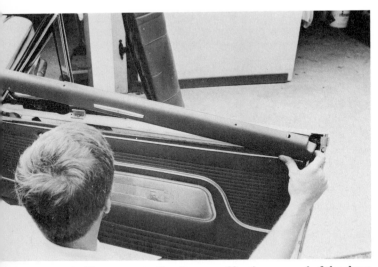

6. Now move to the doors and begin removal of the door panel hardware. Start with the door lock knob and, if necessary, the upper garnish molding. Remove the window cranks using the procedure outlined for the quarter trim panel removal. The doorhandle on GM models is removed in the same manner as the window crank. Ford and Mopar doorhandles may require using a screwdriver. Remove the vent window crank on models so equipped.

1. To remove the headliner, begin by disassembling the dome lamp assembly by popping the lens out of the bezel. To remove the bezel, use a screwdriver to pry the socket contacts to one side and carefully pull the connector out of the back of the bezel. Some models are equipped with roof rail courtesy lamps, which are removed in the same manner.

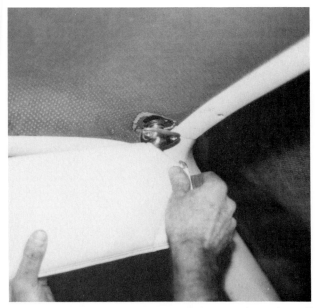

2. Now remove the sun visors and the rearview mirror if it is attached to the upper header panel.

4. The backglass garnish moldings are retained by either clips or screws. On some GM models the moldings simply snap into place: use care in removing them.

3. Unscrew the windshield garnish moldings. With the garnish moldings out, the pillar trim moldings may now be removed. Remove the roofrail molding that extends to the rear of the quarter trim panel in the same fashion. Don't forget any coat hooks, usually retained by Phillips-head screws.

5. Before removing the package shelf, remove rear window defoggers, rear lamp monitors or other accessories such as speaker grilles if so equipped. The package shelf is removed by either removing clips that hold it in place or it may be glued and require careful tugging. Chances are the package shelf is sun-faded or water-stained and will have to be replaced. Reproductions are usually available. If not, keep the old panel for a pattern to construct your own.

6. If the courtesy lamps are located in the C-pillars, remove them by carefully taking out the lamp lens and then removing the screws holding the bezel. On cars equipped with sail panel covers, remove the complete panel. Usually, it is simply clipped into place; however, in some models the panel may be held by glue.

8. If you plan to reuse the headliner, make sure you mark and number the headliner bows and headliner bow holes. Mark the bows, numbering them from front to rear and right to left. Also mark the headliner-bow retaining holes so that you get the headliner bows in the correct holes upon reassembly.

7. Carefully extract the staples from the headliner and remove the headliner from the car. You can expect the soundproofing padding to crumble as you remove the headliner.

9. A rear headliner retaining wire runs along the roofline; do not overlook or lose it as you'll need it when reinstalling the headliner.

10. If so equipped, remove the shoulder belts and retainers by unscrewing the harness take-up cover. Remove the shoulder-belt retaining cover clip and slide the cover off of the belt. Unbolt the shoulder-harness assembly and store it away: you'll ship these off with the seatbelts for refinishing. Cars of the shoulder-belt vintage are usually also equipped with one-piece headliners. Thus be careful when you remove the shoulder-belt retainers, because the headliner will now drop from the roof supports. You can now remove the headliner as well as the coat hooks and sail-panel retaining screws and pull the sail panels. Also remove the rear trim side covers.

Carpet and trim removal

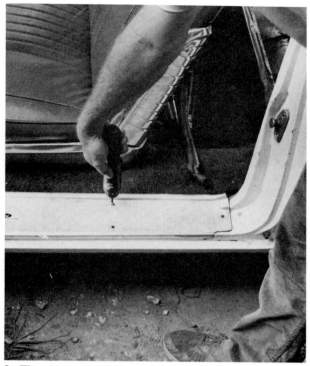

2. The door sill plates hold the carpet in place. The plates are retained by Phillips-head screws.

1. With the seats removed, the seatbelts are taken out before the carpet can be pulled up. Remove the bolts holding the seatbelt anchors to the floorpan. If the belts are worn or damaged, send them out for restoration. Companies like Sssnake Oyl (15775 North Hillcrest, Suite 508–541, Dallas, TX 75248) do an excellent job restoring belts correctly. Reusing your old belts with their date codes intact is all part of a proper restoration.

3. With the door sill plates out, you can remove the front and rear carpets. Some models may have screws through the carpet attaching to the floorpan.

39

4. Remove the carpet underlayment and watershield. These are often well-worn so be careful when lifting them out. Unless reproductions are available, you may need the old pads as patterns to make new ones.

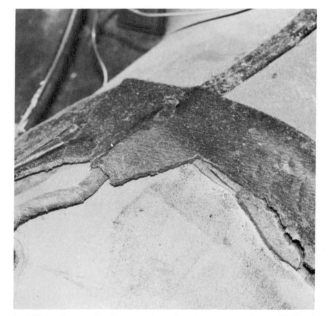

5. With the underlayment and jute removed, you'll find wiring harnesses running along the floorpan. One will travel to the rear of the car. If your car is equipped with a console, you'll find a similar harness to this on the top of the transmission tunnel. Leave these for now; when you remove the instrument panel main harness, you'll take the rear and console harnesses out as well.

Steering column removal

1. Begin removal of the steering column by unbolting the flexible coupler that attaches the column to the steering gearbox. Unplug any wiring harnesses feeding from under the dash to the steering column such as turn signal or emergency flasher wiring.

2. The steering column is secured by a bracket at the underside of the instrument panel; there is also an insulator cover at the base of the column at the floorpan. Remove the attaching bolts at the base first, then unbolt the retaining bracket bolts under the instrument panel. Leave the steering wheel on so you can pull the column out.

3. Carefully extract the steering column from the instrument panel. As you remove the column shaft, make sure the coupler and flange assembly at the end of the column doesn't snag on any underdash wiring.

4. With the column out of the car, you can now place it on your workbench and remove the steering wheel, coupler, insulator, and turn signal and tilt lever stalks. If the stalks need to be rechromed, send them out for rechroming now. If you don't need to disassemble the column, refinish it by taping the exposed wiring harness and plug to protect it, hit the column lightly with fine sandpaper and spray it the correct color. The shaft should be finished with Eastwood's Bare Metal paint to retain the correct appearance and protect it from rust.

Instrument panel removal

Disassembling the instrument panel requires organization and care. As you remove each component and its attaching hardware, label and bag it for future identification.

For many restorers, the instrument panel wiring harnesses are like a bundle of snakes. It looks difficult to understand and harder to remove and reinstall. If some simple steps are taken during removal, installation will be much easier later on.

The trick here is to study the harness carefully before removal. Crawl up under the dash with a light and inspect the harness, how it is routed and the way the bundles are positioned. Make a diagram of the harness and how it is laid out. Your parts book or assembly manual will also show how the harness is routed and the manner in which the leads go to each component.

As you disconnect the harness from each component, label small hang tags and tie them onto the plugs or bulbs. Months from now, when you reinstall the harness, determining where each plug or connector goes will be a snap. Or, if you plan on installing a reproduction harness (available from companies like M&H Electric Fabricators, 13537 Alondra Blvd., Santa Fe Springs, CA 90670), the tags can be transferred to the new harness prior to installation.

Instrument panel design varies depending on year, make and model. Cars built before 1962 usually don't have a dash pad, while models built from 1963–1967 generally have a pad bolted to the top of the panel which is easy to remove. Cars built after 1968 most likely will have padded housings that are one-piece units that can surround the instrument cluster or could be a one-piece design that incorporates the entire instrument panel. These are more difficult to disassemble and must be done carefully so the pad isn't damaged.

Twenty year-old pads are usually fragile and can crack easily. Depending on the condition of the pad, several heavy coats of protectorant like Armor All, allowed to soak into the pad, might make it more pliable and less prone to damage upon removal.

The parts book illustrations here are representative of late-sixties and early seventies GM instrument panels, showing the different designs used. Study your service manual, parts book or assembly manual before disassembling your instrument panel. The instrument panel shown in this disassembly section may not be the same design as yours, however it will show you the proper sequence of steps to take for removal.

1. Begin the instrument panel disassembly by removing the lower windshield garnish molding.

2. If the speaker grille is removable from the top, take it off now and remove the speaker. If the speaker is removed from inside the panel, remove it once the heater-control assembly and defroster ducting have been removed.

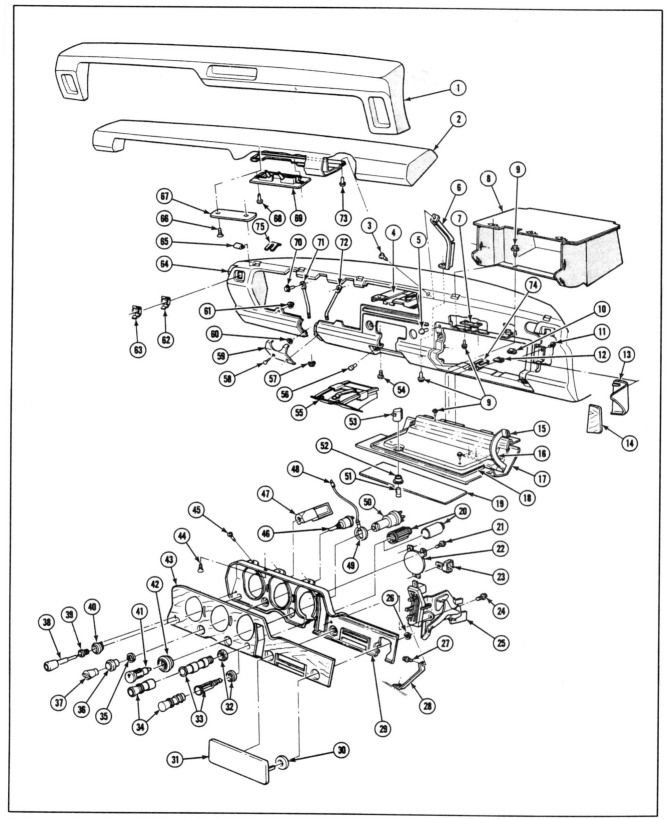

Parts book breakdown for a 1968 Pontiac Tempest
instrument panel.

43

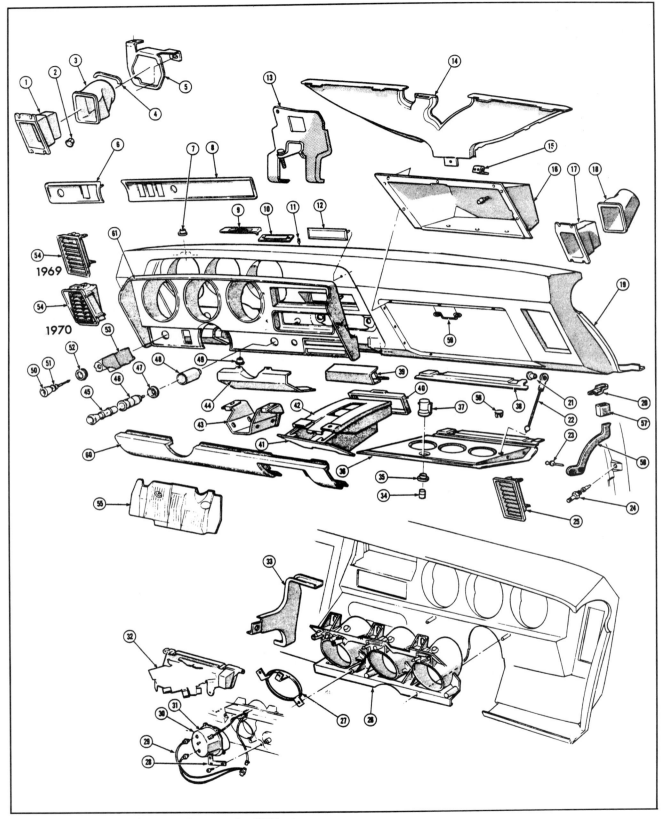

Parts book breakdown for an early seventies GM instrument panel.

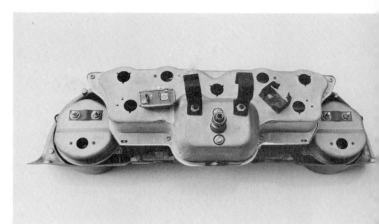

5. Store the cluster for now, taking care not to scratch the faces of the instrument lenses. You'll be disassembling and restoring the cluster later.

3. Usually, the steering column is removed before the instrument panel is removed. Remove the screws retaining the instrument cluster to the panel. These screws are easily accessible from the front on most cars.

4. Once the cluster is loose, carefully pull it forward and disconnect the wiring from the instruments. On some models, the wiring can only be removed by crawling under the dash and disconnecting the harnesses and speedometer cable. Once the harnesses have been disconnected from the cluster, it can be removed from the instrument panel.

6. On some cars, the switches and accessories are integrated into a pod containing the instrument cluster. On others, the switches and accessories are in a separate panel. Begin removing these components one at a time, disconnecting any harness as you remove them. The cigar lighter usually has one lead to disconnect, and then the lighter unscrews from a retainer and is removed. An Allen wrench is needed on some makes to remove instrument knobs. Wiper switches are usually held in place by a center retainer and bezel. Remove the knob and then loosen the center retainer. Slip it over the knob and the switch will pull out from the back of the dash.

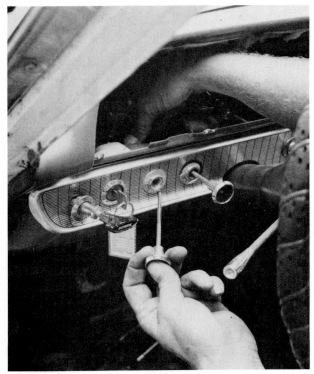

7. To remove the headlamp switch, press the switch knob release button located on the rear of the switch assembly. That releases the shaft. Now pull the knob and shaft out of the light switch.

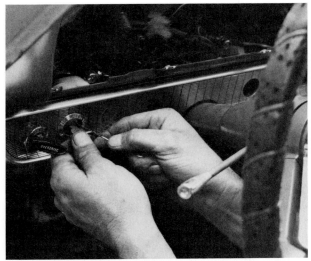

9. To remove the ignition switch lock cylinder and keys, straighten a paper clip and insert it into the small hole on the right side of the ignition switch. While pushing in the paper clip, turn the lock cylinder and key to the accessory side of the switch. You will feel the switch release as you turn to the left. Once the switch is released, you can pull the lock cylinder out of the switch. Most ignition switches are held in place by a spring and collar. Firmly grasp the back of the ignition switch, push it toward the outside of the dash and twist. It will release from the ignition switch bezel and you will be able to pull the switch out from the back of the dash.

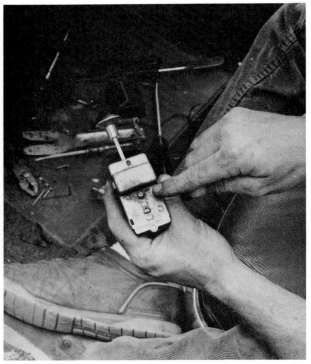

8. The switch knob release button is clearly visible on the removed assembly.

10. The heater control panel assembly is usually retained by four bolts or speed nuts which must be removed from the rear. Once freed, pull the panel forward and remove the control cables, which are usually retained by clips or small nuts. Remove the lamp harness. If the car is equipped with air conditioning, the controls are vacuum activated. Carefully remove the hoses, and the panel can now be stored for later refinishing.

11. Disconnect the speaker and lamp harness and pull the antenna lead from the radio. Remove the radio by pulling off the knobs and using a deep-well socket to unbolt the retaining nuts from the shafts. The radio will now drop out from the rear. If so equipped, remove the clock by disconnecting the power and lamp harness. Unbolt from the rear and remove.

13. If the radio speaker drops from beneath the dash, take it out now. After removing all dash equipment, defroster ducts and any wiring that attaches to the dash, undo the dash retaining screws and remove the dash from the car.

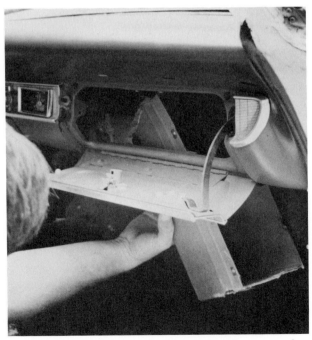

12. The glovebox liner is usually retained by screws that are removed by using a stub screwdriver. Once the liner is out, the glovebox door and any other remaining dash controls can now be removed.

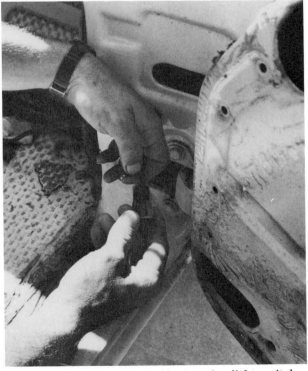

14. Don't forget to remove the interior light switches located in the door pillars.

Hood removal

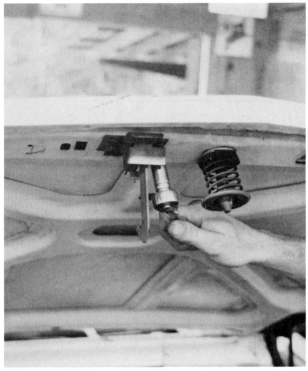

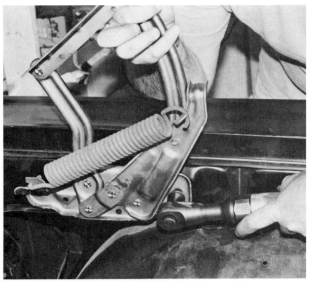

3. Depending on manufacturer, hood hinges and springs are either painted or coated. To refinish hood hinges that are natural steel, begin by removing the hood hinge springs. Clean and bead blast both the hinges and springs. For natural metal-appearing hinges, spray them with Seymours Stainless Steel Paint or DIX lacquer spray. After the steel paint has dried, apply a coat of dry clear. To make clear spray on dry to give a low-gloss look, just add more air to the mixture at the spray gun. The more air at the gun, the lower the gloss, hence dry clear. For cars with black hood hinges, mix black paint with a flattening agent to produce a thirty-percent gloss finish and apply.

1. Remove the hood latches and any moldings, lettering, ornaments or scoops. Note whether the latching components are plated or natural metal in appearance: you'll want to refinish them in the same fashion. Remove the catches and safety mechanism as well.

Grille and bumper removal

2. Prop up the hood with a rod or dowel; this way it can be removed by just one person. Place towels at each rear corner of the hood and then release the hinge-to-hood bolts and remove the hood.

1. Loosen and remove the bumper-to-frame bracket bolts. With a helper, remove the front bumper.

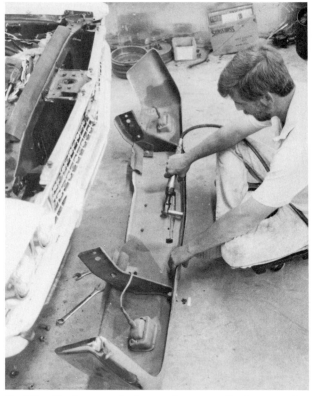

2. After the bumper is dropped, remove the bumper-to-frame brackets and turn signal lamp assemblies and harnesses. If you plan to reuse the old bumper, send it out for rechroming now.

3. Remove the headlamp doors and grilles.

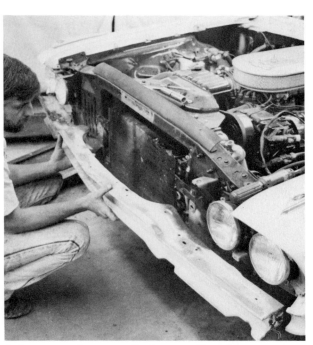

4. Loosen and remove the lower grille valance.

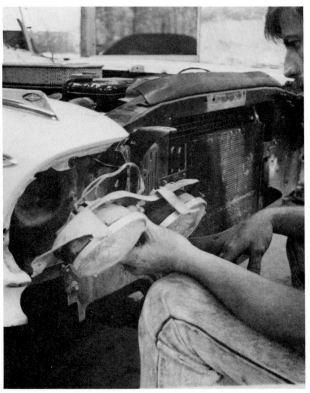

5. Remove the headlamp bucket assemblies and set them aside for cleaning and refinishing. If any of the headlamps are original, you'll want to save them. Remove the rear bumper the same way the front bumper was removed and disassemble in the same fashion.

49

Exterior trim removal

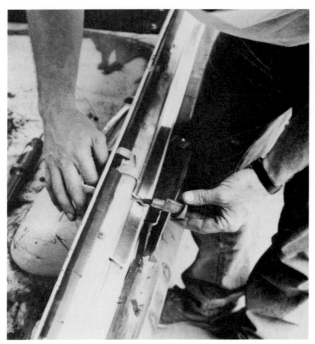

1. Remove the trunk latch mechanism and unbolt the trunk lock assembly. Once it is loose, pull it out.

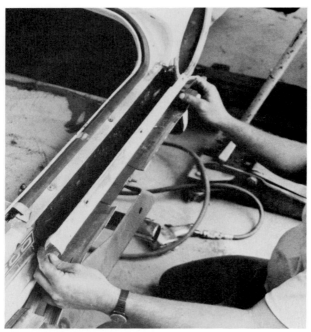

2. Remove moldings, letters or other ornaments from the taillamp panel. These are usually retained by speed nuts. Unscrew the taillamp bezels and remove. Take out the taillamp lenses and housings. The housings are usually attached by speed nuts. If the fuel filler door is located in the taillamp panel, remove it now as well.

3. The trunk molding is retained either by speed nuts or clips. Remove the molding. If there are any letters, emblems or ornaments on the deck lid, use a nut driver or deep-well socket to remove the speed nuts securing them.

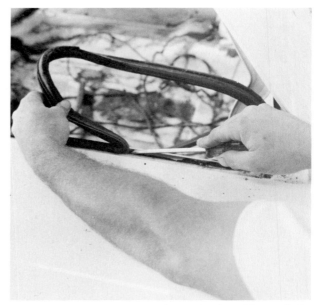

4. Remove the trunk weatherstripping. Most of the weatherstripping will come off by using a flat-blade screwdriver under the rubber and peeling it off. 3M also offers an adhesive remover that facilitates weatherstrip removal.

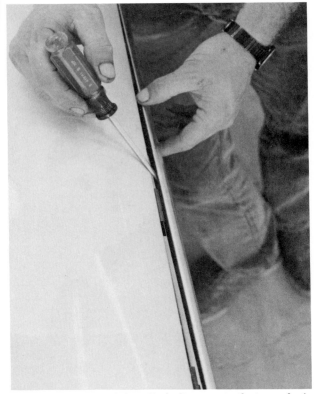

7. Cars with the top painted a different color, equipped with a vinyl top or convertibles with pinchweld moldings have bright trim. These moldings are retained by screws, speed nuts accessible from the trunk or are secured by clips.

5. Loosen any retaining clip bolts or nuts that may be in the trunk and carefully remove the molding from the retaining clips. The molding will either slide off the clips or must be pulled up from the bottom of the clip and then removed.

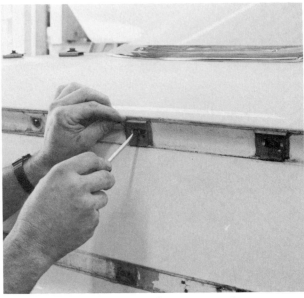

6. Once the moldings have been removed, unscrew or pry off the clip retainers and take them off the body. If there are moldings on the front fenders, remove them and the retaining clips in the same fashion.

8. Unbolt the lock mechanism on the door and then remove the striker plate at the doorjamb.

51

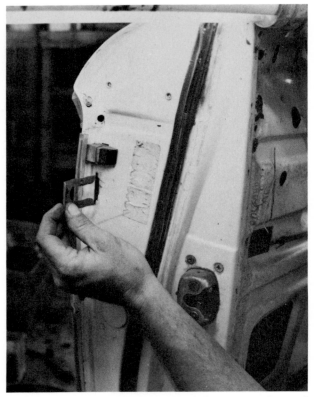

9. The doorhandles are retained by screws located either at the edge of the door or through the door skin. Disconnect the button shaft from the lock mechanism inside the door. A clip retains the assembly. Remove the clip and take the lock assembly off the door. Unscrew the door lock mechanism from the door and remove. If there are moldings on the outside of the door, remove them and unscrew the clips.

10. Remove the roof rail weatherstripping. Don't plan on reusing this; removing the weatherstripping to access the retaining screws will destroy the stripping. Once the weatherstripping is out, remove the Phillips-head screws retaining the roofrail molding to the door and roof pillars.

11. After the screws have been removed, pull the roofrail moldings off. On some cars, it is a one-piece molding. On other makes, several moldings are used from the front to the rear.

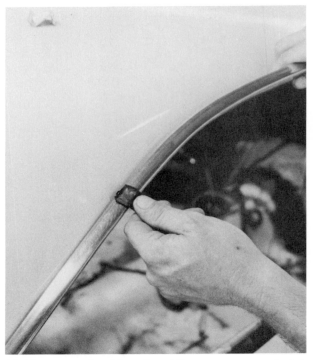

12. To remove the drip rail moldings, wrap some electrical tape around the curved end of a bottle cap opener. Use the lip on the underside of the opener under the molding and carefully lift up on the molding—a little at a time—working toward the rear.

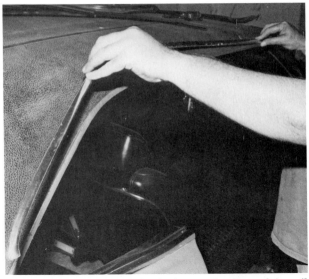

13. Models equipped with vinyl tops also have drip rail moldings that are removed in the same way. Once the drip rail molding has been carefully pried off the drip rail, remove it, taking care not to bend the molding.

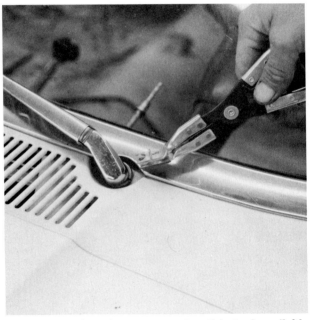

15. Remove the wiper arms, using this tool available from Eastwood. Insert the tool under the wiper arm and squeeze the handles. The tool will pop the wiper arm off the motor shaft. Don't try to pry the wiper arms off with a large screwdriver; it will scar the pot-metal arm and dent the cowl cover.

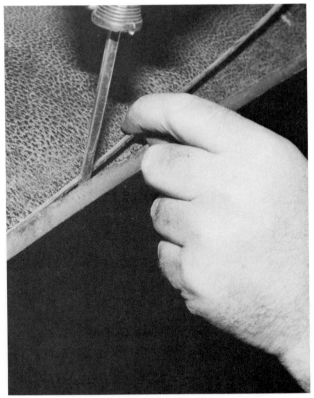

14. Once the molding is removed, there is a retaining strip known as a scalp molding tucked into the drip rail that secures the vinyl top. Carefully remove this strip, being careful not to bend it. After the front and rear window glass moldings and glass have been removed, the vinyl top can be stripped off the car.

16. Remove the windshield washer nozzles and washer hoses from the cowl if so equipped. Some cars also have a rubber molding along the edge of the cowl that seals against the back of the hood and must be removed. The cowl and wiper transmission cover is retained by bolts. Remove the bolts and take the cover off the car.

53

Rear quarter glass removal

1. To remove the rear quarter glass, begin by unscrewing and removing the rear quarter lower seal.

3. Remove the lower channel retainer, and then unbolt and remove the rear channel.

2. Reinstall the window crank so you will be able to roll the window down if necessary. Remove the front and rear window stops.

4. Remove the window regulator arm retaining clips from the glass channel and then remove the arms from the channel.

Door glass removal

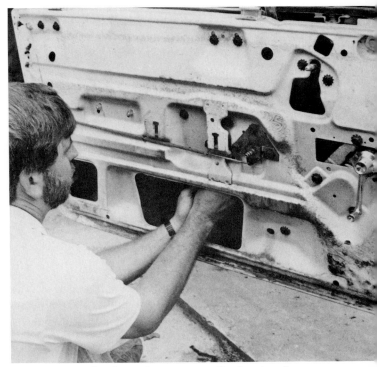

5. Remove the window crank, and loosen and remove the front channel. Work it down to the bottom and take out. Immediately mark the side and location of all components as you remove them. Bag or box all the mounting hardware, nuts and bolts, and identify them for reinstallation.

1. To remove the door glass, remove the front and rear window stops, and then unbolt and remove the lower window stop.

6. You can now remove the glass. Let the back of the glass drop down at the rear and pull it up at the front and then out.

2. Remove the regulator-arm retaining clips.

3. On some cars, the vent window is operated by a crank. If so equipped, remove the vent window regulators.

5. Carefully lift the door glass up and out of the door. Be careful when clearing the lower channel past the window opening in the door.

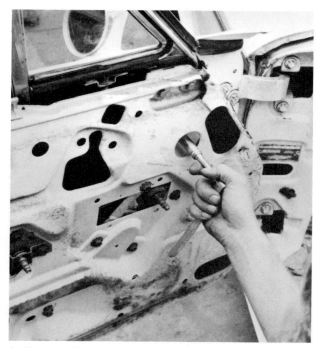

4. Remove the vent window frame screws and bolts. On some GM cars, there is a bolt at the front of the door frame that retains the vent window front frame. There are also other bolts, some of which are hidden. The rear of the vent frame serves double duty as the front glass run channel and reaches down towards the bottom of the door frame, where there is a retaining brace and nut. Loosen and scrape off the vent window or door weatherstripping if so equipped.

6. With the front window glass out, now you can easily remove the vent window assembly. On some GM cars, you will have to twist the frame 90 degrees outward, as there is a kink in the frame that won't clear the opening if pulled straight up.

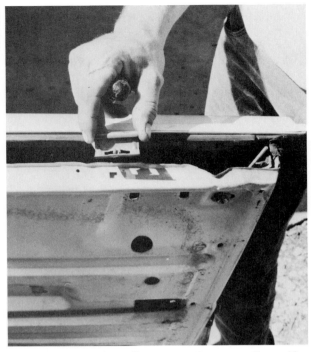

7. If garnish molding clips are used, remove them. Also remove the upper door reveal moldings, if so equipped. Find the screws retaining the window felts and remove them and take out the felts. Take care not to drop the screws down into the door.

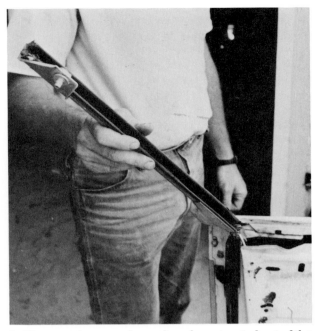

9. The rear glass run channel can be extracted out of the top of the door.

Vent window disassembly

8. Loosen and remove the rear glass run channel. Remember that some of the attaching bolts are hidden behind plugs.

1. After the vent window assembly has been removed, it must be disassembled for restoration. Begin by removing the division bar. Remove the screws at the top and side of the vent window assembly. Some division bars are also riveted or spot welded in place. The rivets or welds must be drilled out. After all screws, rivets or welds have been removed, hold the vent window assembly firmly in place and pull the division bar up and out from the bottom.

57

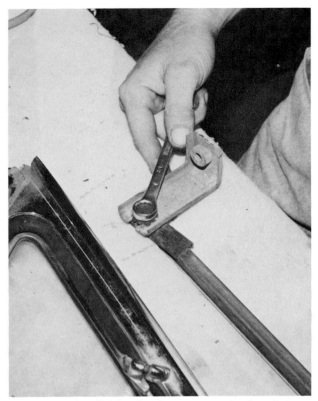

2. Remove the division bar lower mounting bracket.

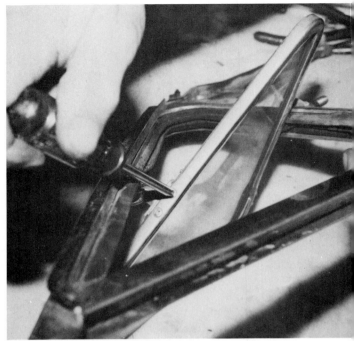

4. The upper pivot assembly is retained by screws. Remove them and take the assembly out. With the assembly removed, the vent glass can be pulled out.

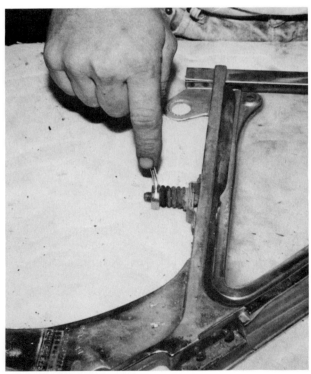

3. Use penetrating oil on the lower pivot nut to loosen the pivot nut so it can be removed, along with the spring, washer and spacer.

5. Remove the vent window weatherstripping. It is held in place by screws, rivets or brads. If brads or rivets are used, they will have to be drilled out. Screws can be used to reattach the weatherstripping when reinstalled. Also remove the vent window vertical division bar weatherstripping. It is held in place just like the vent weatherstripping and is removed the same way.

Front and back glass removal

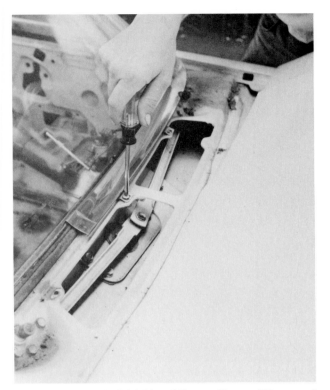

1. Remove the windshield moldings, pillar moldings, and top windshield and lower windshield moldings.

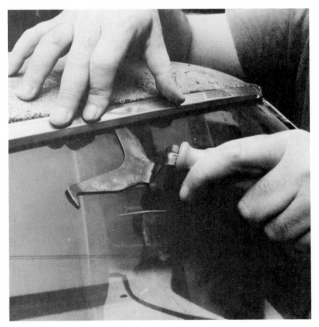

2. This Y-shaped tool is a windshield molding clip removal tool and is available from Eastwood or from most automotive supply stores. If the inside rearview mirror is attached to the windshield, remove it now.

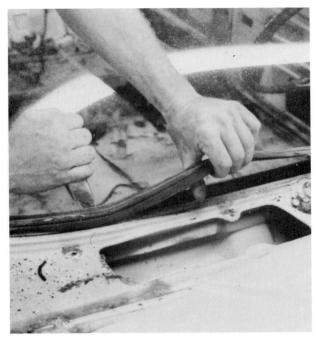

3. Use a utility knife or a razor blade and cut the window weatherstripping away from the glass. Remember when you do this the weatherstripping cannot be reused. Make sure that you can obtain new weatherstripping before performing this task.

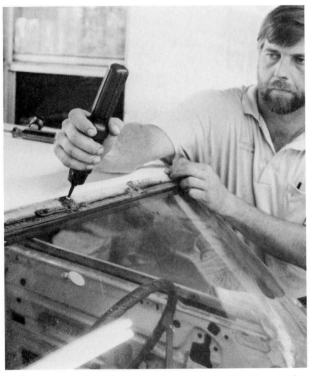

4. Remove any molding clips that retain the glass to the body. Clips are also used to retain moldings around the front and rear glass. Make sure these have also been removed.

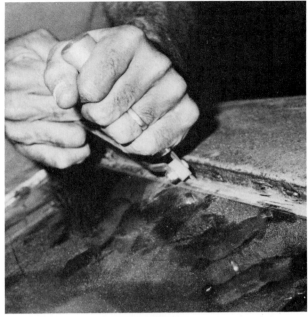

5. It may be necessary to break the seal between the caulking and the glass. To do so, use piano wire run from the inside out and dragged along the windshield edge. This removal tool is another route to separating the glass from the molding.

6. After you have removed any clips, cut away the weatherstripping and broken the seal between glass and caulking, carefully push the glass out from the inside. After it clears at the top, pull the glass up and out of the windshield opening. Some cars have a rubber seal between the window channel and the glass. Remove this seal and discard. You'll replace it before installing the new glass.

7. With the windshield removed, you can now remove the windshield wiper transmission bezel and nuts and remove the transmission assembly.

8. In most cases, each transmission arm is clearly marked left or right. If not, mark them now so you can identify them for reassembly later.

Fender removal

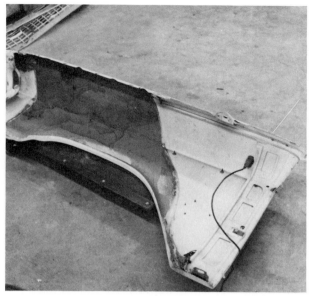

3. With the fender removed from the car, take off the antenna assembly and wire lead. Emblems are usually attached to the fenders by speed nuts. Remove them now that the fender is off and the nuts are accessible.

1. Loosen and remove both front fenders. Remember there are bolts on the wheel opening lip that attach to the inner fender.

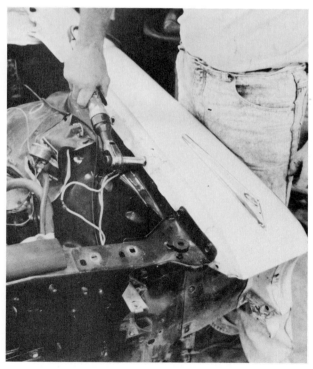

2. Other bolts are hidden in the cowl area or below the A-pillar on most cars.

4. The inner fenders attach to the core support and the firewall. Many GM cars have a firewall-to-inner fender brace that will need to be unbolted before the inner fenders can be removed. Remember to remove all wiring and vacuum lines.

5. Drain any fluids and remove the upper and lower hoses from the radiator first. If the car is equipped with a water-cooled automatic transmission, remove the transmission cooler lines from the lower radiator tank. Remove the radiator from the core support by removing the upper fan shield and lifting it from the mounting brackets at the bottom of the support. Remove the battery tray and windshield washer bottle and mounting bracket. Now unbolt the frame-to-support bushings and remove the core support. On unibody cars, this is not removable.

Engine and transmission removal

1. Before the engine can be pulled, remove all the engine accessories possible. Unbolt, label and bag all the hardware and attaching nuts and bolts for the fan and accessories such as power steering pump, alternator, air-conditioning compressor and emissions pump. Also pull the water pump cover and pump. Remember to disconnect the accelerator linkage from the firewall, and check for other connections from engine to firewall such as ground straps.

2. Remove the valve covers and then the intake manifold bolts. Use a pry bar or wide blade screwdriver and carefully pry the intake away from the heads and block.

3. With the manifold loose, carefully remove it. Remember on some cars the intake is made out of cast iron and is quite heavy. On this type of intake, it may be advisable to use an engine hoist to easily remove it.

62

4. Bring in the engine hoist and attach it to the block. Use a spreader bar to keep the chains an even width apart so the engine assembly will be balanced. Make another check to be sure all linkages, connecting cables or brackets have been disconnected.

6. Block the wheels so the car cannot roll and then start to pump up the engine hoist. Put some tension on the engine. Now carefully loosen and remove the transmission crossmember. Keep tension on the engine because the tailshaft of the transmission will drop. Now, gradually raise the engine. As soon as you have enough height to clear the oil pan over the front crossmember, start to pull the engine hoist away from the car. You will have to raise the engine and move forward a little at a time, but just keep repeating this procedure until the engine clears the car. On unibody cars, this procedure works the same way, however you need a hoist that will raise the engine above the core support. In some cases, you may have to remove the transmission before you remove the engine.

5. Remove the motor mount bolts and the rear engine or transmission mount bolts at the crossmember. Disconnect the driveshaft from the transmission. If you haven't drained the transmission, put a plastic baggie around the transmission tailshaft to keep transmission fluid from leaking. Unbolt the shifter from the tailshaft, or if an automatic transmission, disconnect the shifter cable.

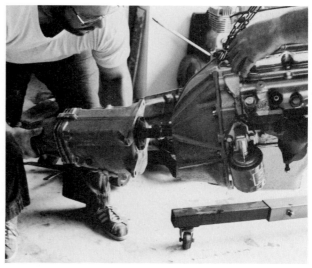

7. Roll the hoist over to a work area and remove the transmission linkages and shifter mounting plate. Now unbolt the transmission from the bellhousing and remove.

8. Set the engine down and secure it. Unbolt the exhaust manifolds and cylinder heads and remove them from the block.

9. Reattach the engine to the engine hoist and lift it up to remove the bellhousing.

10. On manual transmission-equipped cars, unbolt the clutch, pressure plate and flywheel. On automatic transmission-equipped models, the torque converter came off when the transmission was removed. All that remains to be taken off is the flex wheel. Now bolt the block to your engine stand.

Underhood component removal

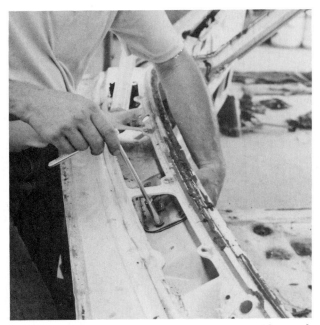

1. On some makes, the wiper motor is located beneath the cowl and is removed once the window glass is out. The wiper motor can also be found on the firewall. Remove it now.

2. Both the engine wiring harness and the front chassis harness attach to a connector block found on the firewall. Unplug the harnesses and remove. Also remove all other harnesses or leads at this time, including the rear body harness and console harness if so equipped. Make a diagram of how they are routed and their connections.

3. Remove the tabs retaining the firewall connector block and push it back inside of the car. On some cars, this will have already been removed, as it also serves as the main harness fuse block and is integral to the under-dash harness.

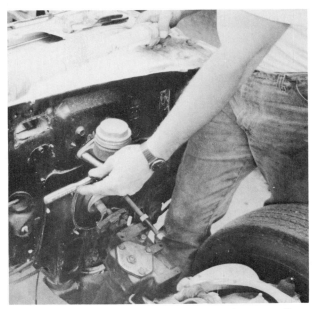

4. Remove the master cylinder and booster if so equipped, horn relay, voltage regulator, harness tabs and any other components mounted to the firewall. Take photos of where the components are located and how they are mounted. You'll refer to these pictures when you remount them on the firewall. Remove the heater plenum cover retaining nuts. Remove the cover and unbolt the core and case. Then remove them and the motor from inside the car.

5. Mark the holes used to mount components and hardware onto the firewall. This will allow you to identify any holes that have been drilled into the firewall over the years that are not correct. These extra holes will be filled before the firewall is painted.

Lifting the body from the frame

Removing the body from the frame is one of the major jobs in a restoration. It also signals a milestone in the project. With the body off the frame, you now have complete access to the chassis and its components. You now also have two different restorations going on at once: the body and paint work and the mechanical restoration of the drivetrain and chassis.

Chances are, you'll be working on both at the same time, so organization of your time is essential. Keeping track of what is being farmed out, such as rechroming, machine work and upholstery work is important, because you'll want to coordinate these subprojects so, hopefully, everything will be done at the same time. In other words, you'll want the chassis to be completed when the body comes home (if you're having a shop do the body and paint). You don't want a painted body sitting around gathering dust while you're sandblasting and painting mechanical parts.

We're going to show you one method of removing the body, and it requires only two people to do it. Don't do it alone; have someone else assist, especially if you get into trouble and need an extra set of hands. Or, if you prefer, have six helpers lift the body off the frame after you have removed all the body-to-frame bolts. If the body is to be lifted manually, make sure your helpers wear work gloves or use towels to protect their hands from sharp metal edges.

1. Remove the gas tank before pulling the body from the frame. You should have already drained the tank. To remove, position a floorjack with a few towels in the jack saddle under the tank, then unbolt the straps that secure the tank at the front. The straps then slip out at the rear. Lower the floorjack as a helper steadies the tank. Notice the rubber seal that separates the gas tank from the trunk pan. Generally, this is where the build sheet was installed on most GM cars, however this car didn't have one.

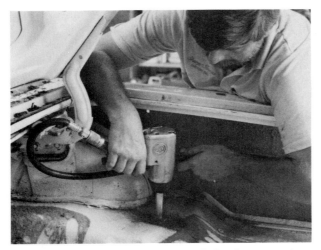

2. To begin removing the body, pull the floorpan plugs and remove the body-to-frame bolts. Then remove the trunk floor plugs and remove the bolts.

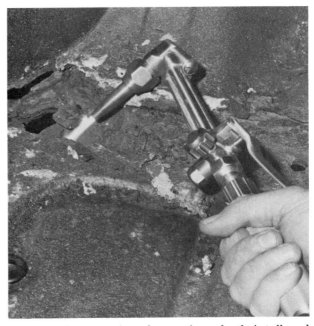

3. Years of water, salt and corrosion take their toll, and some bolts aren't going to come out easily. In most GM A bodies (Chevelle, LeMans, Cutlass and Skylark), body bolt number 5 on the left-hand side near the wheelhouse-trunkpan weld will require a little persuasion. A torch works best, however the faithful hammer and chisel will also get the job done. Remove the body-to-frame bolts at the firewall last.

4. In some cases, the bushings will be in reasonably good shape; however, you'll probably encounter some that will shear off when you apply torque to them, and the bushings and cushions will fall apart when removed.

5. Imagine all the years you've been driving the car on these body bushings? Obviously, you'll be installing new bushings and bolts.

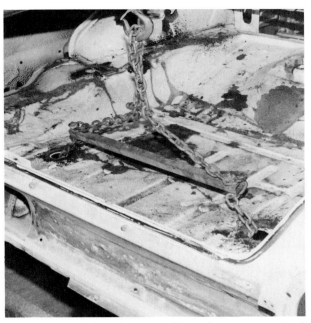

7. If the trunk floor is in excellent shape or you don't want to drill holes in the pan, use this method. Place a 2x10 or 4x4 about 3 ft. wide with two eye hooks on each end under the trunk floor. Run the engine hoist chains down through the trunk floor holes and attach them to the 2x10 or 4x4. Slowly jack up the engine hoist and raise the rear of the body off of the frame.

6. After removing all of the floorpan and trunkpan bolts, place a 2x10 or 4x4 board across the body between the frame rails and under the firewall. Using a floorjack, lift the body up as high as the jack will go. Place another 2x10 or 4x4 (make sure it's about 2 ft. wider than the car) on both sides on top of two jack stands. Put the stands on their higher points with the 2x10 or 4x4 on top. Slowly lower the body down on the 2x10 or 4x4 and the jack stands.

8. Place another 2x10 or 4x4 board (make this one 2 ft. wider then the car on both sides) between the frame and the body. Place the 2x10 or 4x4 on top of the jack stands set at their highest point and rest the body on the 2x10 or 4x4.

9. If the trunkpan will require work (or you don't mind filling in two small holes), use this method. Drill a ⅜ in. hole through the trunkpan at the next-to-last forward hole in the fuel-tank mounting ribs.

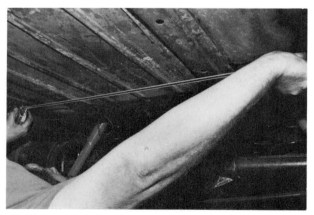

10. Measure between the frame rails, and cut a length of 2x10 or 4x4 board 2 in. less than that distance. Position the 2x10 or 4x4 under the tank mounting ribs and have a helper mark the board with a pencil through the ⅜ in. holes you just drilled. Now drill ⅜ in. holes through the board at the marks.

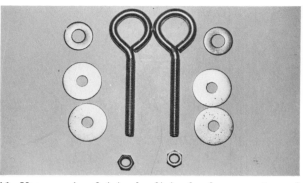

11. Use a pair of 4 in. by ⅜ in. hookeyes, nuts and washers. Drop the hookeyes through the drilled holes at the top of the trunk with a washer above and below the trunkpan.

12. Position the 2x10 or 4x4 and thread the hookeyes through the board, using a third washer and the nuts to secure them. Notice how the board distributes the weight. This method can be used on even severely rusted trunkpans.

13. Use a set of S hooks at the end of an attaching chain and hook this to your engine hoist. You'll have to adjust the chain length several times so the taillamp panel doesn't interfere with the hoist arm as you lift the rear. Do not lift the body if the doors have been removed as the body will flex. Damage to the body will result.

14. Slowly raise the body high enough to position a 6 ft. length of 2x10 or 4x4 under the body and use 35 or 50 gallon drums to support the board under the body. Don't place the boards under the quarter panels, as damage will result to the sheetmetal. Lower the body onto the 2x10 or 4x4 and remove the chain. Now go to the front of the car, attach the S hooks to the firewall at the body bolt access holes and lift the front of the car with the hoist, moving the hoist rearwards as you lift to prevent the body from sliding forward on the rear 2x10 or 4x4. Once the front is high enough, again place a drum on each side of the car, slide a 6 ft. length of 2x10 or 4x4 under the car and lower the body. You can now roll the chassis out from under the body.

15. Before you remove anything from the chassis, take pictures—lots of pictures. Documenting everything on film is absolutely essential. Photograph line routing, positioning of components, any unusual markings, paint dabs or other details that will be destroyed as you dismantle the chassis and refinish it. It will be months before you reassemble the car, and chances are you won't remember how things appeared when you took the car apart.

Front suspension removal

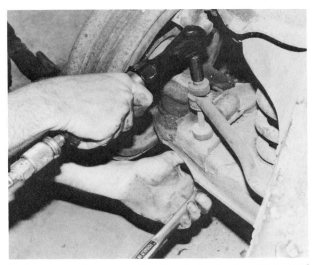

1. Loosen and remove the front shock absorbers, and then loosen and remove the sway bar end link kits.

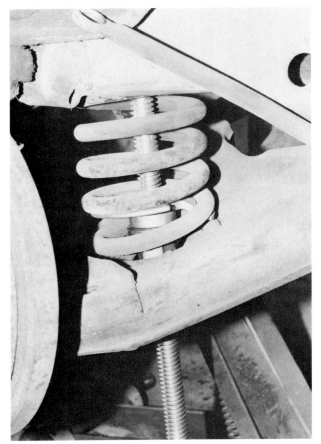

2. Use a coil spring compressor to remove the springs. Don't use chains or other devices, as they may break, causing the spring to fly out and cause personal injury. If you don't have a spring compressor, they are usually available from tool rental companies. Loaded coil springs are extremely dangerous, so use caution when working around them. To install the spring compressor, thread it through the spring and tighten. This will compress the spring. You can now safely remove the front brake drum, brake assembly and backing plates.

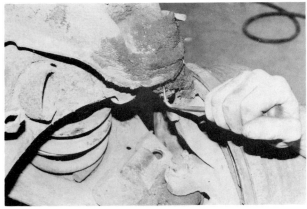

3. Remove the upper ball joint cotter key using a cotter key removal tool like this and loosen the upper ball joint nut. Do not remove the nut.

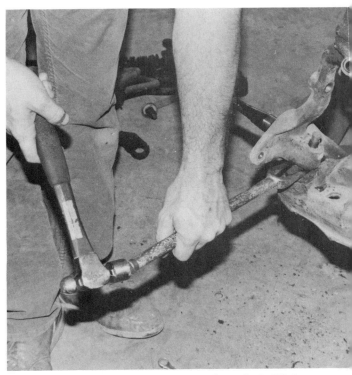

4. Remove the bottom ball joint nut and use the ball joint fork to loosen the ball joint from the spindle.

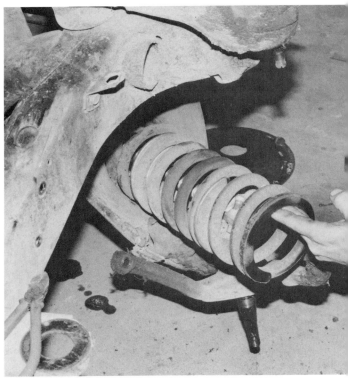

5. After the lower ball joint has been loosened from the spindle, let the control arm swing out of the way and remove the compressed coil spring.

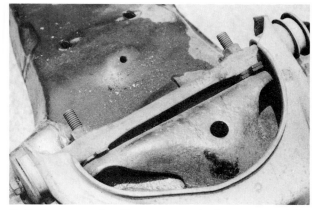

6. Before removing the upper control arms, count the number of shims and their location and record this information for reassembly. Now loosen and remove the upper control arm bushings and remove the upper control arm.

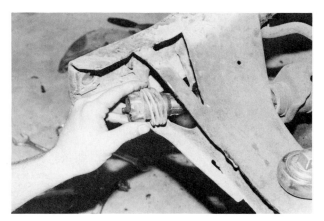

7. Loosen and remove the lower control arm bushings and nuts. This varies from car to car: some have bushings and shafts, some have shafts and nuts. After you have removed the nuts, remove the control arm.

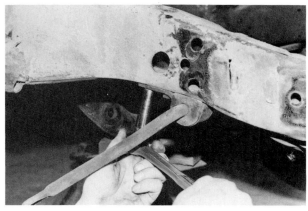

8. Remove the front sway bar bushing and bracket assemblies by unbolting them from the front frame rails.

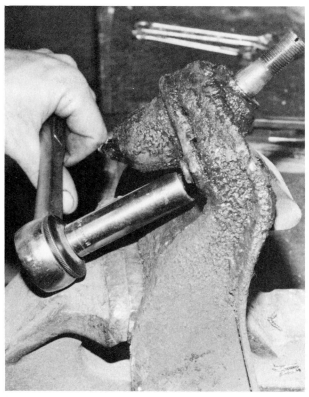

9. Remove the control arm bumper if so equipped. You can reuse the bumper if it's in good shape by bead blasting it and soaking it in protectorant. It will then look as good as new.

10. If the ball joints are original, they will be riveted to the control arm. Use an air chisel to remove the head of the rivet.

11. You can also remove the ball joint rivets by drilling through the head. Then you use a punch to drive the remainder of the rivet out.

Removing torsion bars

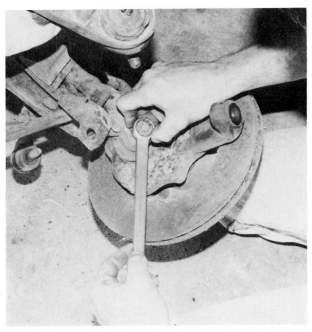

1. To disassemble Mopar front suspensions, begin by removing the front brake assembly following the same procedure outlined in the coil spring front suspension teardown.

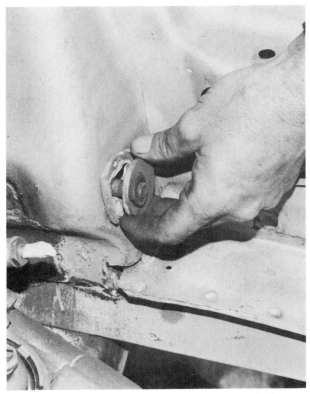

2. Unbolt and remove the upper control arm shaft nuts.

3. Remove the upper control arm shafts.

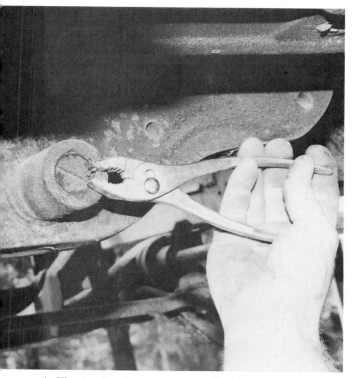

4. The torsion bars are secured with snap rings. Use a pair of pliers to remove the ring.

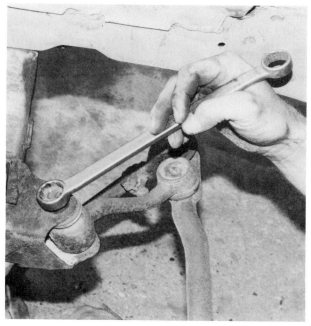

6. Now the idler arm and center link can be unbolted and removed.

5. Once the snap ring is removed, the torsion bar can be removed from the front suspension.

7. The engine crossmember is known as the K-member. It is bolted to each side of the body. Loosen the bolts. Place a hydraulic jack under the K-member. With an assistant helping to balance the K-member on the jack, remove all of the retaining bolts.

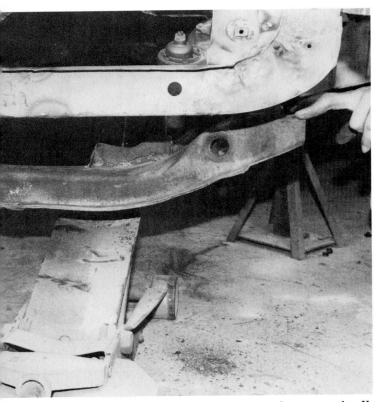

8. Now carefully lower the jack and remove the K-member for final disassembly.

Removing Mopar front suspensions

2. Drive out the upper control arm bushings by placing the control arm in a vise and hammering out the bushing.

1. To remove the upper ball joint, you will need a Chrysler ball joint socket. This tool is available from most parts houses and tool dealers. Remember to check which size ball joint you have, because these sockets come in two different sizes. The early models used one size, the later models another. Once you have the proper tool, loosen and remove the upper ball joint.

3. Use a chisel and split the lower control arm bushing. After it is split you will be able to remove it.

4. Remove the lower ball joint attaching bolts from the spindle and remove the lower ball joint.

Removing the steering linkage and steering box

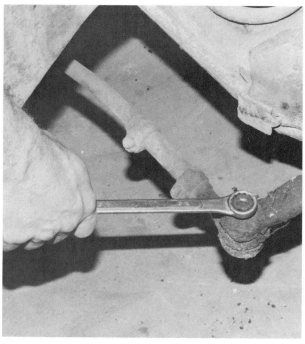

1. To remove the steering linkage, begin by loosening and removing the outer tie rod end nuts.

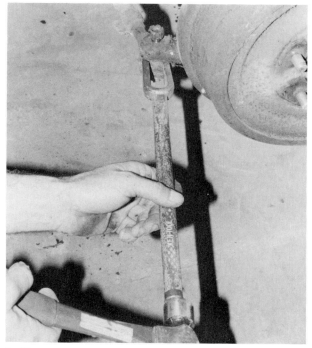

2. Use a tie rod fork to remove the tie rod end knuckle from the spindle arm.

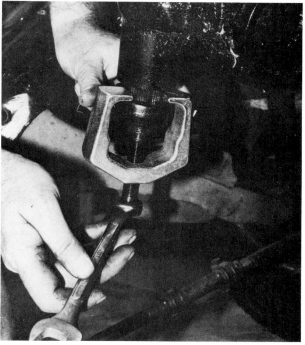

3. Remove the Pitman arm from the steering box. This may require the use of a Pitman arm puller, available from any parts house or tool rental store. Now remove the center link and the other tie rod end from the other spindle arm. Also remove the idler arm from the idler arm bracket. Now the whole steering assembly can be removed.

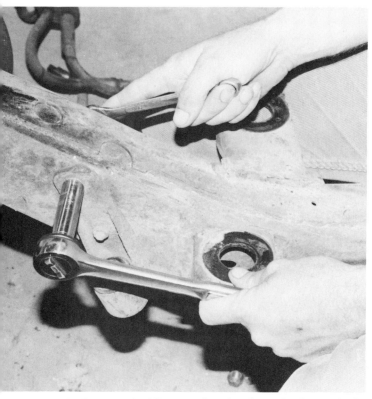

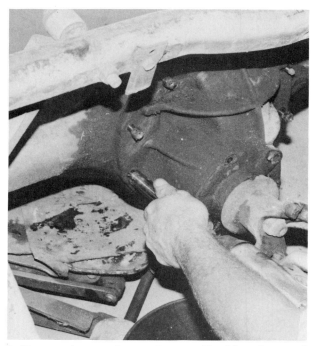

1. Remove the rear drums, shoes and backing plates and remove both axles. On cars with removable center sections, loosen and remove the center section nuts and remove the center section. On cars with an inspection cover, remove the axle keepers. Remove the axles and then pull out the gear assembly.

4. Remove the idler arm bracket from the frame. Make sure you keep track of the bolts and nuts because in some cases they are special-application nuts and bolts and difficult to replace.

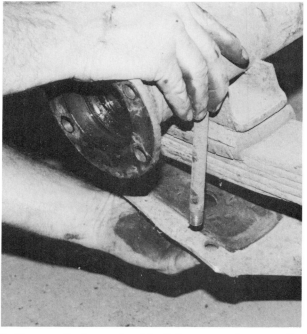

5. Remove the steering box. If the car is equipped with power steering, have plenty of rags handy, because as the box is removed it will probably leak fluid from the fitting holes. On GM boxes, fabricate a loop from the old power steering hoses and screw the fittings into the pump to eliminate fluid leakage. Keep track of the bolts because they are also special in most cases.

2. Remove the lower shock bolt. Loosen and remove the rear end U-bolts from both sides.

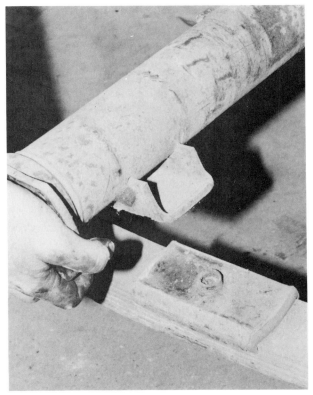

3. Now remove the axle housing from the rear springs.

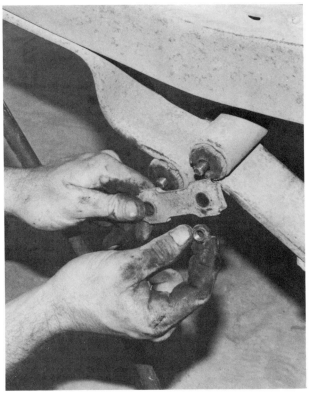

4. Loosen and remove the rear shackles.

5. Loosen and remove the front hanger out of the rear spring assembly.

6. Turn the spring on its side and slide it out of the front hanger.

Rear coil spring suspension removal

1. The four-link rear coil spring suspension uses upper and lower control arms to hold the rear axle in place. Use extreme care when working with coil springs, as they are under tension. Loosening the springs can cause them to fly out and cause personal injury.

2. Position a floorjack under the differential case and raise the rear suspension. Unbolt the upper control arms at the axle. Unbolt the upper shock absorber mounting bolts. Lower the floorjack to unload the coil springs.

3. Remove the coil springs and unbolt the shock absorbers at the lower mount. You may now remove the lower control arms from the axle and the frame. Unbolt the upper control arms from the frame.

4. Position the rear axle assembly on a sturdy set of jack stands and remove the brake drums, brake components, backing plates and axles. The control arm bushings can now be removed.

Brake and fuel line removal

1. Take pictures and make diagrams of all brake and fuel lines, how they route, which ones are wrapped and what type of clips are used and where they are located. Use a quality 35 mm camera with a good lens. Get in close and use a flash to eliminate any dark spots. After teardown, it will be months before you reassemble these components. Unless you possess a photographic memory, you won't recall where and how these components are routed and attached. The pictures allow you to document everything.

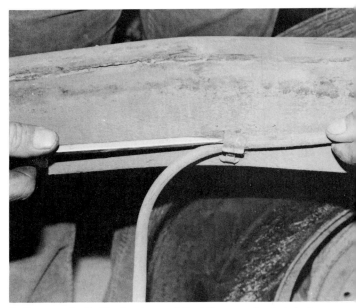

2. Remove both the brake and fuel lines and retaining clips routed along the frame rail. Make a diagram of each line, noting where it went and how. Also note how the clips were installed.

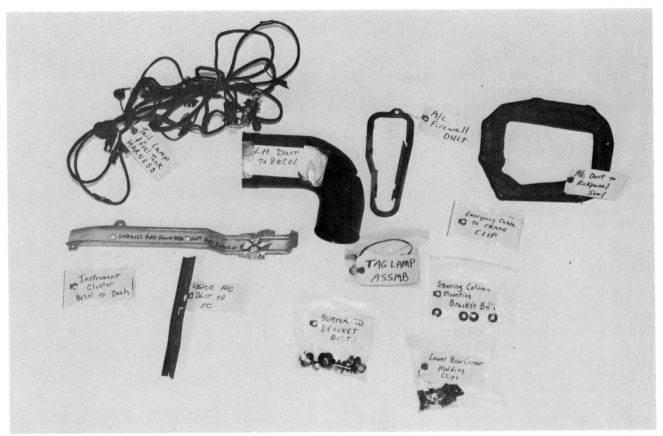

It's difficult to be too organized when undertaking a restoration project. There are thousands of pieces that go together in one way and one way only to make up a musclecar, and when you disassemble the car in the fall and reassemble it in the spring, it's too easy to forget where every last nut and bolt goes. Here's a sample of a well-organized disassembly job.

4

Engine, Transmission and Rear Axle Restoration

With the engine securely bolted to the engine stand, begin a total disassembly of all components. Carefully inspect those components that you'll be reinstalling. Many restorers make the mistake of cutting corners during the engine rebuild. Don't make that mistake. Plan to invest some money in the engine. Pulling the engine apart gives you the opportunity to upgrade engineering that the factory left out.

For example, if you plan on driving your car (especially if it will see some hard revs) ask your machine shop to install hardened exhaust valve seats. Cars built before 1971 were designed to run on leaded gasoline and are dependent on lead lubricating the valve seats. Without the lead, valve seat wear and damage are a possibility if the car will see any kind of hard service—and a few blasts down the drag strip to "see what she'll do" constitutes hard service. Under normal use, seat wear is negligible, however you may want to talk to your machine shop about installing hardened seats.

2. Remove and retain the timing chain cover as it's date coded.

1. If you decide to retain the original flywheel, have the machine shop resurface and balance it. Don't reuse the old flywheel bolts. Install new ones.

3. Plastic timing chains were used by some manufacturers. Any engine with high miles will have a worn out timing chain like this one.

6. This engine also suffered from a leaking head gasket. Check for burnt areas between the cylinders. The engine teardown is the ideal time for an autopsy, letting you know what will be needed during the rebuild.

4. Camshafts are also prone to wear. The lobes on this cam are extremely worn, as were the lifters.

Engine components to be checked, repaired or replaced:

Cylinder bore	Main bearings
Deck plane	Oil screen
Camshaft bore	Fuel pump
Camshaft	Oil plugs
Crankshaft journals	Oil passages in block
Timing chain	Pistons
Oil pickup	Rod bolts
Freeze plugs	Cam bearings
Distributor driveshaft	Pushrods
Connecting rods	Rod bearings
Wrist pins	Oil pump
Rings	Water pump
Lifters	

Taking your engine to the machine shop

Choosing a machine shop is a difficult and serious decision. Which machine shop you use depends on where you live: you may have one or ten shops to chose from. If you belong to a local car club, it's a good idea to ask your fellow club members for recommendations. Check if any shops specialize in your type of engine—Pontiac, Ford, Chevy, Mopar and so on. Whatever you do, don't shop price, and try to stay away from machine shops located behind parts stores, because you'll get what you pay for. These shops tend to do general work and having them rebuild your engine can be a disaster.

Before ordering machine work, decide exactly what kind of service your engine will see. Will it be used strictly for show, will it be trailered, or will it see average driving? Since most musclecars of the era had an advertised compression ratio of 10.0:1 or higher, consider lowering the ratio to survive on today's low-octane fuels. This will require replacing the pistons with lower-compression units or having the machine shop mill the piston tops to lower the compression. If you plan on driving the car,

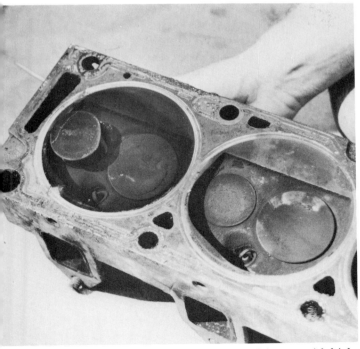

5. Because musclecars were designed for use with high-octane fuels, burned valves are often a problem. Hard use on low-octane fuel generally causes this condition. Switching to stainless-steel valves is the best solution.

7. Big ends of connecting rods should be magnafluxed, and checked for size and alignment during a quality engine rebuild.

8. Don't skimp during an engine rebuild—especially on the top end work. Valve guides should be replaced and a valve job performed.

9. Balancing engine components is important to engine performance and reliability.

consider having the machine shop install hardened exhaust valve seats. A forged, replacement-style piston is recommended with all compression ratios from 9.5:1 or higher. Forged pistons are much stronger and can withstand detonation better than cast units.

Depending on the tools available to you or your engine building experience, you should decide how your engine will arrive and depart from the machine shop. If you have the tools and experience to completely disassemble the engine, you can save some money on the machine shop bill. If you don't have the experience and the necessary tools such as micrometers, dial indicators or balancer installers, it would be to your advantage to have the machine shop completely reassemble the engine.

Don't rely on a buddy who has been working down at the Ford dealer to put your Dodge engine back together. If a mistake is made on reassembly, the machine shop will not warranty the repair. Most reputable machine shops will warranty complete engines for at least one year or 12,000 miles.

When you take your engine to the machine shop, there are some specific things you should ask for. The bores and pistons should be checked for flatness and the align bore checked. The crankshaft should be magnafluxed, checked for size and straightness. If necessary, the shop will grind the crank. The big ends of the rods should be magnafluxed, and checked for size and alignment. The cylinder heads should be disassembled, magnafluxed and checked for flatness. The guides and valves should be checked and the springs should also be tested.

Have the attaching engine parts such as the oil pan, front cover and intake manifold degreased. Their equipment can do in minutes what it would take you hours of scrubbing to do. Remember that a concours restoration should not have any aluminum engine parts or accessory brackets sand blasted as it will destroy the natural finish and texture—and cost points on judging.

Once all the parts are checked out by the shop, ask for a parts and labor estimate, predicated on the amount of reassembly you want the shop to perform. For a twenty-year-old musclecar engine that was built for high performance, expect to spend $1,500 to $2,500 for a complete, stock-type rebuild with assembly.

Follow the advice given by the machine shop on which parts should be rebuilt or replaced. A rule of thumb in most machine shops is all blocks require boring, decking and align honing. All rods need bolts and rebuilding, most cranks need turning and all head surfaces need surfacing. They will also recommend the guides be replaced and a valve job be performed.

It's a good idea to have the block finish-honed with torque plates installed. This creates the same stress on the block as when the cylinder head is bolted on. Many restorers have the misconception this is a process reserved for race engines only. It's an essential part of *any* engine rebuild.

If the connecting rods need to be rebuilt, this is the time to replace the rod bolts and nuts. If it is done after the rods are rebuilt, the big ends will distort and have to be rebuilt again. If the pistons are to be replaced, the engine should be balanced. Undue engine stress can be caused if pistons of different weights from the originals (forged in place of cast, for example) are installed.

Bronze valve guides will wear better than iron and should be considered an option in your engine rebuild, as should hardened exhaust valve seats to be compatible with today's low-octane fuel. If the exhaust valves are to be replaced, use stainless-steel replacements. If not already equipped, the cylinder heads should be machined and fitted for a positive type of valve seal, such as teflon or rubber-teflon type. If a higher-than-stock-lift camshaft is being considered, the valve springs should be checked for coil bind and retainer-to-guide clearance and the seal should be checked.

By all means have even a stock replacement camshaft degreed when installed in the engine. Tolerances in cam and crank gear machining alone are enough to throw off the camshaft timing and it is important that the cam timing events happen as designed to piston placement and crankshaft rotation.

Armed with this knowledge, good machine work, quality parts and attention to detail on assembly, you will have all and more of the power that was designed into your musclecar's engine by the factory.

Engine finishing

If you decide to reassemble the engine yourself, follow the factory service manual for step-by-

10. Finishing the engine and components in the proper colors is essential to a concours restoration.

step instructions and torque specifications. There are also a variety of books available that show how to reassemble engines, available from Motorbooks International. These books will specify the necessary parts, tools and techniques needed for engine reassembly.

While the engine has been at the machine shop or once you've completed the rebuild, you can begin refinishing the external engine parts such as intake and exhaust manifolds, attaching nuts and bolts, brackets, pulleys, bellhousing, alternator, power steering pump and other components.

Parts like aluminum brackets, alternator housings and aluminum intake manifolds should be bead blasted and given a coat of dry clear to preserve the finish. Glass-bead blast other parts like brackets and pulleys. Some brackets, like fuel filter brackets, are zinc-chromate in appearance; chrome shops can apply a zinc-chromate plating to these parts. Most attaching brackets are either painted engine color, like the throttle cable bracket, or sixty-percent gloss black, like the alternator bracket. Pulleys are also painted sixty-percent gloss black.

Air cleaners are either chrome plated or painted sixty-percent gloss black. Those cars with Ram Air or other air induction systems usually used a foam rubber seal, which are available from a variety of reproduction companies such as Year One (Box 2-23, Tucker, GA 30085).

We recommend sending out your carburetor for rebuilding and refinishing to specialists like Carbs Unlimited (19332 Briarwood, Mt. Clemens, MI 48043) or the Holley Custom Shop (Holley Replacement Parts Division, 601 Space Park No., Goodlettsville, TN 37072). Not only can they correctly rebuild the carburetor, but they can replate the air horn and throttle body to duplicate the original factory finish. If you want to refinish and reassemble the carburetor yourself, send the air horn and throttle body to the chrome shop for zinc-chromate plating. They will come back with a shiny, rainbow appearance, which can be dulled down by spraying on dry clear. One thing to remember is that gasoline will eat away the clear, so it will be necessary to touch up the carburetors on a regular basis.

Preparing and painting the engine

1. Begin by taping over or stuffing rags in all open holes such as the valvetrain, intake and exhaust ports, and coolant passages. Install the oil and freeze plugs and screw in the old sending switches. Don't put on a junk set of valve covers to cover the rocker arm assemblies. Using old covers prevents paint from reaching the edges of the head. Rust can then appear and stain your painted heads and intake.

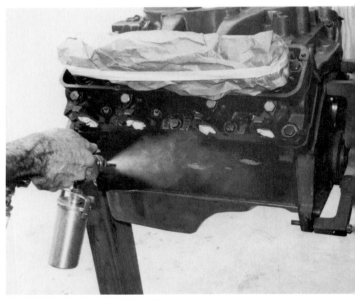

2. Use either Prep-Sol, Pre Kleeno, tar and wax remover or lacquer thinner to wash down the engine before painting. Do this at least three times. After you have sprayed the engine with one of the above do not touch it with your bare hands. Oils in your skin left on the metal surface will cause poor paint adhesion and it may lift off.

3. Plastic-kote is the leading producer of engine paint, and their products duplicate exactly the proper engine color. Paint is manufactured in batches, which means that pigments vary from batch to batch. For this reason, paint manufacturers number the batches. The batch number can be found on the bottom of the can. When you purchase your paint, buy at least six cans, and check the underside of each can to ensure they all contain paint from the same batch. Buy enough for painting the block, heads and intake, as well as the attaching parts that are also painted engine color. The remainder will be used for matching touchup work after restoration and the car is driven and shown.

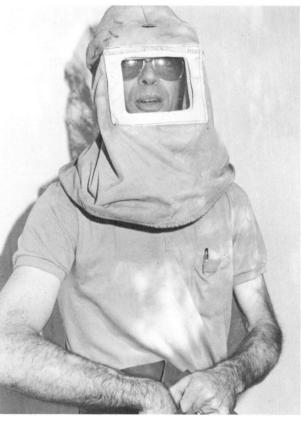

4. Apply the paint using light, even coats. Spraying on heavy coats will cause runs and paint buildup in corners and crevices. Vary your spray angles: top to bottom, bottom to top, side to side. Remember to check all corners and crevices, especially around the freeze plugs. It's also recommended to use a drop light to check for uniform paint coverage. You want an even coat all over— no high and low or dark and light spots.

5. Allow the paint to dry between coats. Don't forget to get behind the harmonic balancer, up under the oil pan rails and valley cover. If necessary, paint the intake manifold off the car to reach areas not accessible with the intake on the engine. Clean and spray all the engine parts that are the same color as the block, following the same procedures for painting the block and heads.

Restoring exhaust manifolds

1. Refinishing the exhaust manifolds starts by sandblasting them. Always wear protective gear like a hood and heavy gloves when sandblasting.

2. Do your sandblasting outside because the sand will get everywhere. Use a gravity- or pressure-type sandblaster or a bucket-feed sandblast unit. Make sure you have a water separator on your compressor because wet sand won't spray well and doesn't remove surface rust. Don't try to beadblast exhaust manifolds. Beadblasting leaves the surface too smooth and the stainless-steel paint does not adhere properly. Sandblasting leaves a much rougher surface finish that paint can adhere to.

4. Eastwood's Stainless Steel Coating provides a correct finish and is resistant to high engine temperatures.

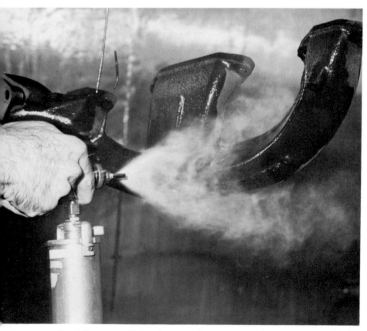

3. After sandblasting, make sure you have gotten all the sand particles out of the manifolds. Use lacquer thinner to clean the exhaust manifolds. Do not touch the manifolds after you've cleaned them.

5. Pour the stainless steel paint directly from the can into the paint jar. Use 55–60 lb. of pressure at the gun for spraying.

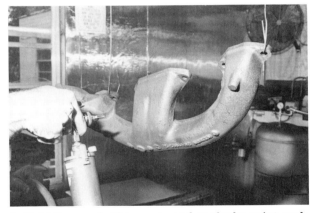

6. Hold the gun 6–12 in. away and apply the paint, making sure you get coverage in all the corners and on both sides. Apply thin coats, allowing ten minutes drying time between applications. Four or five coats will complete the job.

7. The completed exhaust manifold will have an even appearance that won't burn off. If touch up is necessary once the manifold is installed, it can be done with a small brush.

Refinishing nuts and bolts

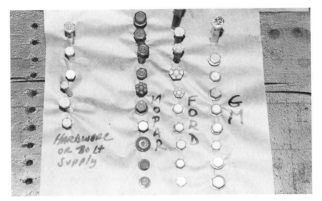

1. There is a considerable difference between Mopar, Ford and GM engine bolts and common graded bolts. The correct method for refinishing the bolts, as well as cables, brackets, driveshaft and transmission yokes is to use Eastwood's Spray Gray or Seymours Stainless Steel paint. Both are sold in spray cans and are easy to use.

2. Make sure you have thoroughly cleaned the bolts before spraying. Beadblast or wirebrush each and every bolt, bracket, cable, anything that you are repainting. Then clean with Prep-Sol or lacquer thinner before spraying. Don't think you can beadblast or wirebrush bolts, brackets and other parts and then simply shoot them with clear. This method will not preserve them from rusting. The steel will rust under the clear and then appear as a brown stain running all over your paint. The only way to cure this is to beadblast the clear off and start the entire process all over again. Save yourself a lot of time and aggravation by doing it right the first time.

3. Set the bolts in some type of retainer, such as a large board with various size holes drilled in it so the bolts will stand up when painted. Spray the bolts using Eastwood's Spray Gray or Seymours Stainless Steel paint. Make sure you spray in all directions to get even coverage. Use a catalyzed clear to give the bolts, brackets and other painted parts a dull sheen. Spray the clear dry, adjusting the spray gun to flow more air pressure and less paint. Practice on a few items before you try it on a finished product. The clear will protect your Spray Gray-covered parts from most chips caused by installation. Spray the clear from all directions just as the Spray Gray was applied.

Restoring engine components

1. If the engine has an aluminum intake manifold, bead blast it and then blow out all bead particles from the intake.

2. Spark plug brackets are refinished by bead blasting, then taping the end that attaches to the engine. Dip the other end in black Plastic Dip, available from Eastwood. The Plastic Dip looks exactly like the factory rubber coating.

3. The starter and solenoid are painted gloss black, as are any attaching brackets. On some cars, the brackets are natural metal appearance. Remember to use the correct number of shims to match the starter to the flywheel gears.

4. It's little details that make a restoration a show winner. Heater and vacuum hoses should have the correct markings and be routed correctly in their brackets.

5. Use the correct plug wires, air filter and coil. These are clearly marked and will add points to your restoration.

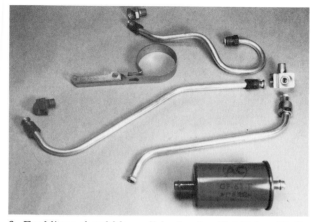

6. Fuel lines should be polished using Met-Pol or Mothers to remove scratches. Brass fuel fittings should be cleaned and the correct fuel filter installed.

7. When installing the carburetors, carefully bolt them down, taking care not to damage the finish on the bolts and screws. Install the fuel lines and fittings, using a line wrench so as not to round off the soft brass fittings. Note small detail items, such as throttle clips and return springs. Make sure these are painted or plated properly. Many small parts are plated in black cadmium instead of painted black.

8. Many carburetors have identification numbers stamped on them, such as this Holley 4174. There are also numbers stamped into the carburetor, such as date codes and part numbers.

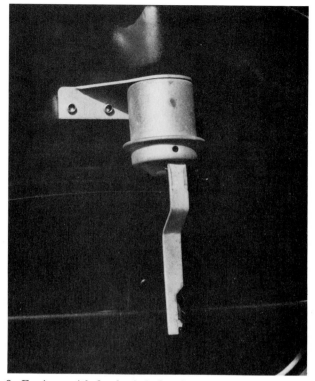

9. Engines with fresh air induction systems often use a solenoid to open a seal or scoop. These solenoids are natural metal in appearance and should be refinished with Eastwood's Spray Gray or Seymours Stainless Steel paint.

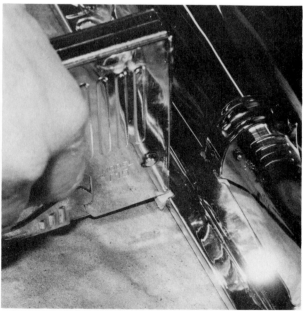

10. Early Ford valve cover gaskets were held in place by staples, not glue. To install, set the gasket in place and, using a heavy-duty stapler, staple a ⅜ in. staple across the valve cover tab.

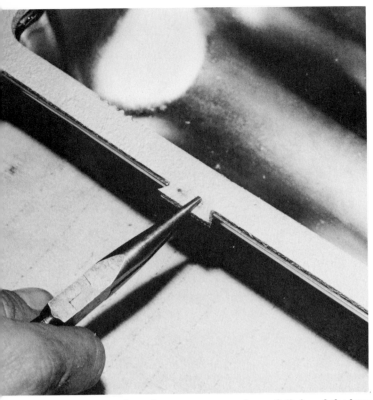

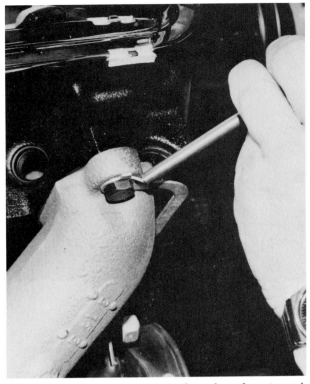

11. Turn the valve cover over and carefully bend the legs of the staples in toward each other.

13. Some engines use a locking tab on the exhaust manifold bolts. Depending on the engine and manufacturer, some are a combination lock and some are a single tab.

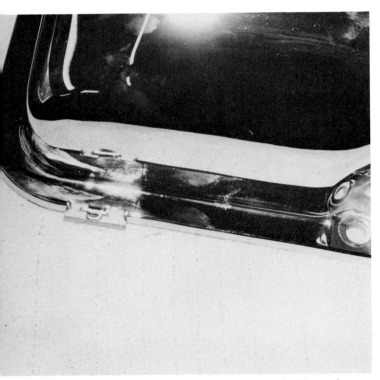

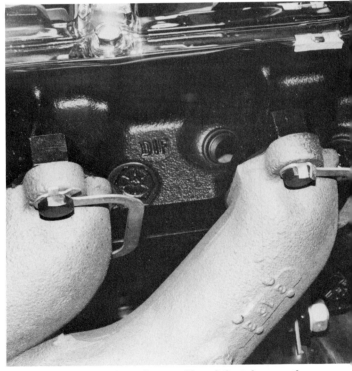

12. The finished product looks exactly like a factory installation.

14. Place the lock tab in place and bend the tabs over the bolt.

Rebuilding distributors

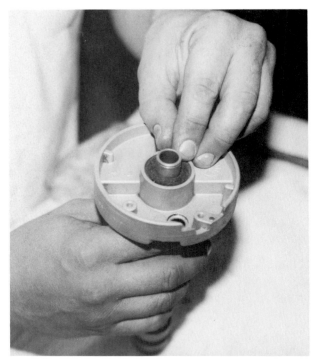

1. One of the components you will be rebuilding is the distributor. After disassembly, bead blast the distributor housing. Most GM cars have a red band around the lower housing tube that must be carefully removed and cleaned before the housing can be blasted. Depending on manufacturer, the housing will either need to be painted with Spray Gray, Stainless Steel or gloss black.

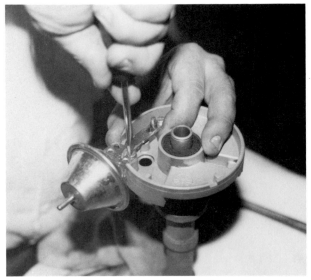

2. Install the felt washer and attach a new vacuum advance unit. Now insert the primary wire through the bottom of the housing.

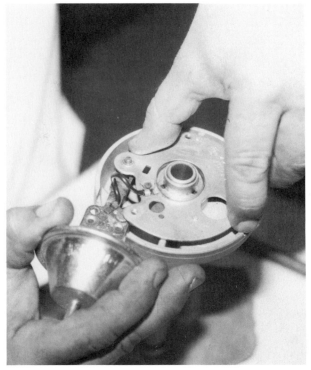

3. Install the distributor mounting plate, attaching the ground wire to the vacuum advance diaphragm link.

4. The distributor mounting plate is retained by a ring that snaps in the groove around the top of the housing tube.

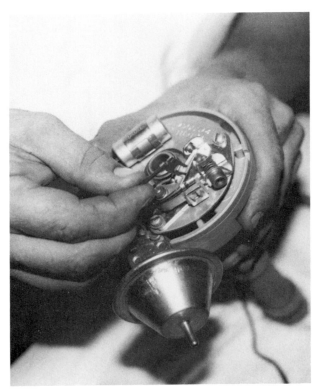

5. Install the points and condenser.

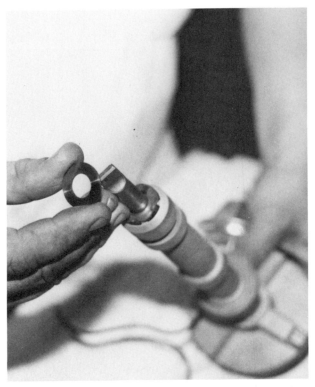

7. Install the distributor housing-to-shaft lower washer and retainer.

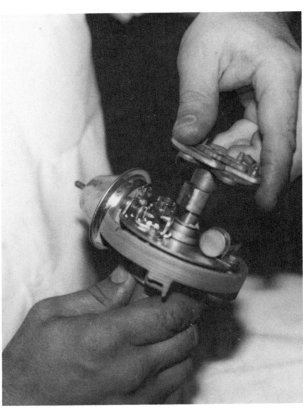

6. Apply lubricant to the distributor shaft and slip it into place.

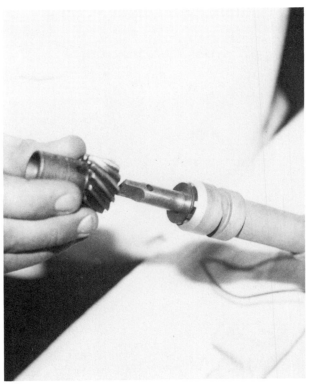

8. Install the distributor drive gear.

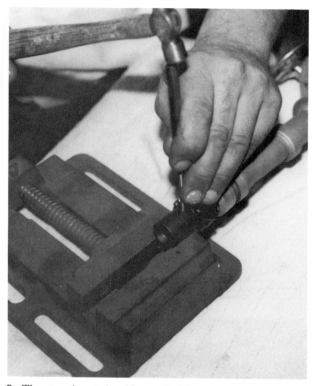

9. The gear is retained by a pin. Place the shaft in a vise, insert the pin and tap it into place.

1. After draining any remaining fluid, begin disassembling the power steering pump for refinishing by removing the steering pump pulley retaining nut.

10. After adjusting the points, install the rotor and snap the distributor cap into place. Don't forget to install the distributor gasket or seal on the shaft housing.

2. On some units, the pulley can be removed by carefully using a breaker bar. You'll need a pulley remover for pumps with tapered shafts.

3. After the pulley is removed, carefully take off the keyway. Check it for wear or grooves. If it's marked or worn, replace it.

5. Check the shaft seal. If it is worn or leaking, replace it.

4. Remove the bracket or brace.

6. Cap off all of the hose fittings and openings. This will prevent fluid from leaking out of the unit.

7. Now thoroughly clean the pump, pulley, attaching bolts and bracket in the parts washer. Make sure you keep an eye out for any assembly line markings. If any are present, make notes of their location and appearance so they can be duplicated when the pump is reassembled.

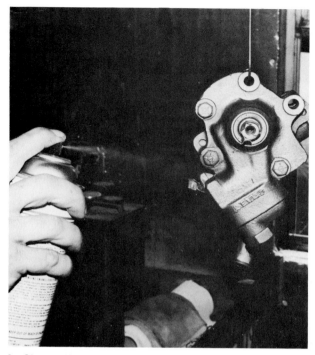

9. Clean off all of the glass beads and hang the parts for refinishing. Cast-iron pumps (Ford) are usually painted with Spray Gray. GM and Chrysler two-piece pumps are usually thirty-percent gloss black, and mid- to late-sixties Ford two-piece pumps are painted a special Ford Power Steering Pump Blue. It's available from most Mustang parts dealers.

8. Now beadblast the pump housing, pulley, bracket and attaching bolts.

10. Depending on manufacturer, the pulleys are either natural or thirty-percent gloss black in appearance.

95

11. Most brackets and braces are thirty-percent gloss or semi-gloss black.

12. Any parts that are painted with Spray Gray should be sprayed with a coat of dry clear.

13. Don't forget to refinish the attaching bolts. They should receive a coat of Spray Gray or thirty-percent gloss black, depending on manufacturer.

14. Before reassembly, refer to your notes and then duplicate the paint markings and codes you found on the power steering pump before you refinished it.

15. Reassemble the pump unit by installing the bracket or brace onto the pump.

16. Reinstall the keyway and then place the pulley onto the pump. Note the paint dab placed on the finished pump.

17. Tighten the pulley bolt to the torque specifications found in the factory service manual. The pump assembly is now ready to be installed on the engine.

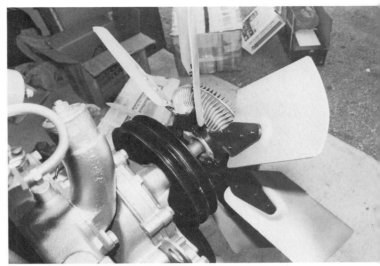

18. The pulleys and balancer for the crank and the water pump pulley are usually painted thirty-percent gloss black by the manufacturer. Clutch fans are sometimes finished with black hubs, natural blades and natural-finished clutch assemblies. Seymour Stainless Steel paint provides an excellent finish for the fan blades.

19. When no clutch fan is used, the fan is painted thirty-percent gloss black. All straps or braces supporting the alternator and power steering pump are usually painted thirty-percent gloss black, however later models use aluminum brackets for mounting the power steering pump and emissions pumps. These should be glass beaded and coated with dry clear. Alternators are date coded. It is possible to repair your alternator yourself by disassembling and glass beading the case. Alternator rebuilding kits are available from parts houses. They consist of diodes and other components that should be replaced. If you don't want to tackle an alternator rebuild, there are many companies that provide the service. Remember to have them rebuild your alternator, not exchange it. You want to keep the correctly dated alternator for authenticity.

Transmissions

Manual and automatic transmissions are complex mechanisms. It's recommended that you farm out the rebuilding of the transmission to an experienced transmission shop. A rebuild will be guaranteed for at least 12,000 miles. Once you get the transmission back from the shop, you can refinish the case and apply any paint dabs or codes.

1. A Mopar A–833 transmission, which was enclosed in a cast-iron case. To duplicate the original cast-iron appearance, you can respray the case and tailshaft with Eastwood's Spray Gray.

2. Eastwood's Aluma Blast spray paint works well on aluminum to replicate the original finish. It also is good for restoring a bright cadmium finish.

Transmissions vary greatly between manufacturers. Some use aluminum cases, such as the GM Muncie series, while some have cast-iron cases, like the Mopar A–833. Others use a combination of cast iron and aluminum. All must be detailed accordingly.

If you are not going to disassemble the transmission, start by draining it and then thoroughly cleaning the exterior with mineral spirits or Prep-Sol. If it's cast iron, use a steel-bristle brush to clean it. If the case is aluminum, use a nylon-bristle brush to avoid scratches.

If the case is cast iron, you can respray it and the tailshaft with Eastwood Spray Gray. Make sure you spray from side to side and top to bottom for complete coverage. You will also have to detail all of the bolts. To do this, remove every other one on the side or top cover and every other one that retains the tailshaft to the case. Clean, degrease and refinish to the correct color. Most of these bolts were either natural steel or cadmium plated. For a natural steel appearance, use Eastwood's Spray Gray. After they are dry, reinstall them and then remove the other remaining bolts and refinish them the same way. Now reapply any factory paint marks or stencils. After they have dried, apply a coat of dry clear to the exterior transmission case.

If the transmission is aluminum and cast iron, you'll have to tape off the aluminum case and spray just the tailshaft. Remove and refinish the bolts as outlined above. Now apply any factory paint codes and apply a coat of dry clear to the entire transmission.

If the transmission has been disassembled, you'll be able to sandblast or bead blast the case and tailshaft. If the transmission is cast iron, sandblast the case and tailshaft. If it's aluminum, bead blast the case and tailshaft. If the transmission has both cast-iron and aluminum sections, bead blast the aluminum and sandblast the cast iron. After you have finished, make sure you clean the inside of the transmission case and tailshaft thoroughly. When it's clean, refinish them as outlined above, then reassemble and dry clear the entire transmission exterior.

Automatic transmissions should be checked by a competent transmission shop. Make sure they inspect the transmission thoroughly, as well as the torque converter. Tell the shop you will detail the transmission case after it is assembled. Instruct them to make sure to clean the case and pan thoroughly so it can be refinished. Also ask for an extra pan gasket. When you get the transmission back,

3. Most Ford and Mopar manual transmissions were coded by the factory by using paint dabs and letter codes.

4. Restoring the factory paint dabs and letter codes is all part of a thorough restoration. Make notes and take photographs of the transmission markings before refinishing so you have a record for the restoration later.

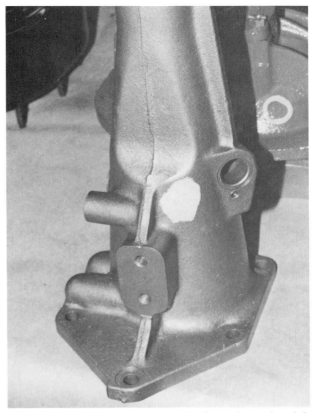

5. Most transmissions also received a color paint dab code on the tailshaft to identify which speedometer gear was used.

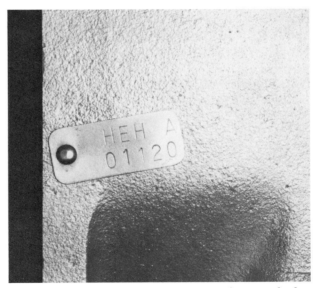

6. There are several codes either stamped or attached to the transmission. Most manual transmissions had the VIN sequence numbers stamped into one of the ears or collar. To identify transmission type, application and date code, others received a tag bolted to the side cover or an assembly bolt. Automatic transmissions usually have a plate on the side with the same type of information.

set it up so that you can remove the pan and refinish it and the pan retaining bolts. Most pans are either thirty-percent gloss black or natural. For a natural metal appearance, use Seymours Stainless Steel paint, then dry clear for protection.

Once the bolts are refinished, reinstall the pan and the new gasket and clear the transmission case, which should have a natural metal appearance. Remember, automatic transmissions also have paint markings and identification tags that need to be restored.

When you take your automatic transmission to the rebuild shop, make sure they understand you don't want an exchange transmission. If your transmission is original, the numbers on the identification tag will match the car. You don't want to lose it in an exchange. If you get an exchange transmission, it could be from any year or model that also used the same transmission as your car. For example, the M40 GM Turbo Hydra-matic was used in all GM divisions for a number of years. Your 1970 GS Buick could end up with the M40 out of a 1975 Impala, and the numbers won't match.

Hurst shifter and linkage rebuilding

Most stick-shift musclecars were equipped with Hurst shifters. Minor rebuilds of the shifter mechanism can be performed, allowing you to clean the components, lubricate them and install new bushings. Better yet, you can send your entire Hurst shifter to Hurst for a total teardown and rebuild. For around $35, Hurst will replace worn parts, align the neutral gate and check the shifter for operation. Any extra parts or rechroming requires additional charge. The shifter comes back to you as tight as the day Mr. Hurst built it. For more information, contact the Hurst Performance Division of Mr. Gasket Company (8700 Brookpark Road, Cleveland, OH 44129-6899).

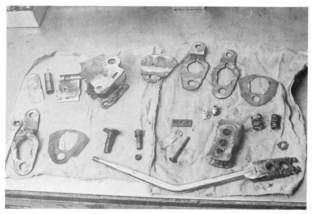

1. Before: The Hurst shifter after teardown . . .

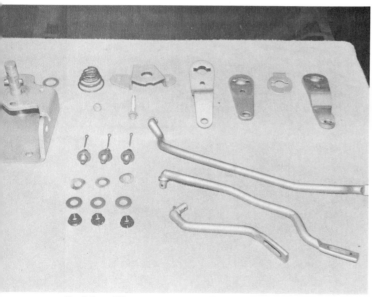

2. After: If you own a non-Hurst unit, or you want to do a minor rebuild of the Hurst unit, disassemble it, have any parts rechromed, plated and painted. Here all the components are laid out before reassembly.

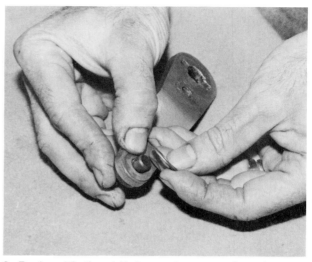

3. Begin with the shift levers, because when they are installed on the mechanism, it can be difficult to install the shift rod attaching studs. Place a washer on the shaft.

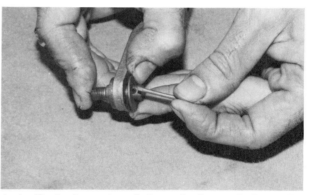

4. A clip is then pinned through the stud above the washer to secure it.

5. Line up the shift lever and the shift mechanism shaft and slide the lever into place. Remember to apply plenty of lubricant to the shaft for smooth operation. Hurst offers an excellent shifter grease, however Lubriplate will also work well.

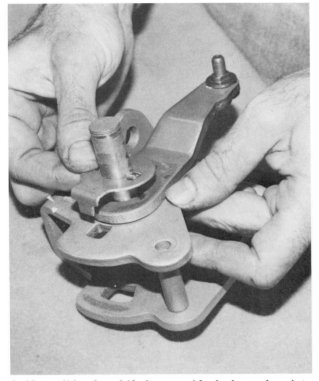

6. Now slide the shift lever guide lock washer into place—don't force it. Make sure the mechanisms are well lubricated.

8. With all the shift levers in place, you can now install the shift lever retaining plate and bolt it into place.

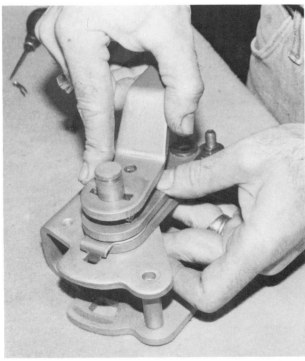

7. Slide the next lever into place and then the final lever. On a four-speed shifter, make certain you install the levers in the correct sequence.

9. Install the tension spacer, the retaining washer and the snap ring onto the mechanism shaft.

10. Install the nuts to the ends of the shifter levers. The shifter is now ready for installation on the tailshaft of the transmission. Some shifters are attached to a shifter mounting plate. This plate is usually aluminum. To refinish, bead blast it and spray with clear and mount it to the tailshaft.

Ford T-handle four-speed shifter rebuilding

Replacement parts for Ford T-handle shifters have never been available, and when the internal reverse lockout cable snapped or the T-handle broke, the only solution was to go find another shift lever assembly. There is, however, a simple way of repairing the T-handle. It requires having several old shift levers on hand to supply the necessary replacement parts. This repair procedure also applies to other makes like Mopar and Chevrolet that used the T-handle-style shift lever.

1. To remove the cable, spring, washer, T-handle and collar, this pawl must be heated and then removed.

2. Place the shift lever in a vise and grip the pawl with a pair of needle-nose vise grips. Apply heat to the center of the pawl. While heat is applied, pull the pawl up and out of the shifter. Run water over the pawl to cool it so it can be handled without burning your hands.

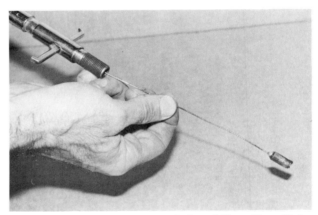

3. After the pawl is removed the shift cable will be exposed. Push it down using a thin, flat-blade screwdriver or an icepick. You can now remove the cable.

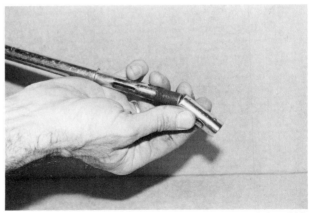

4. With the cable out, slide the T-handle out of the shift lever collar and take the collar off the end of the lever.

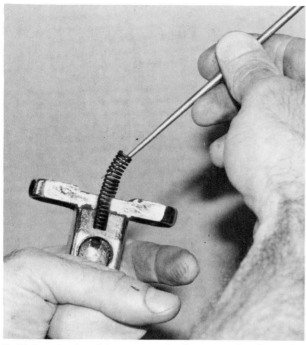

5. Using the icepick, remove the lower spring from the bottom of the lever. The spring seats to a washer that will fall out when the lever is tapped on the workbench. Don't lose this washer; it keeps the lower pawl reverse lockout spring from going up into the lever.

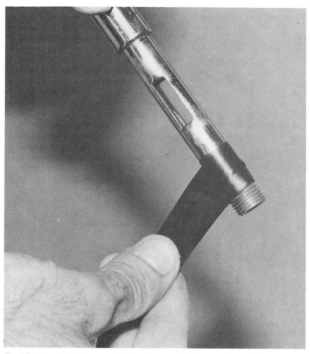

7. If you need to send the lever off for rechroming, cover the threads on the shift handle with electrical tape. This protects the threads from chroming. By not taping the threads, the chrome would have to be removed from the threads, causing the chrome to chip, peel and ruin the nylon bushing in the collar.

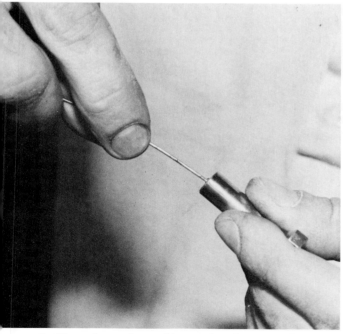

6. Clean the spring, cable, pawl and washer. Flush the old grease out of the lever tube (don't use solvent in the lockout collar). Polish the pawl and cable with a Scotch-Brite pad or wire wheel. Work the polished cable into the pawl to make sure it slips in and out smoothly.

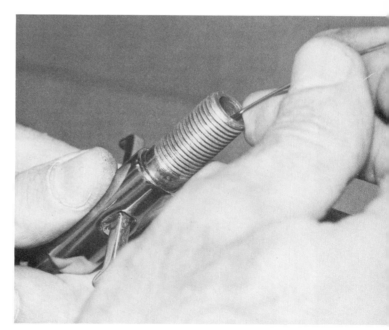

8. To reassemble, install the shift collar and T-handle first. Feed the cable with the anchor end facing the top of the lever through both and then out from the bottom of the shifter. Pull on the T-handle: if it won't pull out, the cable is properly installed.

103

9. Now push the cable down until the anchor end bottoms against the T-handle. The bare end of the cable will now be visible at the bottom of the shift lever.

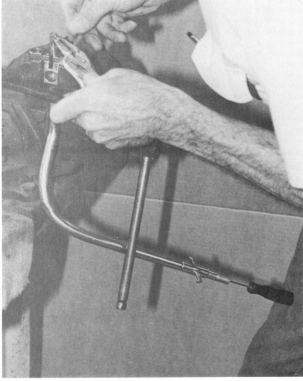

10. Have a helper use a screwdriver to keep the cable anchor from dropping out of the top of the shift lever while the unit is upside down in the vise. If you don't have a helper, push the screwdriver into the shift lever with your knee as shown.

11. Work the washer over the cable into the housing.

12. Then drop the spring over the cable onto the washer.

13. Drop the pawl back into the lever, making sure the top lays below the surface of the bottom of the lever. Heat the pawl and braze the cable into place.

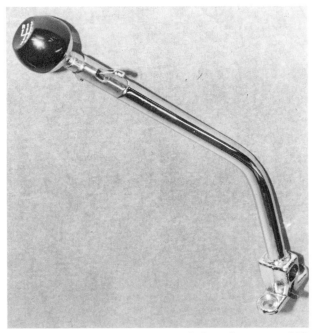

14. Polish the lever assembly and thread on your shift ball. The shift lever will now be ready to install in the car later on.

Driveshaft rebuilding

1. If you're using the driveshaft out of another car the same make and model as yours, have it balanced by your machine shop. Balancing won't be necessary if you're using the original driveshaft. Remove the universal joints and sandblast the driveshaft. After you've blasted the shaft, clean it by spraying with Prep-Sol or lacquer thinner. Then apply Spray Gray or Stainless Steel paint to the driveshaft. After you have finished painting it in one direction, turn it over and spray it again. You'd be surprised how many areas you miss if you don't do this. If your car has a black driveshaft, spray it with sixty-percent gloss black.

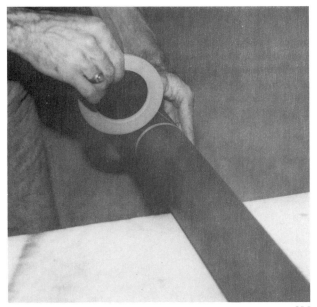

2. If your car has paint codes on the driveshaft, use 3M Fine Line ¼ or ½ in. masking tape to line off the areas that will have the stripe codes. Color codes and locations are usually listed in your factory service, parts or assembly manual.

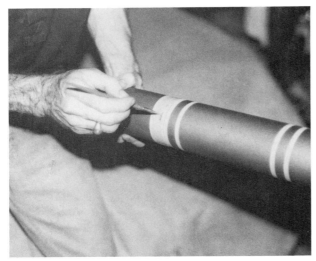

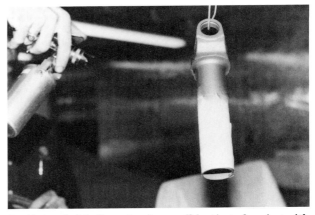

5. Also refinish the yokes by sandblasting, cleaning with Prep-Sol and painting. Depending on manufacturer, the yokes will either be sixty-percent gloss black or natural metal in appearance, which you will duplicate by spraying it with Spray Gray or Stainless Steel paint and then with the dry clear.

3. Mix the color needed and paint the stripes. Sign Painter's 1 Shot Lettering Enamel paint is excellent for reproducing the stripes. Once the paint has dried, carefully remove the tape.

Rear axle refinishing and reassembly

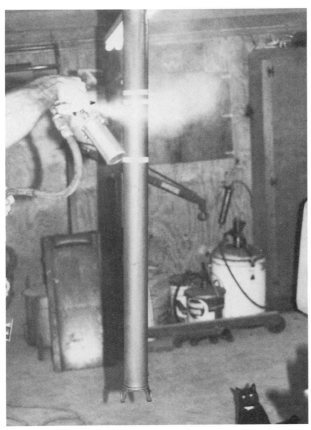

4. Now clear the driveshaft using a catalyzed clear. Spray the clear dry for a dull sheen. Spray from top to bottom. As soon as the clear gets tacky, turn the driveshaft around 180 degrees and respray for total coverage. Remember to use more air than paint to produce a dull sheen.

1. Disassemble the rear axle assembly by draining the differential and removing the cover. If you removed the rear axle as one assembly, remove the front hangers from the springs and remove the springs from the axle. Consult your factory service manual for teardown instructions regarding removal of the axle retaining clips (if so equipped) and other information on disassembling the gears. Remove the pinion nut and take off the companion flange. Remove the axle shafts by unbolting the axle flange nuts (as used on Chrysler products). Inspect the rear for any factory paint dabs, codes or markings and note them. Once all the parts have been removed from the rear assembly, sandblast and refinish. Most rear assemblies are painted completely semi-gloss black, sixty-percent gloss black or high-gloss black.

2. On 1960–1972 Fords, the rear end center is painted red oxide primer. Use a non-sanding primer, such as Ditzler Ferrochrome DPE-1202, for ease of application and finish.

3. Red oxide primer is mixed in a ratio of approximately two parts primer to one part paint reducer or thinner. Spray the mixture at 50 to 60 psi, and apply three or four good, even coats to obtain total coverage. Set the center section up on a 4x4 in. board so you'll be able to get complete coverage from the top to the edge of the section. Remember to do the pinion flange at this time so that both the housing and the flange will match colors.

5. Paint on the color codes. Try to duplicate the number and letters in the exact style and location as the original markings.

4. Reinstall the yoke. To replace the markings obliterated when you sandblasted and repainted the rear, use Sign Painter's 1 Shot Lettering Enamel in the appropriate colors and a fine artist's paintbrush to apply the paint.

6. Replace any worn rear gear components. After you have assembled the ring gear to the carrier, press the side bearings into place. If you are unsure about rebuilding the rear, send it out to your local machine or speed shop to have the rear set up.

7. Place the race on the side bearings and install the ring gear assembly into the carrier.

9. Now install the side carrier locks and set into place.

8. Set the side carrier bearing retainers in place and adjust the side load as per the specifications in your factory shop manual.

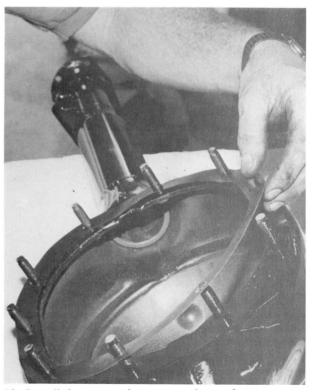

10. Install the rear end center section gasket.

11. A rear end tag similar to this was used on Ford products showing ratio, date and applications. Other makes, when equipped with limited-slip rears, may use a similar tag specifying use of limited-slip differential fluid.

13. Remember to install the differential tag, using it as a washer on the driver's side bolt. Do not use a washer with the tag. The fluid instruction tag on Pontiacs is installed on the lower right-hand bolt and hangs away from the center section.

Rear axle installation

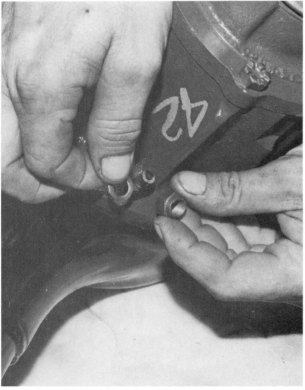

12. When assembling a Ford or Mopar rear-end assembly, always use a copper washer and nut to hold the center section to the differential housing.

1. Carefully press new bearings onto the axle. Remember to install the axle flange retainer on the axle first, or you're going to have to start all over again.

2. Most axles are also color coded as to the number of splines and applications.

4. Before you install the rear backing plates, make sure you have the correct ones for each side. They are either marked right and left or are numbered. Usually, if the last digit is even, it will be for the right-hand side; odd digits are generally placed on the left-hand side.

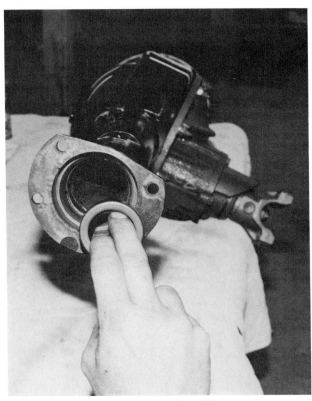

3. Remember to install new axle seals.

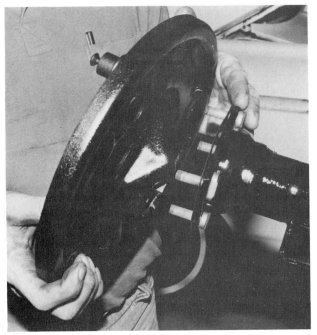

5. Install the backing plate retaining studs and gasket. Then install the correct backing plate, which you have already blasted and repainted using either thirty-percent or sixty-percent gloss black depending on manufacturer. Refinish the axle ends and flanges in either natural or Spray Gray, depending on manufacturer.

6. Install the axle. Carefully seat the axle onto the center section and then tighten the axle flange retaining nuts using the specifications found in the factory service manual.

7. The axle assembly is now completed and ready for installation when the rear suspension is reinstalled in the completed chassis. Notice the assembly line code on the center section.

5

Restoring the Rolling Chassis

No part of the restoration is as critical as the reconstruction of the frame, suspension and braking systems of your musclecar. Since all of your work is literally riding on the quality of the components you install, don't cut corners by using cheap parts. Avoid bargain-priced brake parts and by all means make sure the parts you install throughout the car are for the correct application. To hold inventory costs down, many parts houses have one-size-fits-all components that may or may not be correct for your musclecar. Utilize those companies that have the correct parts designed for your specific make, year and model. Remember, all of the work and money you have tied up in the project will be riding on your frame, brakes and suspension. Not only that, but your personal safety is also on the line.

When working on the car, make sure the floorjack, jackstands, coil spring compressors and other tools you're using are of top quality. Too many people have been killed or injured when the valve in a $39.95 drugstore floorjack failed, or a cheap jackstand gave way with someone underneath the car. There's a natural temptation to cut a few corners here and try to save a few dollars there on tools and equipment. Don't do it. The quality of your restoration and your personal safety are at stake.

The following chart will assist you in determining the proper appearance of the chassis and attaching components. This chart applies to the majority of musclecars built in the sixties and early seventies, however there may be occasions when you'll run into variations. Keep in mind that each assembly plant built cars a little differently, even within the same company and car line. Also keep in mind that manufacturers sourced parts from a variety of suppliers during the course of a model year and run. It wasn't unusual for different vendors to supply components that differed in appearance and finish. When the parts arrived at the assembly plant, they were placed into bins next to the assembly line. If parts from one vendor were mixed in with parts from another, it's conceivable that different-appearing—yet identical as far as the manufacturer was concerned—parts could be installed on the same car. While this was more prone to happen in engine compartments and exteriors, suspension and brake components could differ from car to car in the same model run.

Some car clubs will only accept certain colors on suspension components. If you are going to compete in one club's concours event only, then follow their guidelines.

Chassis color chart				
Assembly	**GM**	**Ford**	**Mopar**	**AMC**
Frame	CB	CB	—	—
Front unibody subframe assembly	30% GB	30% GB	Body color	Body color
Inner fenders	30% GB	30% GB	Body color	Body color
Firewall	30% GB	*	Body color	Body color
Core support	GB	GB	Body color**	—
Transmission components				
Transmission	N	N/CC	N/CC	N/CC
Driveshaft	N/CC	N/CC	N/CC	N/CC
Transmission and driveshaft yoke	N/CC	CI/CC	N/CC	N/CC
Differential housing	GB	30% GB	SB	SB
Clutch linkage	N	N	N	N
Brake components				
Brake drums	SB	SB	SB/N	SB
Disc brake shields	N	N	N	N
Calipers	CI	CI	CI	CI

Assembly	GM	Ford	Mopar	AMC
Master cylinder	CI	CI	GB or CI	GB or CI
Axle and suspension components				
Axles	N/CC	N/CC	N/CC	N/CC
Third member	GB	Red oxide primer	SB	SB
Upper control arms	30% GB	30% GB or N	30% GB	30% GB
Lower control arms	30% GB	30% GB	30% GB	30% GB
Inner and outer tie rods	MP/CC	N/CC	N/CC	N/CC
Tie rod adjustment sleeve	SB	SB	SB	SB
Center link	MP/CC	MP/CC	MP/CC	MP/CC
Idler arm, bracket	MP/CC	CI/CC	CI/CC	CI/CC
Strut rods	CI/CC	CI/CC	CI/CC	—
Torsion bars	—	—	30% GB/CI/CC	—
Coil springs, front	GB/CC	GB/CC	—	GB/CC
Shocks	Gray***	SB/CC	SB/CC	SB
Coil springs, rear	SB/CC	—	—	—
Trailing arms	GB	—	—	—
Rear end U-bolts	N/CC	N/CC	N/CC	N/CC
Rear leaf springs	SB/CC	N/CC	N/SB/CC	SB/CC
Front and rear spring shackles	N	N	N	N
Backing plates	30% GB	30% GB	30% GB	30% GB
Spindles	CI/CC	CI/CC	CI/CC	CI/CC
Antisway bars	MP/CC	N/CC	N/CC	N/CC
Steering components				
Pitman arm	CI/CC	CI/CC	CI/CC	CI/CC
Steering box	N/CC	CI/CC	N/CC	N/CC
Power steering control valve	—	30% GB	—	—
Power steering cylinder	—	30% GB	—	—
Exhaust system				
Muffler hangers and clamps	N	N	N	N
Exhaust system and mufflers	N	N	N	N
Gas tank components				
Gas tank	N	N	N	N
Gas tank straps	30% GB	30% GB	N/30% GB	—
Gas and brake lines	N	N	N	N

Legend

CB .... Chassis black
GB .... Gloss black
CI .... Cast-iron gray
N .... Natural steel or aluminum
SB .... Semi-gloss black
MP .... Manganese phosphate
CC .... Color coded

*Some firewalls were painted body color, some were thirty-percent gloss black, while others were thirty-percent gloss black and body color. The appearance differed between assembly plants. After 1964 all Ford firewalls were thirty-percent gloss black.

**It has been discovered that some Mopar core supports were body color on the engine side and semi-gloss black on the grille side.

***Most GM shocks were Delco spiral shocks painted gray; however, some were also thirty-percent gloss black, depending on model and year.

Restoring the chassis and chassis components is a time-consuming job—especially when you are trying to refinish all the parts to the correct factory colors.

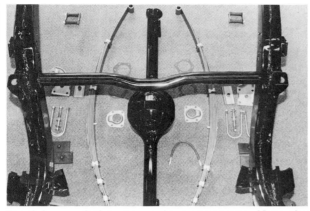

Breakdown of the rear axle components. Note the numerous different finishes—and you can bet that a concours or show judge will spot any discrepancies!

Frame inspection and refinishing

Before any restoration on the chassis can begin, take the frame outdoors and inspect it carefully. Although the frame will be covered with grease, grime and rust, look it over for signs of chalk marks or other markings that may have been applied by the assembly plant. If you want, wash the frame down with solvent to remove the heavy dirt and take a closer look for any markings.

2. Bring the frame back inside and set it on jackstands. Thoroughly inspect the frame for rust. Don't overlook this, because a rotted frame is dangerous and should be repaired before you begin installing suspension and steering components. Also scrutinize the frame for collision damage. Bent rails, dents from hammer work and other marks are a tip-off that the car has been in an accident and the frame was bent. If the frame is rotted, have the rusted metal cut off and new frame sections welded into place. If you have any suspicions that the frame was bent due to an accident, take it to a frame shop. The frame shop can check the frame and straighten it to specifications if necessary.

1. Before sandblasting the frame, put on protective clothing and a hood. On areas over the rear spring perches, the rust may have attacked the frame and scarred the metal badly. This is where the heaviest rust accumulation will be and it will require extra time to clean the surface. Once you have sandblasted the frame, clean it thoroughly to remove all sand, especially within the cavities where the frame is boxed for reinforcement.

3. Once the frame is ready for refinishing, begin by applying POR 15. POR 15 is used as a rust inhibitor on numerous chassis and underbody components as well as the frame. It's available from POR 15, Inc. (Box 1325, Morristown, NJ 07960). Follow the instructions and spray or brush POR 15 on. You'll notice that POR 15 fills in some of the open pores of the frame where rust has scarred it. Remember POR 15 is not a top coat. Even the clear POR 15 must be covered by some other paint for full protection. Once the POR 15 is dry, spray the frame gloss black.

Flaring and bending fuel and brake lines

1. To flare a line, first install the line end even with the lip of the flaring tool and adapter.

2. Place the flare adapter on top of the line and use the flaring tool to make the first flare.

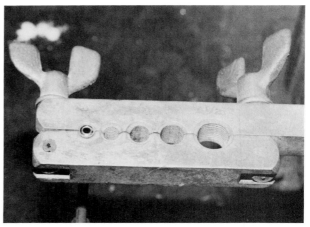

3. Remove the flaring tool and adapter and slide the line down even with the tool vise and reclamp it into place.

4. Reposition the flaring tool and now reflare the line.

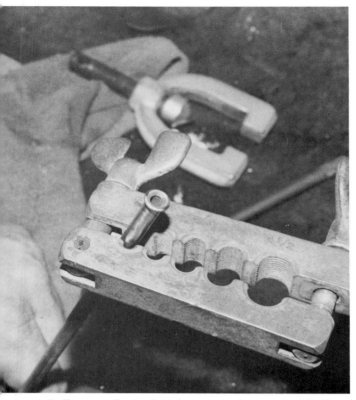

5. Remove the tool and you now have a double flare. Practice on some scrap line until you perfect the flare and double flare technique.

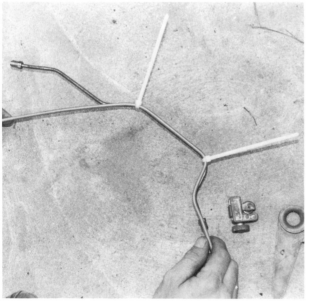

6. To bend tubing, use wire ties to hold the lines together, allowing you to follow the curves of the old line as you bend the new piece. Duct tape will also work, but not as well as wire ties in holding the lines together. As you make the needed bends, continue to tie the line with the wire ties.

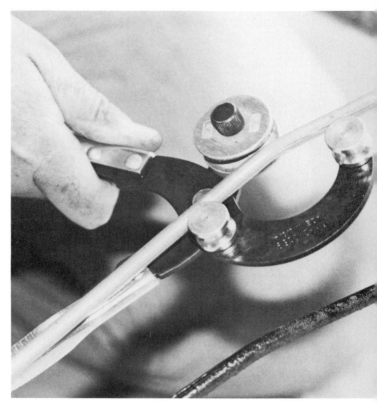

7. Use a line bending tool and several screwdrivers to bend the frame fuel lines and brake lines to copy the slight dips in the original lines.

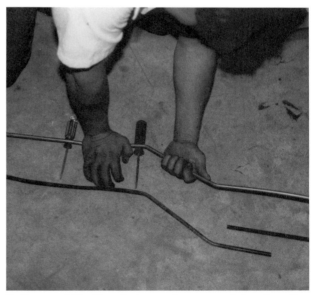

8. Suspend the lines between two screwdriver handles and press down until the correct curve is achieved. If the old line is still complete, use it for a pattern. Remember all brake and fuel lines at the frame are one piece from the factory, not pieced together. Fuel and brake lines are available from any auto parts store in 20 and 25 ft. lengths.

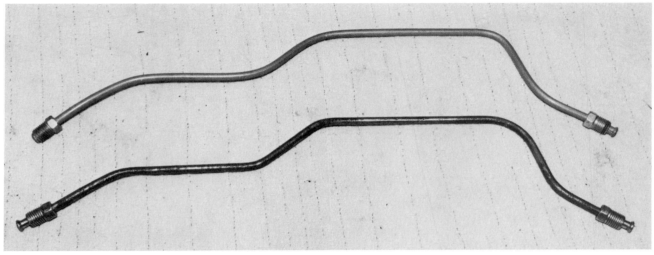

9. Using this technique to bend fuel and brake lines will result in near-perfect reproductions of the originals.

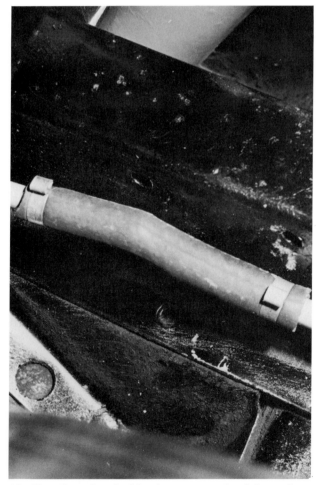

10. Short lengths of rubber hose are used to join sections of metal lines. Note the correct crimp-type fuel line clamps shown here. The factory never used worm clamps for fuel or brake hoses.

11. Bead blast and repaint the fuel and brake line clips or replace as necessary.

Replacing bushings

Today's restorer has a choice of bushing composition for control-arm and antisway-bar bushings when reassembling the suspension of a musclecar. Car makers in the sixties and seventies used rubber, which is compliant and flexes as the suspension works. Rubber also deteriorates, causing the bushings to crack. This further reduces the car's handling and safety.

With the advent of new compounds in the mideighties, restorers now can install an alternative to rubber bushings—polyurethane bushings. There are advantages to using polyurethane bushings, but there are also disadvantages. While polyurethane bushings are as hard as rubber, they are less compliant, which improves handling. Polyurethane also has a longer service life. From an appearance standpoint, it's hard to identify black polyurethane from rubber, so it's perfect for the restorer who wants to upgrade a musclecar's handling without compromising a concours appearance.

The downside to using polyurethane is that it does stiffen the vehicle's ride characteristics. Polyurethane bushings can also squeak. To combat this annoyance, manufacturers now impregnate the polyurethane with graphite, a compound called polygraphite. Proper installation is also critical when using polyurethane or polygraphite bushings, as they will still creak when the car is driven over undulating road surfaces.

When you're considering the type of bushing compound to install, talk to vendors and ask questions. If possible, ride in a restored musclecar that's had polyurethane bushings installed before making your decision. Once installed and the car completed, you don't want to tear it apart again because you don't like the stiffer ride characteristics inherent with polyurethane components.

2. If you want to install the new bushings yourself, there are tools available that mount in a bench vise such as MATCO's BJP-7025 clamp press.

1. While it's possible to pound out the old bushings and hammer in the new ones, you'll find it much easier to take your control arms to the machine shop. The cost to have the old bushings pressed out and the new ones installed is minimal.

3. There are a variety of companies that offer complete front end rebuilding packages that includes either rubber or polyurethane bushings, rebound bumpers and antisway bar bushings, along with new tie rod ends, and upper and lower ball joints.

4. Don't laugh—keep the new bushings stored right next to the Gatorade and Pepsi until it's time for installation. Cold bushings are contracted and will slip into the control arms much easier. Once they warm up to room temperature, they'll be snug and secure.

Cleaning and refinishing suspension parts

It's time to take that pile of parts you've removed from the frame and clean and prepare them for paint. Few restorers relish this part of the job; it's tedious work scraping, brushing and washing years of grime, grease and dirt off of components. If you have a parts washer or a large bucket of solvent (such as mineral spirits or kerosene), allow the parts to soak in the solvent. This will cut most of the heavy gunk off the parts and make cleanup easier. Keep in mind that these solvents are highly flammable. Don't smoke or weld near an open container of solvent and always keep the area ventilated.

After the parts have soaked, inspect them carefully for factory paint codes or marks. Many times there are paint codes dabbed on or numbers stenciled or written on the components. If you detect any markings or color dabs, make careful notes as to their location, size or color; you'll want to duplicate these after the part has been refinished and before it's installed back in the car.

Now scrub the parts with a stiff wirebrush to remove the remainder of the paint and grease. To

achieve a satisfactory surface refinishing, sandblast hard metal components like control arms. Bead blast other parts that are made of softer metals, like aluminum. Sandblasting affects the texture of the metal surface, and the appearance of soft metal parts can be ruined by sandblasting. Bead blasting using glass beads or walnut shells is less abrasive and won't damage surface texture.

Once the parts have been blasted, wipe them with lacquer thinner or Pre-Kleano as preparation for painting.

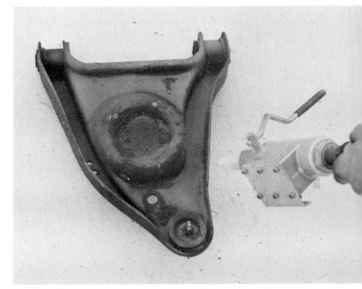

1. Sandblasting parts removes all traces of surface debris and beats using lots of elbow grease and a wirebrush.

2. Depending on the finish (see component refinishing chart), paint or coat the components and allow them to dry before installation. Apply any color code paint dabs or markings now.

Assembling the front end

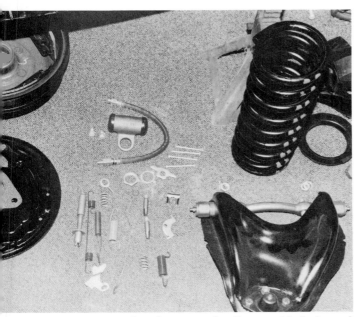

1. There are a lot of parts you've disassembled, cleaned and refinished, and now it's time to begin reassembly. Before you start, lay out all the components you'll be working with. Also prepare your tools so you won't be stopping the installation process to constantly go to the toolbox for another tool.

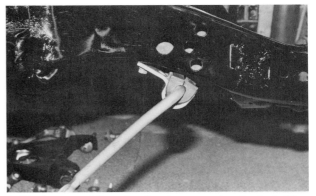

2. Begin assembling the front suspension by installing the antisway bar bushings in their brackets. Slide the antisway bar through the bushings and bolt the brackets to the frame.

3. Install the completed lower control arms with bushings and shafts in place. Tighten the shaft and nuts. Tighten and adjust the front nut and bushing to the factory specifications found in the service manual.

4. Install the completed upper control arms and shafts and tighten the upper control arm down. Remember when you removed the upper control arms you counted the number of shims and their location and recorded it? Bead blast, clear and now put them back the same way they came out.

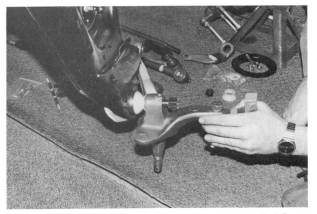

5. Attach the spindle to the lower ball joint and tighten the nut.

6. Compress the front coil spring. Install the upper coil spring insulator and slide the spring into the spring socket.

7. Place the upper ball joint into the spindle and attach the ball joint nut. Now tighten the upper and lower ball joint nuts to factory specifications and carefully remove the coil spring compressor tool.

8. Install the antisway bar end links by first placing a washer and then a grommet on the bolt and sliding the bolt up through the lower control arm. Place another grommet on the bolt, followed by another washer.

11. Install the wheel cylinder. If you decide to use the original wheel cylinder, disassemble it, clean, bead blast and refinish with Eastwood Spray Gray. The cylinder will have to be honed and a wheel cylinder rebuild kit installed (see the brake installation section for more detail). If you're not concerned about originality here, it's much simpler to buy a new wheel cylinder. It will also prove to be more reliable than your rebuilt cylinder.

9. Install the sleeve, another washer, grommet, antisway bar end, grommet, washer and nut. Tighten partially. You'll be torquing the end link package once the car is back on the ground and the bar is loaded.

12. Now install the front brake hose. Don't forget to use a copper washer between the hose fitting and the wheel cylinder.

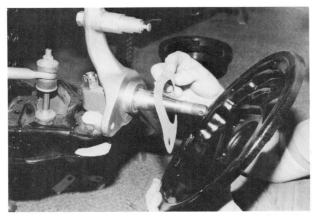

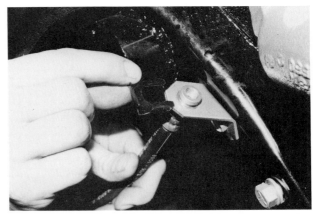

10. Install the backing plate gasket first and then the refinished brake backing plate.

13. Attach the new replacement front brake hose to the brake hose bracket.

14. Install the steering box. For the correct steering box finish, refer to the component refinishing chart.

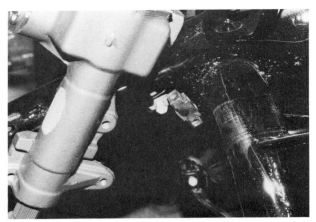

15. Install the front brake line junction block. If it hasn't been damaged, the brass block can be bead blasted, polished and clear coated.

16. Install the idler arm and bracket to the frame. Depending on manufacturer, the arm and bracket may or may not have a color code paint dab. Note the paint dabs used on Ford products.

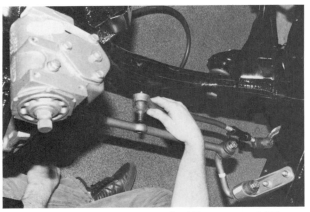

17. Attach the center link to the idler arm and Pitman arm.

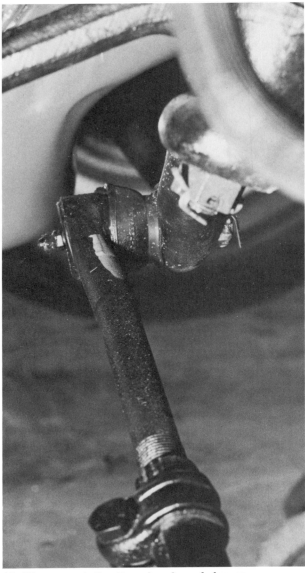

18. Then attach the tie rod ends and sleeves.

19. Assemble and install the front brake shoes as per the manufacturer's shop manual. Refer to the rear brake installation section for some tips on assembling drum brakes.

Installing unibody front suspensions

1. Begin by assembling the upper control arm shaft package. Install the upper shaft grease fittings before installing the upper control arms. As you assemble the upper control arms, make sure you turn the inner shaft so that the mounting bolts can be installed.

2. Install the upper control arms. After they are in place make sure they are torqued to specifications found in the manufacturer's service manual. Notice that the replacement ball joints were bolted on and not re-riveted. Also notice the factory paint code marks.

3. Now install the lower control arms assembly and torque to the specifications found in the factory service manual. Note the special cam bolt unique to this type of lower control arm.

4. Install the spindle and backing plate to the upper and lower control arms using the same procedure as outlined for composite body-frame front suspensions.

5. Install the new washers and bushings on the strut rod. Shown is the proper sequence for bushings and washer installation on strut rods.

6. The strut rod is installed by first bolting it on the right-hand control arm bracket. Place the grommet on the rod against the outboard side of the bracket, then the washer and nut and tighten.

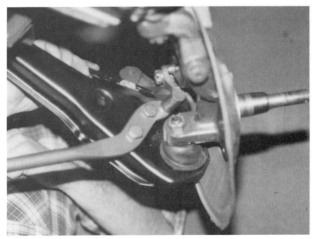

7. Now move to the left-hand lower control arm and tighten the rod to the arm. Remember to install the strut rod with the wheel stop toward the backing plate.

8. Begin installing the front antisway bar by bolting the bushing brackets to the car.

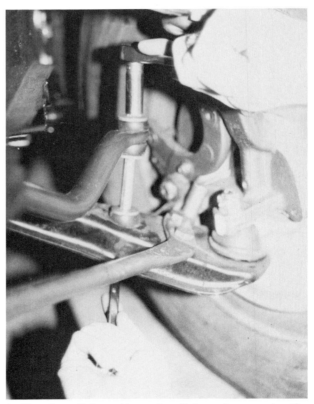

9. Now install the antisway bar link packages, using the same procedures outlined in the composite body frame front suspension installation section.

10. Front coil spring with upper insulator. Notice the color code on the spring. This is applied by dabbing the proper color paint on the springs with a paintbrush. The spring color code information is listed in the factory parts book. Moog offers a special compressor tool for use on unibody front coil springs.

11. Tool installed and spring compressed. Carefully align the compressor tool up and through the top opening in the front subframe. Align the spring on the control arms and carefully unscrew the tool. In a matter of minutes the new spring will be in place safely and without any damage to the car or yourself.

Installing unibody car steering components

1. Begin by installing the new steering linkage and idler arm to the subframe. Index the nuts so they face the engine.

2. Install the steering box. The box attaches to the subframe with three bolts. Tighten these to the specifications listed in the factory service manual.

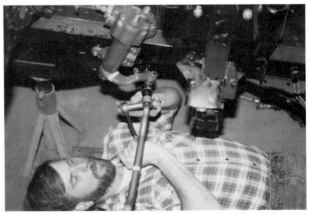

3. Install the center link (also called the drag link). On Ford products, install the power steering control valve and tighten the clamp.

4. Assemble the tie rods and tie rod ends prior to installation. Install the tie-rod assembly and attach it to the center link and spindle arms. Leave all adjusting clamps and bolts loose. When the car is totally assembled, you'll need to adjust the front end. That's when you can tighten all the adjusting clamps and bolts.

5. If you've removed the side cover on GM power steering boxes for restoration, you'll have to adjust the steering gear lash once the car is assembled and back on the ground. Follow the instructions in the factory service manual for this procedure.

Assembling the torsion bar front suspension

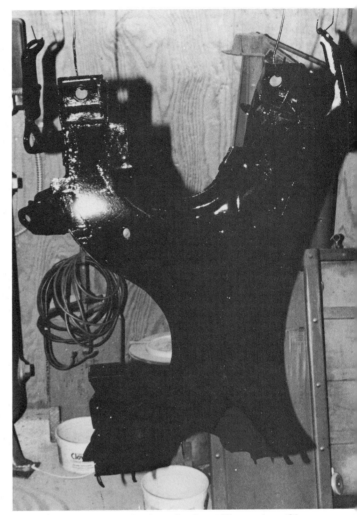

1. Everything is attached to the front K-member. Glass bead the K-member and the upper and lower control arms and paint thirty-percent gloss black. Glass bead the ball joints and torsion bars and then paint them with Spray Gray and a coat of dry clear.

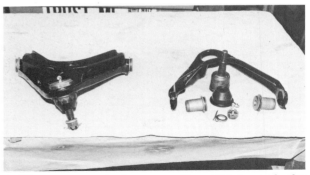

2. The upper control arm on the right is ready for assembly. On the left is a completed upper control arm.

3. This homemade control arm bushing installation tool is constructed of ⅝ in. threaded rod, two ⅝ in. nuts, two large washers and one rubber washer.

4. Assemble the bushing installer in a large vise as pictured. Tighten the nut against the socket (make sure the socket is large enough for the bushing to fit snugly inside). Tighten until the bushing is fully installed.

5. Install the upper ball joints, using the correct Mopar ball joint socket.

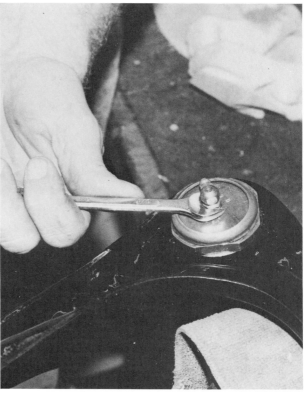

6. Don't install the old grease fittings. Use new ones.

7. With all the components refinished and rebuilt, they can now be attached to the K-member. Install the strut rod, bushings and washers on the K-member.

8. Slide the lower control arm and shaft into place. Install the shock mounting bolt, rubber bumper and torsion rod adjuster. Torque the control arm shaft nuts to the specifications found in the factory service manual.

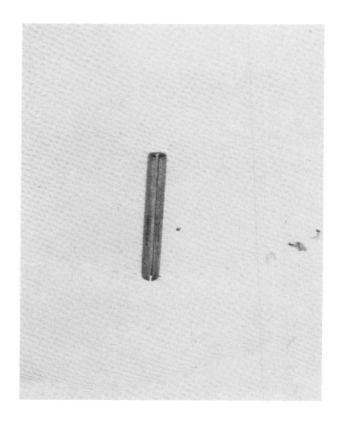

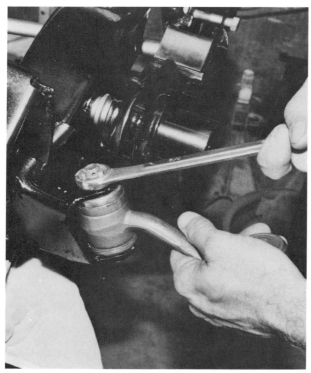

9. Install the idler arm assembly and torque to the specifications found in the factory service manual.

10. Install the strut rod bolt, washer and roll pin. Chrysler products used a roll pin instead of a cotter key on the strut rods.

130

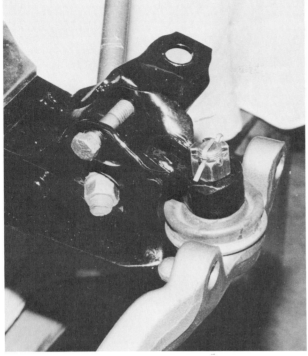

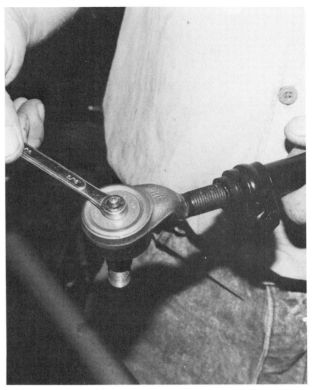

11. Assemble and install the lower ball joints. Notice the new jounce bumper. If the original bumper is in excellent condition, it can be glass beaded, dressed with Armor All and reinstalled.

12. Assemble and install the tie rods, tie rod ends, tie rod sleeves and center link.

13. Now install the spindles.

2. When the new bushings are pressed in, make sure a spacer is placed in the control arm to prevent the arm from becoming bent. You can pound the arm straight again, but why go through the bother when a spacer will prevent the damage in the first place? Once the bushing is in place, tape it off and paint the control arm.

14. Install the steering box. The attaching bolts should be natural finish. Torque the bolts to the specifications found in the factory service manual.

Installing rear axle and control arms

1. Restoring coil spring rear suspensions begins by replacing the upper and lower control arms bushings before the control arms have been painted. While you can remove the old bushings yourself using the tried-and-true hammer-and-chisel method, you will save considerable labor by simply taking the arms to your local machine shop for a short workout on their press.

3. Most manufacturers identified coil spring usage for assembly line workers by color code. Each spring received paint dabs with particular colors for particular applications. Most factory parts books or service manuals list the correct color code for each model and suspension. Don't be a Rembrandt and make it a work of art. The paint was literally dabbed on.

132

4. Prior to applying POR 15 and painting the rear axle assembly, mask off the bushing holes with tape. The POR 15 is virtually impossible to remove once dried, and it won't make the bushing installation any easier if the hole isn't clean metal.

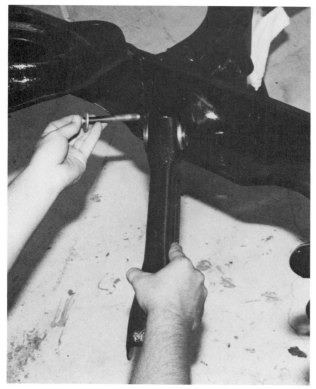

5. Reassembling the rear suspension begins by attaching the upper control arms to the frame. Thread the nut onto the bolt but don't tighten it yet.

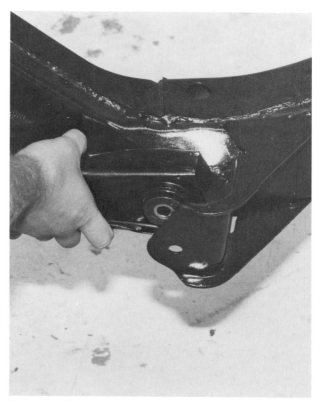

6. Install the lower control arms next. The new bushings will require you to work the control arm into place, and the holes for the bushing and the brace will have to be carefully aligned so the bolt can be slipped into place. Thread the nut onto the bolt but don't tighten it.

7. Most GM musclecars with coil spring rears used a frame reinforcement bracket on each side that attached to the upper and lower control arm mounts. The slotted end attaches to the lower arm. Thread the nut onto the bolt but don't tighten it.

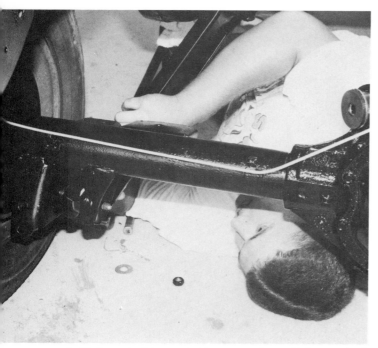

8. Bolt a set of tires onto the rear axles, roll the rear end assembly into place and attach the lower control arms to the mounting brackets on the axle. Note the brake lines that were bent and installed before the rear end assembly was installed.

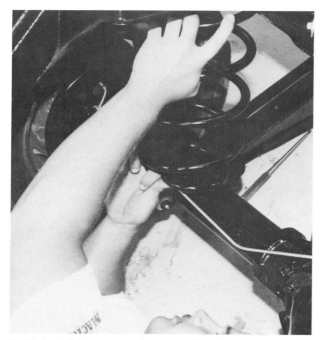

9. To install the rear springs, a coil spring compressor is not needed using this rear suspension reassembly procedure, as they are not loaded during the installation. Install the upper spring insulator, making sure it is properly aligned to the frame. Then slip the springs into place.

10. The spring clamp is next. It fits over the bottom of the spring and is contoured to match the profile of the coil. Bolt it to the axle and torque to manufacturer's specifications.

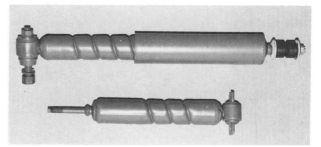

11. While the following pictures illustrate installation of aftermarket shocks, the correct shock absorbers for most GM cars were manufactured by Delco and had a spiral design. These shocks were painted gray or semigloss black.

12. Place a floorjack under the differential and raise the rear-axle assembly. It will be necessary to have a helper sit on the frame to weight it down against the coil springs as you jack up the rear to attach the upper control arms. Once the upper arms are in place, torque down all the control arm bolts to the manufacturer's specifications found in the service manual. At this point, the shock absorbers can now be installed.

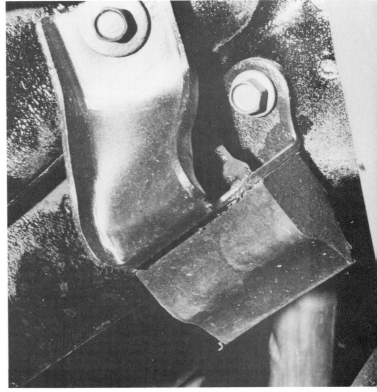

13. If so equipped, install the rear antisway bar at this time. Reinstall the shims you removed when you disassembled the rear suspension.

14. Install the new rear axle jounce bumpers. If your old ones were in good shape, you can glass-bead blast them, apply a coat of protectorant and reinstall.

15. The rear suspension is now complete. The painted limited-slip lubricant tag attached to the lower right-hand differential bolt will be replaced with a new reproduction as part of the final detailing.

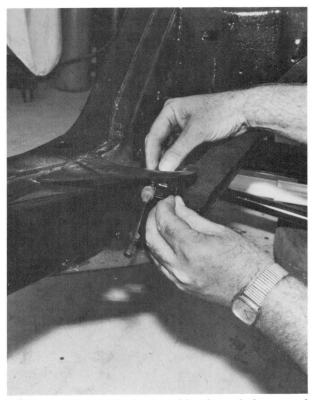

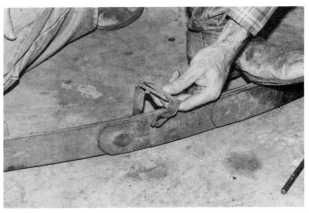

2. Carefully pry back the clamp (if they are to be reused) and remove.

16. Thread the parking brake cables through the control arm brackets at this time and secure them with the proper C-clip.

Rebuilding rear leaf springs

3. After you have removed all the clamps, now remove the spring center bolt using the vise grips on the head of the bolt and the socket on the nut. Retain the nut and bolt for reassembly.

1. To disassemble multileaf rear springs, you'll need a small hammer, chisel, flat-blade screwdriver, vise grips, ratchet and socket. To open the spring clamps, use a large flat-blade screwdriver or chisel.

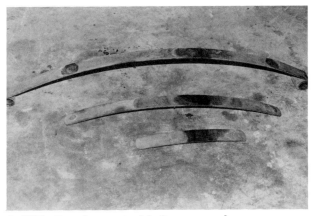

4. With the clamps and bolts removed, you can now disassemble the springs. It's also a good idea to mark the left- and right-hand springs so they are reinstalled on the proper sides.

5. A gravity-feed sandblaster hooked to your compressor will be used to remove surface rust and other debris. When sandblasting, always wear protective clothing and gear. As you sandblast the springs, remember to do both sides and edges.

6. Always be observant when sandblasting. The original paint stripe and inspection codes are clearly visible here. Reproducing these markings is the goal of a correct restoration.

7. Some manufacturers also had casting numbers and date codes stamped into the springs. All Ford products use these stamped codes.

8. Most Ford springs were a natural cast color. GM cars were virtually always black. Mopar springs were either natural or semi-gloss black, depending on supplier. Be observant when cleaning the springs to determine how they should be refinished. Use Eastwood's Spray Gray or Seymours Stainless Steel paint to obtain the correct appearance. After coating them, spray on a dry coat of clear for preservation.

Color coding rear leaf springs

1. In some cases, you can use an everyday office stencil sheet to reproduce some of the spring markings. Cut out the code you need, tape the letters together and then use masking tape to place them in the proper location.

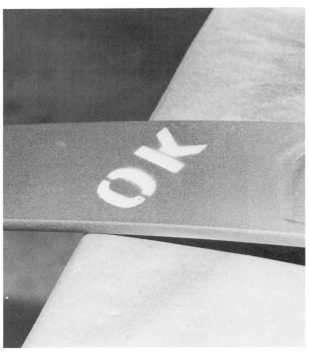

2. Use spray paint to fog over the stencil. As soon as the paint becomes tacky, carefully remove the stencil.

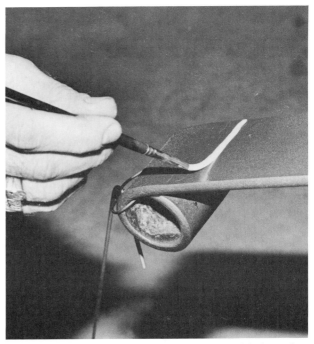

3. If your springs were also striped, use a thin lettering brush and Sign Painter's 1 Shot Lettering Enamel paint to apply the stripe. In some cases, the stripe goes completely around the spring. Some GM cars equipped with leaf springs were also color coded.

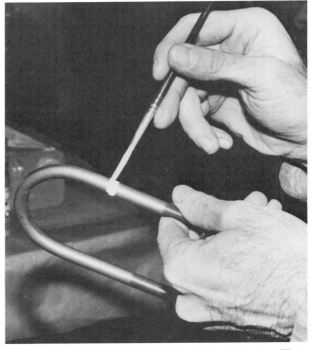

4. The U-bolts are also color coded in some cases. They can be brush coded on the top of the U-bolt on the sides. They can also be spray painted on the legs of the U-bolt. This depends on make and manufacturer.

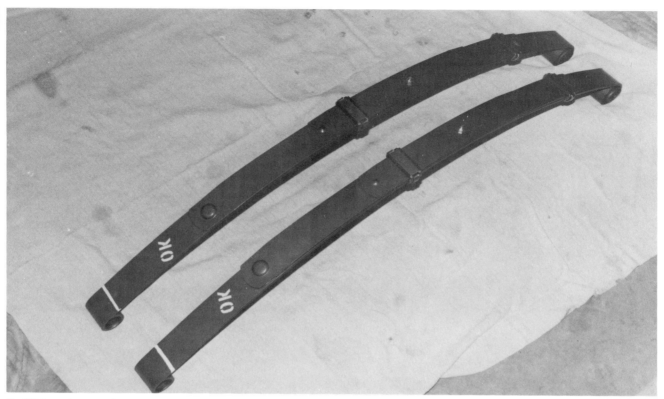

5. With stripes and assembly line paint markings, the assembled and coded springs are now correct and ready for installation.

Reassembling multileaf rear springs

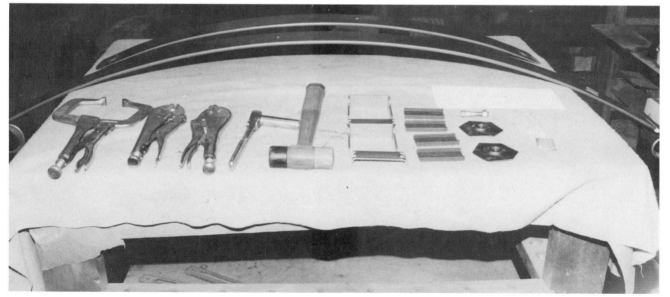

1. Tools needed for multileaf rear spring reassembly include vise grips, ratchet, hard rubber hammer, spring clamps, spring pads and center bolt.

139

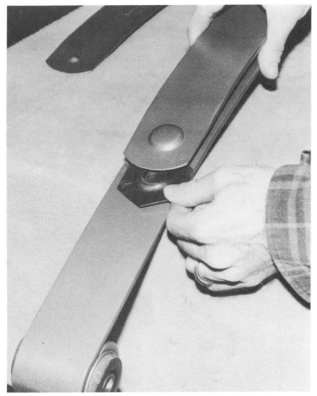

2. Stack the springs together and insert the anti-squeak pads between the long leafs.

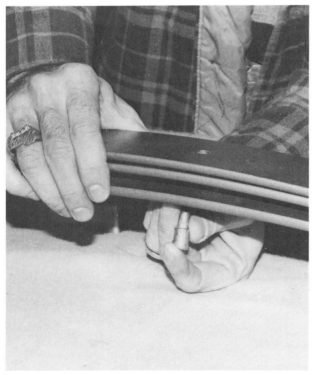

3. Align the bolt holes and insert the center bolt into position.

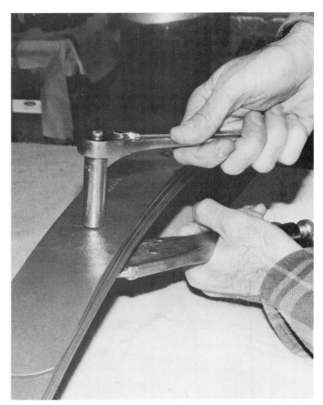

4. Tighten the bolt down.

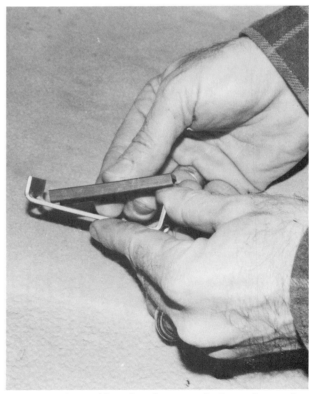

5. Insert the rubber insulator pads into the spring clamps.

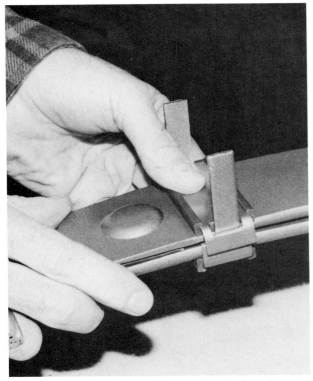

6. Position the spring clamp in the correct location and place both halves of the clamp together.

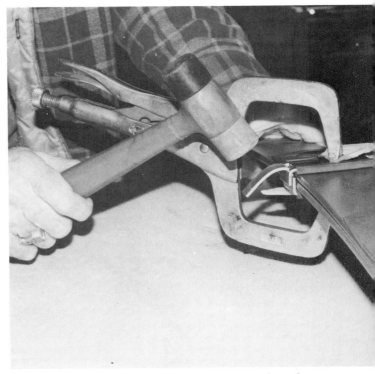

8. With a hard rubber hammer, tap the spring clamp leg into place.

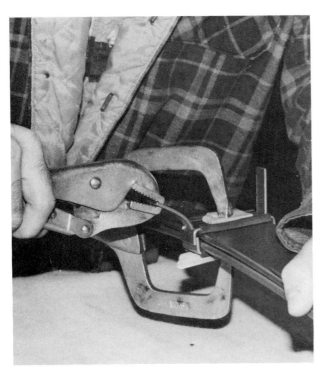

7. Place a small block of wood on each side of the clamp and use vise grips to squeeze the two halves together. Now take another pair of vise grips and turn the clamp legs down approximately halfway.

9. Now turn the spring over and tap any excess clamp leg over onto the top of the clamp. Repeat this procedure on each clamp until all the clamps are installed.

141

Refinishing Mopar rear springs

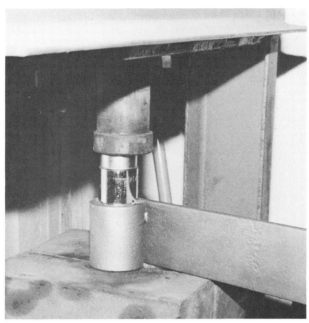

1. Use a solid shaft or arbor to start to push the old bushing out of the spring end.

2. After the bushing is about one third of the way out, remove the shaft and place the new bushing into the spring eye. Make sure it is centered. Now push the old bushing out with the new bushing and install it in one step.

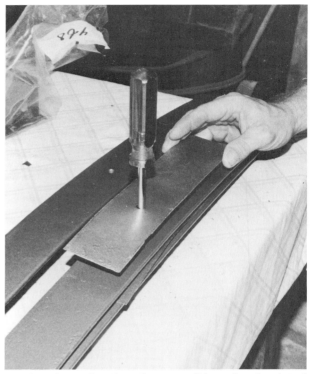

3. After the springs have been sandblasted and painted with Spray Gray, they can be reassembled. Use a screwdriver or punch to line up the rear springs. Remember to use the spacer between the center of the leaves if it was originally installed by the factory.

4. Install new anti-squeak pads.

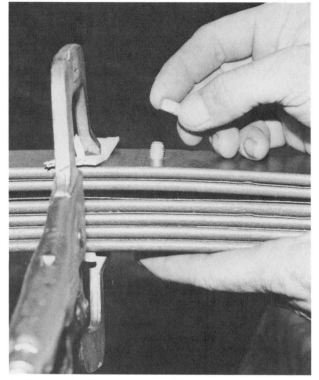

5. Clamp all of the leaves together and install the center bolt.

7. Reclamp the leaves in the correct locations. Don't forget to install the pad in the clamp before you put the clamp into place on the springs.

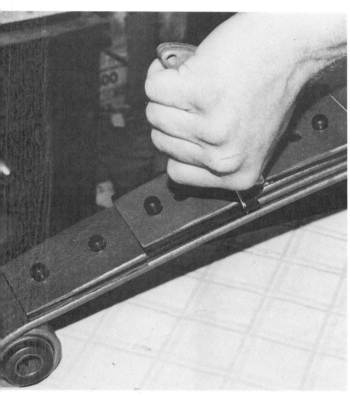

6. Cut off any excess from the anti-squeak pads. Be careful not to nick the finish with the knife blade.

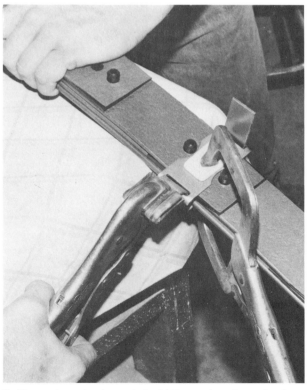

8. Use a vise grip clamp to hold the spring clamp in place and bend the legs of the clamp over.

143

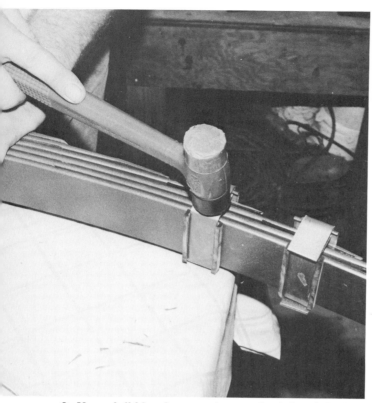

9. Use a dull-blow hammer to completely bend the legs over so they are folded neatly on the clamp.

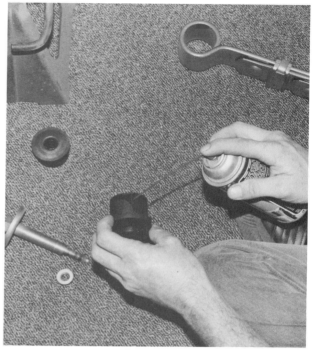

1. Spray silicone on the rear spring shackle bushings and slide them into place.

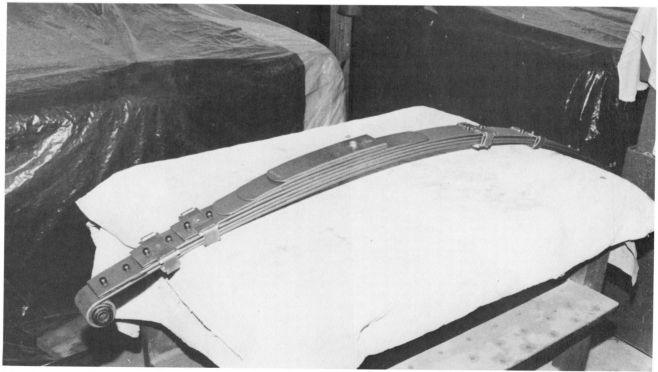

10. The finished Mopar springs are now ready to be installed on the car.

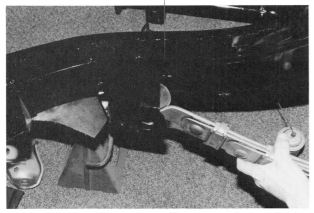

2. Turn the rear leaf spring sideways and place it into the front hanger.

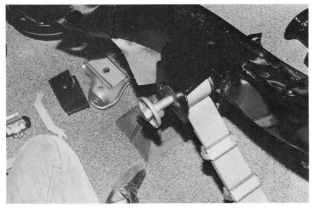

3. Now turn the spring to its correct position, align the bushing to the bracket and install the front shackle bolt.

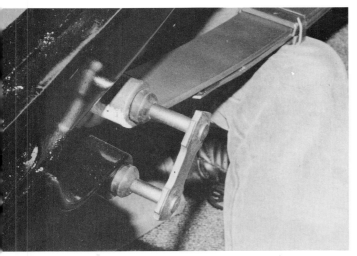

4. With the front of the spring secured, slide the rear of the spring into the rear shackle. Silicone will help ease the parts into place. Now tighten the rear shackle nuts to the torque specifications found in the factory service manual.

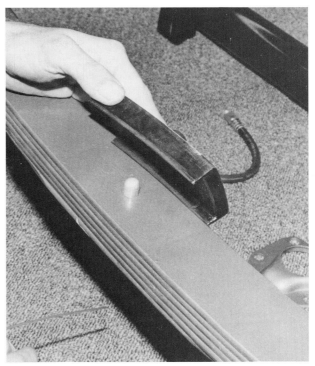

5. Spray silicone onto the rubber pad and install the center spring insulator onto the rear springs. Install the center spring insulator metal alignment plate, if so equipped.

6. Set the rear end housing onto the insulator. Align the insulator pin up with the alignment hole on the axle tube bracket.

7. Install the rear spring U-bolts. Remember to check the length of the U-bolts: some cars use longer bolts on the outside of the leaf spring than on the inside. Torque the U-bolts down to the specifications in the factory service manual.

8. Install the backing plate and gasket and remember to install a new axle seal.

9. Slide the rear axles into the tubes and seat.

Installing rear leaf springs on unibody cars

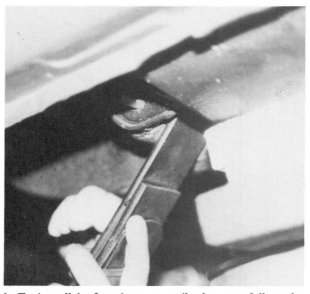

1. To install leaf springs on unibody cars, follow the same procedures as outlined above with the following notes. Place the rear-end assembly on a padded floorjack and slide the assembly under the car. Line the spring pads up with the center spring insulators and start to jack the rear-end assembly up. Install the rear shackles to the frame. Remove the bushings from the lower mount and install them into the spring.

2. Install the leaf spring jounce bumper first, then set the shackle plate in place. Insert the rear spring bushing into the plate, install the lock bolts and torque to the specifications found in the factory service manual.

3. Install the lower center spring insulator into the lower spring mount. Slide the U-bolts in place and then tighten.

Gas tank refinishing and installation

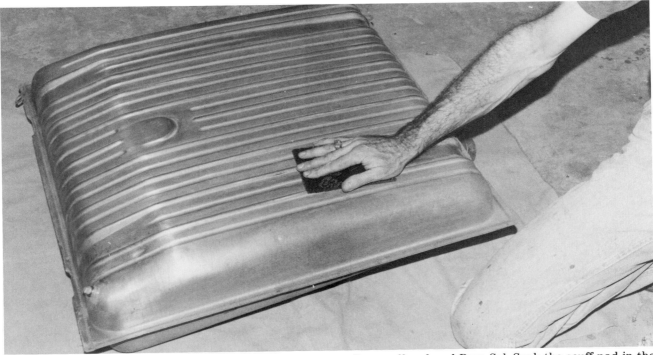

1. In all cases, fuel tanks are galvanized steel, and the only time they are not a natural galvanized finish is when the car has received factory undercoating. If you do not have a new tank for your car but you do have a dent-free tank, you can sometimes bring the finish back by using a fine scuff pad and Prep-Sol. Soak the scuff pad in the solvent and slowly start to scour the tank. Don't press down hard or you will cut through the galvanized finish leaving shiny spots. Keep light, even pressure until the tank is clean top to bottom.

2. After you have let the tank dry thoroughly, spray a coat of urethane clear over it. This will protect the surface and keep the tank looking new. If your tank has some rust spots or the galvanized finish has been worn off, you can possibly save it by spraying a fog coat of Ditzler Non-Smudge Aluminum over the tank, then clearing it with a good urethane. This gives outstanding results.

3. If your car was undercoated by the factory or the dealer, one side of the tank is shiny and the other side is undercoated. If you plan on retaining the undercoating for your restoration, you can restore the undercoating on your tank. After cleaning the tank to remove dirt and grease, if the undercoat is in excellent condition, brush on tire black to enhance the undercoat's appearance. If the undercoating has deteriorated, spray new undercoating on the bottom of the tank.

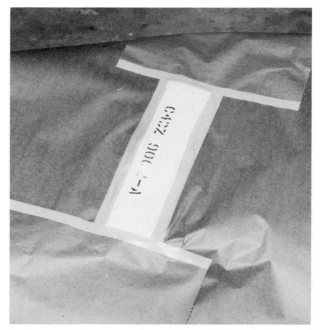

4. Some cars have a part number or date code stamped on them. In most cases, this can be duplicated by using stencils available from most stationery stores. Research which number is correct for your tank. Line the stencil up and tape the letters together, keeping the spacing uniform. Place the code number on the tank in the proper location and use masking tape to hold it in place. Mask off the surrounding area; you don't want any overspray on the remainder of the tank surface.

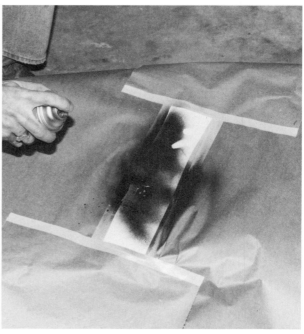

5. Select a semi-flat black paint and spray over your stencil. Two passes will usually be enough to get adequate coverage.

6. Once the paint has dried, carefully remove the stencil and you have a factory-correct code stenciled on your fuel tank.

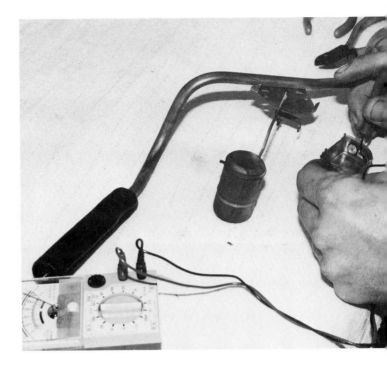

Fuel tank sending unit

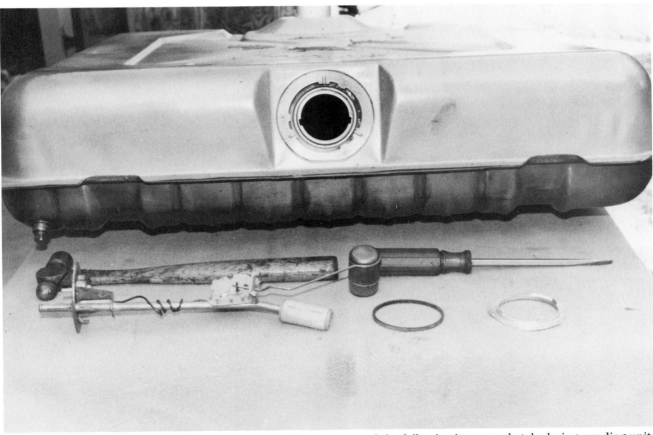

1. Before installing the fuel tank sending unit, check it for proper operation as outlined in your factory service manual. To install the sending unit in the tank, you'll need the following items: gasket, lock ring, sending unit, screwdriver and small hammer.

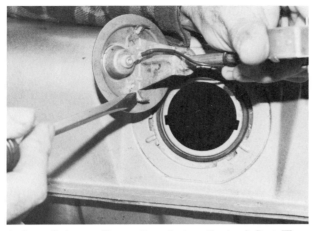

2. Install the sending unit gasket on the tank first. Then line up the sending unit positioning tabs with the slots in the fuel tank. Remember the sending unit pickup tube must be pointed down toward the bottom of the fuel tank.

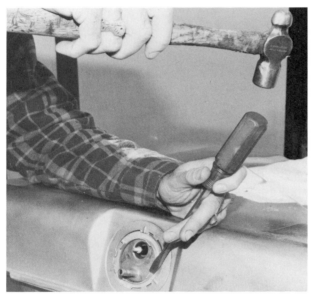

3. Install the sending unit and place the locking ring in position. Use either a flat-blade screwdriver or a drift to tap the locking ring into place. Make sure the locking ring tabs stop at the fuel tank stops. When they do the ring is locked in place. The tank is now ready to be installed once the body is back on the frame.

Restoring drum brakes

Restoring your musclecar's braking system requires a combination of refinishing old parts and installing new ones. This section will concentrate on the restoration aspects. For information on drum or disc brake assembly procedures, follow the instructions outlined in your factory service manual.

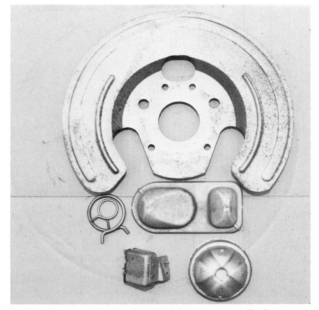

1. Small parts like brake shields, master cylinder caps, and even Corbin clips and relays were plated in gold cadmium or zinc-chromate. It doesn't take long for these coatings to lose their luster and become dull. There is a way of reproducing that dull effect without the expense of plating. Before the parts can be refinished, glass-bead blast them. Then spray the parts with lacquer thinner to remove all traces of dust and residue from the bead blasting.

2. Go to your local auto paint store and order a quart of Ditzler #DDL–43433 Sauterne Sage Poly acrylic lacquer. Mix the paint in your touch-up spray gun jar one part paint to one-and-one-half parts thinner. Add two drops of fish-eye remover and stir.

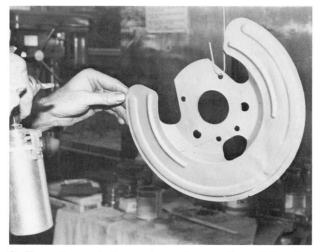

3. Hang the parts from wire and spray the paint, using thin, even coats. Set the air pressure at 35–40 psi and apply five to seven light coats, allowing about five minutes drying time between coats. Those parts that can't be hung up should be placed on a clean surface and painted in the same manner. Once you've applied an adequate amount of coats, allow the parts to dry at least eight hours. They will now take on the appearance of dulled plated parts.

Assembling drum brakes

2. Install the rubber brake lines. The attaching bolt to the frame should be natural metal, the bracket gloss black or natural, and the retaining clip natural or black oxide.

1. Prior to assembling your drum brakes, apply white lithium grease to the brake contact points on the backing plate. Most backing plates have four to six contact points that the brakeshoes ride on. By spreading the grease on each contact point, you'll eliminate the squeaks when the brakes are applied.

3. The rear brake lines should have already been bent and installed on the rear axle and the fittings installed on the backing plate. Depending on manufacturer, the parking brake cable will either be semi-gloss black or natural metal in appearance. Install the parking brake cable through the backing plate.

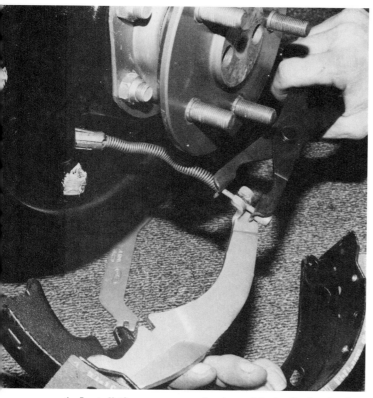

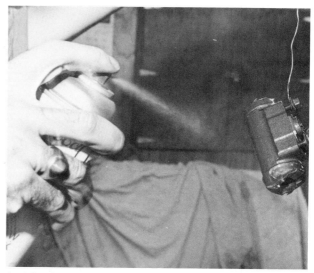

6. After bead blasting, clean the cylinder thoroughly and use lacquer thinner or Prep-Sol to prepare the metal surface for painting. Suspend the cylinder with mechanic's wire and apply Spray Gray, shaking the can often and holding the spray head about 6 in. from the object. More than 6 in. away causes the paint to set with a lower gloss and poor adhesion. Once dry, hone out the bore, rebuild the cylinder and install the new boots.

4. Install the emergency brake cable to the brakeshoe assembly. The tool shown is available from your local auto parts store and greatly eases installation.

5. After years of use, few musclecars retain their original wheel cylinders. If yours is original and you chose to reuse it for correctness, it can be restored to look like new. Remove the internal components and the rubber cups and bead blast the cylinder. If you chose to sandblast, tape over any threaded sections to protect the metal and threads. Don't forget to bead blast the attaching bolts as well.

7. Before you begin reassembly, use masking tape to cover the brake linings. Now you can assemble the brakes without getting grease or fingerprints on the brakeshoes. Contamination of the linings can cause brake noise or make the car pull to one side when the brakes are applied. After you have assembled the brakeshoes and springs, remove the tape and install the brake drums.

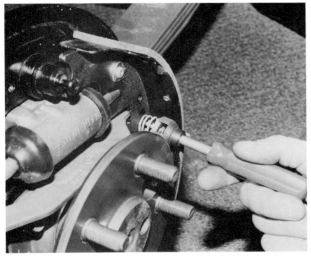

8. Those parts that aren't replaced, such as the levers and struts, should be bead blasted, refinished and cleared. All springs, washers and adjusting parts should be replaced with new parts.

10. Another exception is aluminum drums. GM offered aluminum front drums on several car lines. These should be bead blasted and painted with VHT clear. The VHT clear is designed to withstand high temperatures. On all brakes, remember to replace damaged wheel studs and use new lug nuts.

9. You should have already taken the brake drums to the machine shop for inspection and turning. Once they have been turned, cover the machined inner surface with masking tape and beadblast the drums. Most cast-iron drums should be painted sixty-percent gloss black.

There are some exceptions, however, such as 1966 Pontiac GTOs equipped with Rally wheels; these drums were painted red by the factory. Also, some Mopar drums were natural cast iron.

153

Restoring disc brakes

1. Before rebuilding the disc brakes, take the rotors to the machine shop for inspection. If possible, have the rotors refinished and turned. If there is not enough thickness left, replace with original equipment-style rotors. The first step in the reassembly process is to place the new or re-turned rotors on the workbench and install new packed inner bearings and grease seals. Remember to refinish the inside of the rotors. Don't forget to cover the races when you do so.

2. Pack the outer bearing with grease and install the rotor and outer bearing. Now install the outer bearing retainer, nut and nut retainer. Tighten to the specifications found in the factory service manual.

3. Install the cotter key. Bend back the legs and cut off the excess. Put the grease cap in place. To prevent damage to the cap, use a punch or large screwdriver on the edge of the cap and gently tap on the tool to seat the cap. A large socket that just touches the lip will also work without damaging the cap.

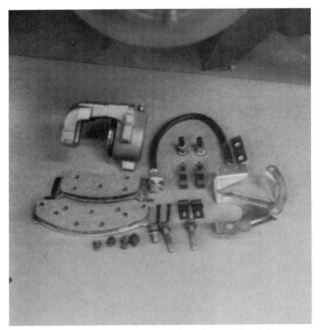

4. Aside from minor clips and brackets, all of the components you'll be installing should be new. We highly recommend the use of stainless-steel liners in the brake calipers. Calipers are manufactured of porous iron, and the bores holding the pistons corrode and wear, reducing brake efficiency. Companies like Stainless Steel Brakes (11470 Main Road, Clarence, NY 14031) supply disc brake parts and systems for GM, Ford, Mopar and AMC cars.

5. Assemble the disc brakes per the instructions found in the factory service manual. Before assembly, apply De-Squeak on the back of the pads.

Refinishing standard and Rally wheels

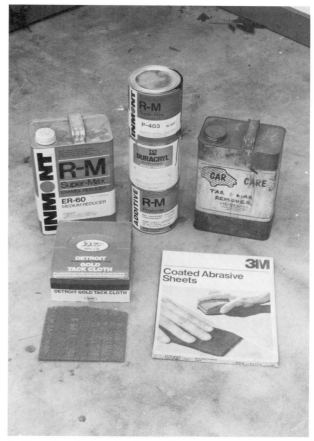

2. To refinish the wheels, you'll need black enamel, flattening agent, enamel reducer, tar and wax remover, 3M Coated Abrasive Sheets (ScotchBrite), tack cloth and Ditzler #DDL–8568 Non-Smudge Aluminum paint.

1. Many musclecars were equipped with optional Rally or road wheels. All Ford, GM and Mopar Rally wheels were painted the same color. Unless the wheels are in bad condition, do *not* sandblast them. Sandblasting will remove the baked-on primer and changes the surface texture of the wheel. Prior to refinishing, remove all wheel weights and valve stems.

3. Thoroughly degrease the wheels by spraying with degreaser. Fantastik or 409 should remove all grime and grease; tar and wax remover will also work well.

4. Using a stiff-bristled brush, scrub the wheel. Get the brush down into the slots and seams to remove all traces of grease and dirt. Scrub the front of the wheel, turn it around and do the same to the rear. Then go back and give the front another workout. Once you're satisfied the wheel is clean, rinse it with water.

5. Soak a fine-texture abrasive sheet with metal-prep or enamel reducer and scrub the wheel again, getting into the seams, crevices and slots. Do this to the front and back side of the wheel. Rinse the wheel thoroughly with clean water and either blow it dry with compressed air or allow the wheel to air dry.

6. Use 600 grit sandpaper to scuff the surfaces of the wheel. Get into the seams and slots. You don't want to sand out all the scratches and chipped paint; going too deep will expose the bare metal. This process is only to prepare the surface for better paint adhesion. After sanding, blow all the dust off the wheel and go back over the wheel again with a clean abrasive pad. Once the wheel surface is entirely done, hit the wheel with compressed air to blow off all dust and debris. Then wipe the wheel down front and rear with a clean tack rag.

7. Cover the front of the wheel with masking tape. You'll be painting the back side of the wheel first to duplicate the overspray pattern when the wheel was new. When wheels were delivered to the manufacturer, they were solid black. The factory would then paint the front of the wheels silver, leaving a silver overspray pattern on the back side of the wheel.

8. Prepare the paint for refinishing the back side of the wheel. Use straight black enamel, mixed one-and-one-half parts paint to one part reducer in a quart paint cup.

10. Spray the back side of the wheel, setting the air pressure at 50–55 psi. Apply three or four light coats, allowing five to ten minutes drying time between coats. After the paint has dried between coats, rotate the wheel 45 degrees, using the valve stem hole to mark the rotation. This assures even paint application. After the wheel is completely painted, let it air dry for at least one hour.

9. Add fifteen to twenty percent flattening agent and four drops of fish-eye remover. You will have to experiment with the amount of flattener depending on temperature and humidity to get the proper mixture. The fish-eye remover is essential for the paint to adhere to any surface contaminants on the wheel surface.

11. Mix Non-Smudge Aluminum paint one part paint to one-and-one-half parts thinner, then add four drops of fish-eye remover. Mix the paint thoroughly. This mixture produces a thin paint that can run easily, so you'll have to apply thin coats. It's recommended that you spray with a spray gun and compressed air, however a paint supply store can mix the paint and put it in an aerosol can for you. Some major reproduction supply companies also offer Rally wheel paint in spray cans, such as Mid-Country Mustang, Inc. (Route 100, P.O. Box 189, Eagle, PA 19480) or Ames Performance Engineering (Bonney Road, Marlborough, NH 03455).

14. A completed Rally wheel can look this good once it's restored. If you are reusing the old trim rings and center cap, polish them to remove superficial scratches. If the caps and rings are damaged, reproductions are readily available from most parts companies like Year One.

12. Remove the masking tape from the front of the wheel and wipe it down with a tack cloth. Spray the aluminum paint, using 40-45 psi, applying five or six light, even coats. Allow five to ten minutes drying time between coats, and rotate the wheel between coats for even paint coverage. Using care not to allow the paint to run, apply the last coat a little heavier than the previous ones. Allow at least two hours drying time before handling the wheel.

13. The overspray pattern previously mentioned is clearly visible here. The aluminum paint has drifted onto the back side of the wheel through the center and lug holes as well as the cooling slots. This duplicates the appearance of the wheel when it was mounted at the assembly plant.

15. Some Rally wheels, such as the Pontiac Rally II, are painted two different colors. Use the same procedures for these wheels as outlined above, however the wheel body is painted Charcoal Gray and the spokes are Non-Smudge Aluminum. This job will require a two-step process, painting the wheel first and then using a stencil to cover the wheel and paint the spoke sections second. The stencil is available from Ames Performance Engineering.

16. Standard wheels are prepared for painting exactly the same as Rally wheels. All standard wheels are painted thirty-percent gloss black on the back. Note the overspray, as well.

17. If your car was equipped with full wheel covers, the front side of the wheel is also painted thirty-percent gloss black. If your car was equipped with hubcaps, the front side of the wheel is painted to match the color of your car's lower body—white, here. The back of the wheel is still thirty-percent gloss black with the overspray of the front color showing through. This applies to all manufacturers.

Refinishing wheel covers

1. To restore wire or disc wheel covers, you'll need a trim hammer, nylon brushes, nut driver, pliers, rubber gloves and a caustic wheel cleaner, such as Auto Magic.

2. Most wheel covers are assembled using ¼ or 5⁄16 in. bolts. Use a nutdriver to remove the ornamental spinner or removable center cap emblem.

159

3. If possible, disassemble the center cap so you can clean and polish the ornament.

4. Place the wheel cover on the workbench and gently tap out any dents with a body hammer or straighten spokes with a pliers. On wire wheel covers, carefully straighten any bent spokes.

5. Take the wheel cover outside and spray it with water to loosen dirt and grime. Remember to wear rubber gloves because the cleaner is usually caustic and can injure unprotected skin. See label for precautions and emergency instructions. Spray the cleaner on the wheel cover. Allow the cleaner to work for about five minutes (make sure the cover stays wet) and use your nylon brush to scrub the covers. Don't forget to also clean the backs of the wheel covers. After you have cleaned the front and the back, rinse thoroughly and let dry. Clean any spacer or insulator for the center cap or ornament.

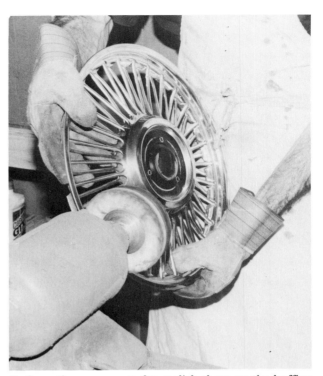

6. Once the covers are dry, polish them on the buffing wheel. Observe safety by wearing eye protection and heavy gloves to protect your hands while working with an electric buffer. Spoke covers will require hand polishing to get into the places the electric buffer can't reach. Also polish the center caps or spinners.

7. If the cover has any painted detail, tape off the area to be painted. Use a fine scuff pad on the exposed area, then use a product like Prep-Sol to remove any grease or oils.

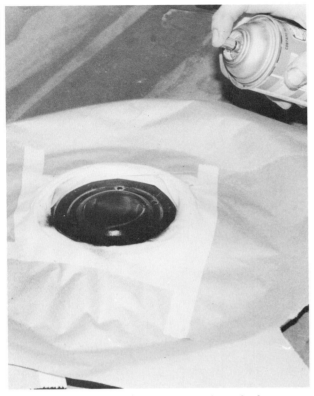

8. Once the surface has been prepped, apply the appropriate color spray paint, using thin, overlapping coats.

9. If the center emblems are plastic, you'll need to clean and polish them using a plastic cleaner and polisher, such as Meguiar's. Start by cleaning to remove any residue or slight scratches. Once the plastic is cleaned and scratch-free, polish the inserts.

10. With all components cleaned, painted and polished, begin reassembly by placing the insulator or spacer on first, then attaching the assembled center cap or spinner.

11. Install and tighten the mounting screws. Don't over-tighten the bolts; they may strip or the cover may distort.

12. The wheel cover is now refinished and ready to install on the car.

Tires

To achieve a concours restoration, installing the correct tires is extremely important. Musclecars were generally offered with high performance tires after 1966, and a variety of manufacturers supplied tires to the auto makers. The best source of information is the factory sales brochures or dealer sales albums to determine the correct size and make of tire.

Today, there are a number of companies that offer reproduction tires. They come in red-line, whitewall or blackwall designs and are identical to the OE tires except they will have the DOT (Department of Transportation) safety information stamped into the sidewall.

1. Early musclecars used standard tires. On some models, like this 1964 GTO, red-line tires were standard equipment.

3. Firestone Super Sport Wide Ovals began appearing on musclecars in 1967. They were one of the first 70–series tires, and were offered in either red-line, whitewall or blackwall applications.

2. Coker Tire (1317 Chestnut Street, P.O. Box 72554, Chattanooga, TN 37407) offers a full line of reproduction red-line tires bearing the Coker label.

4. The Goodyear Polyglass tire was offered in either raised white letters or blackwall design. They were widely offered by car makers in the late sixties and early seventies.

5. When mounting your tires, always have them indexed. Here, the valve stem is indexed over the "s" in Firestone. This was done on all of the wheels so that the tires could be matched up and all the lettering will be located in the same place when the car is shown. Don't forget to have the spare done as well.

Engine installation

With the wheels and tires now mounted on the chassis, and the drivetrain components rebuilt, refinished and ready for installation, you have now reached another major milestone in your muscle car's restoration—installing the drivetrain back into the chassis. At this point, your rolling chassis should have all brake lines and cables installed, along with fuel lines, steering box, motor mount brackets and body bushings.

If you're restoring a unibodied car, you'll be mating the front subframe onto the body and then dropping the engine and transmission into place and hooking up the driveshaft.

Extreme care is necessary during this process, not only for the drivetrain components, but also for your own personal safety. Working around engine hoists, attaching chains and other equipment requires paying attention to detail. Take your time during this process to insure the installation goes smoothly and safely.

Rolling chassis with all brake and fuel lines, cables, steering box, body bushings and motor mount brackets installed.

1. Prior to engine installation, bolt the motor mount brackets and oil filter adaptor onto the engine.

2. Before the engine can be installed, the flywheel, clutch, pressure plate and bellhousing must be installed. Attach the engine hoist chains to the proper mounting tabs on the engine, lift the engine to unload the engine stand bolts and unbolt the engine from the stand. Lower the engine to the ground, placing blocks under the engine to steady it.

3. Install the pilot bushing first. If you don't have a bushing installation tool, you can use a large brass drift to tap the bushing into place.

163

4. If so equipped, install the flex plate. Use a tap to clean out the crankshaft bolt holes before you install the flywheel. You should also clean out all bolt attaching holes on the motor before you attach any brackets or accessories.

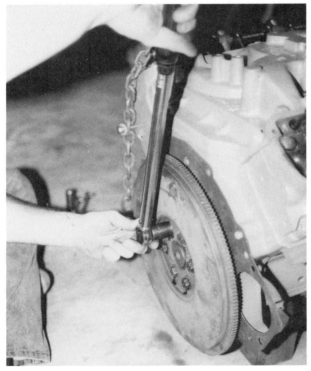

5. Position the new or refaced flywheel and install the flywheel attaching bolts. Do not use the old bolts. Use a torque wrench to tighten the bolts to the correct specifications; consult your factory service manual for this information.

6. Use a Scotch Brite abrasive pad to clean any grease or fingerprints from the flywheel surface and wipe it clean before installing the clutch.

7. Use a clutch alignment tool when installing the clutch pressure plate. Carefully align the clutch bolt holes to the holes in the flywheel and install new bolts. Prior to installation, make sure the clutch and pressure plate have been balanced.

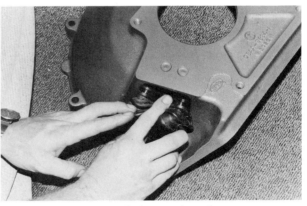

8. All manual transmission-equipped cars use some kind of clutch fork boot. If the original boot was in good condition, it can be glass-bead blasted and reused. Use a spray silicone to lubricate the grooved portion of the boot so it will slip into place easily.

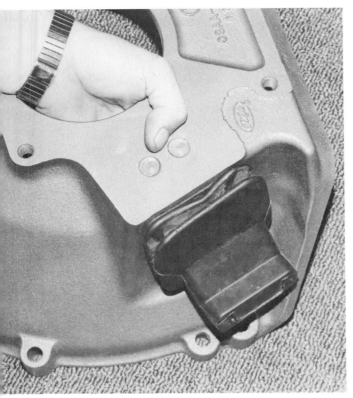

9. Work the grooved portion of the boot onto the bell-housing lip. Reach inside the bellhousing and make sure the boot is seated all the way around the opening.

11. If the engine is being installed in a unibody car, cover the fenders to protect them from possible damage and carefully position the engine into the compartment. Slowly lower it into place and bolt the motor mounts to the cross-member. With a unibody car, you will add the transmission later.

10. Slide the clutch fork in through the boot to check the fit. The clutch fork pivots on a ball on the inside of the bellhousing. A riveted clip retains the fork to the ball.

12. With a non-unibody car, you can now attach the transmission. If you have an automatic transmission-equipped car, install the torque converter and bolt the transmission onto the rear of the engine block. Install any vacuum lines from the carburetor to the modulator and the line-retaining clips. Support the assembly with three jackstands if the assembly will not be placed in the car at this time. Install the exhaust manifolds.

165

13. If you have a manual-transmission car, install the shift linkage. If you are reusing the old rods, they should be replated black cadmium or natural. The new levers, bushings and clips should be installed.

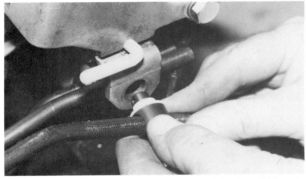

14. On Hurst shifters, a pin is installed in the shifter to lock it in the neutral gate. You then can install the new rod-to-lever swivels or trunions.

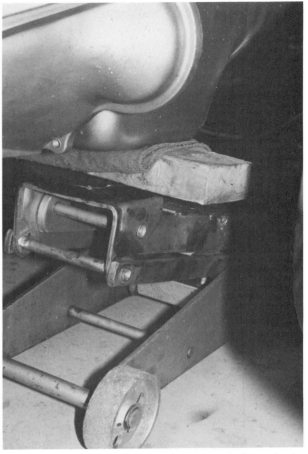

16. If you chose not to install the transmission prior to engine installation, support the rear of the engine with a jackstand, using a block and rag to prevent damage to the pan.

15. On a composite body-frame car, carefully lift the engine and roll the hoist under the front of the chassis. With the help of an assistant, position the engine over the front of the frame. Slowly lower the engine into place, having the assistant position the engine as it drops into the motor mounts. Be extremely careful during this process; many a finger has been caught between a motor mount and the frame bracket.

17. With the engine in position, thread the motor mount bolts through the mounts. It may be necessary to lift the engine slightly with the hoist to slip the bolts through the mounts. Tighten the motor mount bolts to the specifications listed in the factory service manual. Remove the attaching chains and roll the engine hoist out of the way.

18. Install the rubber insulator between the transmission and cross-member and install the attaching bolts. Torque the rear mounting bolts as specified in the factory service manual.

Driveshaft installation

1. Layout all the driveshaft components prior to assembly. Make sure the U-joints you purchase are of top quality and designed for high-performance applications.

2. Put the driveshaft on your workbench and begin the assembly process by placing the uncupped U-joint in the driveshaft yoke. Place a cup on one end. Make sure the cup is centered in the yoke. Put a towel in your vise to protect the detail work on the driveshaft, then place the driveshaft yoke with the cups into the vise. Keeping the cup centered, slowly close the vise and install the cup on one side. After you have finished one side, go on to the other side.

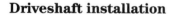

3. Now place a small spacer (even a ⅜ in. nut will work) into the center of the U-joint cup.

4. Slowly close the vise to set the U-joint cup below the retaining clip groove.

5. Some U-joints have external locking rings.

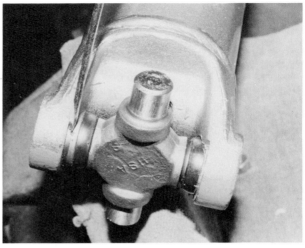

6. Other U-joints have internal locking rings.

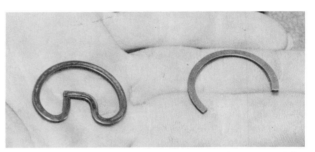

7. External lock ring on left, internal lock ring on right.

8. Install the retaining lock ring using a pair of needle-nose pliers.

9. To center the U-joint, use a brass drift. Place the drift against the center boss of the U-joint and hit it firmly. Do this on both sides of the U-joint.

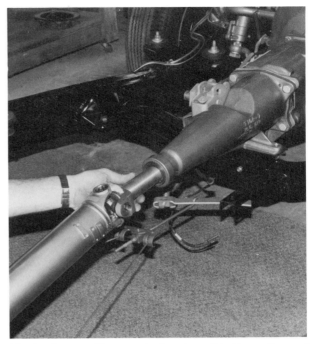

11. Apply a small amount of engine oil to the spline and the outside diameter of the yoke and slide it onto the transmission output shaft.

10. The transmission yoke installs the same way as the rear yoke. With the U-joints and yokes installed, the driveshaft is now ready for installation. The installation will be the same for composite body-frame or unibody cars.

12. Place the rear driveshaft yoke into the rear end companion flange. Make sure the U-joint cups fit into the rear end yoke.

169

13. Install the universal-joint U-bolts, thread the nuts onto the bolts.

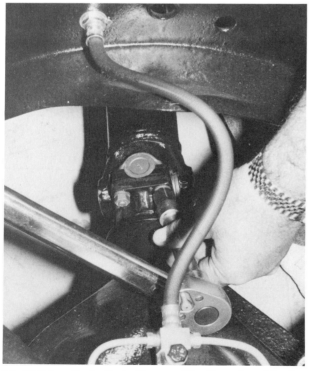

14. Tighten the bolts to the specifications found in the factory service manual. The driveshaft is now installed.

15. At this point, your rolling chassis should have an engine, transmission and driveshaft installed.

Exhaust system installation

1. For a proper restoration, don't use universal hangers that are sold at the corner parts store. Obtain the correct hangers and install them as per the factory service manual or assembly instruction book.

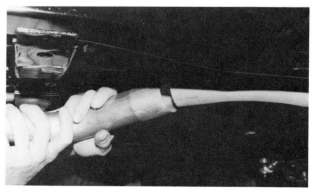

2. Start from the H or Y pipe first, and work towards the rear. Install the H or Y pipe, then install the exhaust pipe.

3. All muffler clamps should point down or to the side, depending on location and manufacturer. Clamps never point up on any factory-installed exhaust system.

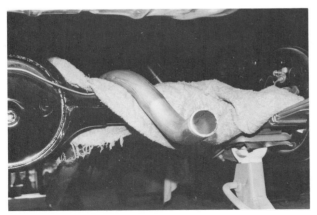

4. When installing the tailpipe where it routes over the rear end housing, put some kind of protection on the axle tube to avoid scraping and nicks to the finish.

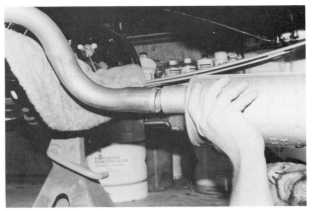

5. Install the muffler to the inlet pipe. If it has lineup tabs, make sure to align them properly.

6. It may be necessary to tap the muffler onto the inlet pipe to obtain the correct length and position. Always use a large rubber hammer for this.

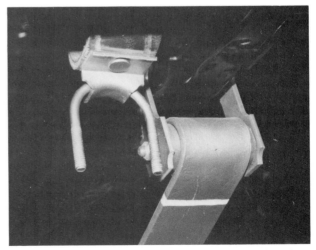

7. Prop up the exhaust system to make sure the pipes are properly positioned and that all of the hangers line up correctly. After you have done this, place the muffler clamps into position, facing downward.

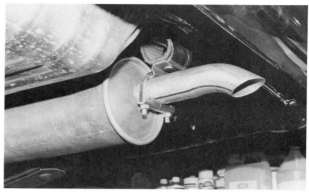

9. Once everything is satisfactory, torque the clamps to the specifications found in the factory service manual.

8. Put the exhaust system into place and snug all your clamps. Check for frame clearance. If the pipes don't clear, adjust the system to obtain the correct clearances.

Halfway point of the restoration

At this point, with the drivetrain and exhaust installed, the rolling chassis is completed. You are now at the midpoint of the restoration. From here on, you'll be working on the body, preparing it to be dropped back on the frame.

If you're working on a unibody car, the drivetrain and exhaust will be installed once the car is painted. Don't let the different processes confuse you; approaching the restoration of a composite body-frame car and a unibody car require different strategies. The end result is the same. The only difference is in the restoration sequence.

The composite body-frame chassis at the halfway point with drivetrain installed.

6

Body and Paint Work

Whether you're restoring a composite body-frame or a unibody car, it is a process completely separate from the mechanical restoration. One of the first things you'll want to do is construct a dolly to move the body easily. It's a simple affair, made from 4x4 and 2x4 lumber. You'll want to use a set of heavy-duty casters so the body can be moved around the garage or outside. After you've determined the proper location for the mounting holes, drill them out and place the body on the dolly. Now insert large carriage bolts through the body-to-frame mounting holes and through the top of the dolly frame. Install the nuts and tighten. The body is now secured to the dolly and easy to move.

Unibody cars can be mounted on frames as well. You may build a dolly similar to the one used for composite bodies, or you can purchase one of the units advertised in *Hemmings*. Either way, you'll find this is a much more convenient way to store and work on the body.

If you plan on having the body and paint work farmed out, now is the time to send the body out to the shop. Depending on the shop, it will take several days to several weeks for the body and paint work to be completed. Picking the shop that will perform the work on your musclecar can be difficult if you aren't familiar with the shops in your area. Ask your fellow club members which shop has the best reputation and inspect their work. Body and paint work isn't cheap, so make sure you've budgeted ample funds to cover the work, and be prepared for the shop to give you a high and low estimate. Forget the low side of the estimate and assume the bill will exceed the high side. An estimate is just that—a projection of the final cost. Regardless of how carefully you inspected the car prior to purchase and how well the shop prepared the estimate, there's really no telling what they'll find once the paint is off and the metal is bare. And if there are some surprises under the paint, the bill will be adjusted upward.

Once the body is at the shop, you'll want to visit regularly to see how the process is going. You're not visiting to make sure the shop is doing the job right (although it doesn't hurt). The important thing is you know how the car looks and what condition it was in once the paint was removed. This is *your* car, and you want to know everything about it, even if you're not doing the work yourself.

If you're going to tackle the body and paint work yourself (and you've never done it before), we recommend you purchase several instructional books on body and paint work. These are available from Classic Motorbooks and other sources.

Stripping and paint removal

1. The easiest method for paint removal is chemical stripping. Always wear rubber gloves and work in a well-ventilated area. Never strip paint in direct sunlight. When applying the paint stripper, always brush it in the same direction and slightly overlap the strokes. After you have applied the paint stripper, do not go back over it until it has finished working. Depending on ambient temperatures, 15–45 minutes are required.

2. As the stripper begins to work, the paint will bubble. You can then loosen it for removal.

4. After the first application, a second may be needed. Apply the stripper using the same method as before. Overlap your strokes and apply in one direction.

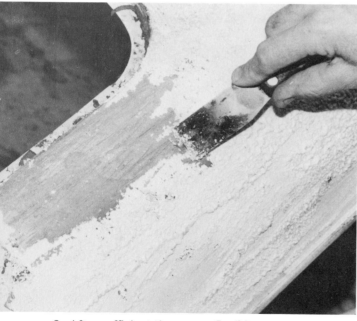

3. After sufficient time, use a flexible scraper to remove the first layer of stripped paint. Don't worry if it all doesn't come off the first time.

5. After the second application of stripper, most of the paint will be removed. To get at the paint in tight areas and corners, use 00 or 000 steel wool.

6. You will now be able to remove the remainder by using a DA sander. This will take everything away down to the bare metal.

7. The surface has been stripped and sanded and is now ready for the body work process to begin. Notice the two types of supports used for the body. The dolly under the

GTO isn't pretty, but it's sturdy, easy to construct and the body is securely attached.

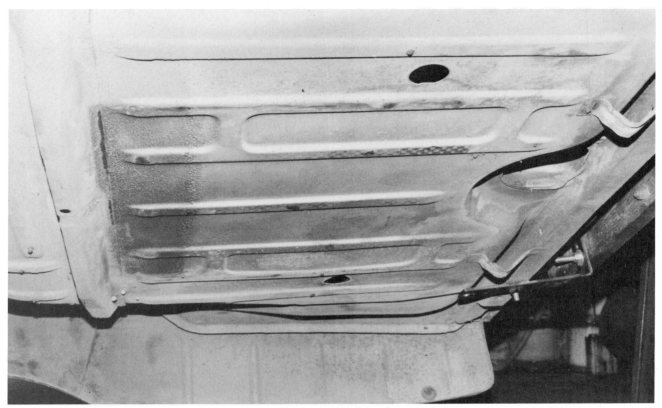

8. The easiest way to remove underbody paint and undercoating is to sandblast. Always sandblast at a 45 degree angle to the area you are blasting and move the sandblast nozzle across the area. Never point directly at a particular area because this will either warp or blast right through the metal. Also use 30/65 sand. It cuts well and doesn't plug up the nozzle. Make sure you use a filter and water trap on the sandblaster. If you don't, condensation will form in the tank and cause the sand to get wet and clog the nozzle.

Body work or panel replacement?

Even the most experienced body man can't detect body damage that is hidden by Bondo and paint. Using the Pro-Gauge and Spot Rot can give you an idea about what's under the paint, but only after the paint is stripped will you get a complete picture of just how good—or bad—the condition of the body really is. Remember, we're dealing with cars twenty through thirty years old. There's no telling what's happened over the years. If there's been accident damage or extensive rust repair, you'll have to decide whether to replace or repair the affected body panels.

When you reach this crossroads, a decision has to be made about what's the best and the most economical choice. Major rust or substantial body damage dictates panel replacement. In the long run, it is cheaper than the hours of work you will have to perform, or pay for, to get new pieces fabricated or repaired. Fortunately, there are several choices when it comes to replacement panels. A number of vendors advertising in *Hemmings* offer solid body panels from the Southwestern region of the country. If NOS (new old stock) panels are available, by all means consider the purchase. However, NOS body panels may be extremely expensive. Used, rust-free panels are cheaper and require little work to be excellent.

The other choice is reproduction panels, and here we must advise caution. Several years ago, the collision repair business began using "off-shore" sheetmetal. These panels are sourced from Asia, and are generally inferior due to impurities in the metal. In many cases, the panels are not accurately stamped out and may often not fit properly. That requires plenty of panel beating to make things fit. The final problem with using repro panels is, because of the inherent impurity and acidity of the metal, some of the chemicals in the metal will eventually rise to the surface. These impurities are then sandwiched between the metal surface and the paint, and begin eating away at the paint. This results in paint bubbling and deterioration. Many times, the metal actually rusts away beneath the paint.

The bottom line to choosing reproduction panels is to question the vendor thoroughly as to where the panels are manufactured and their quality. Obviously, cheap panels are just that—cheap. Unless you plan on stripping the paint, performing body work all over again and then repainting, do it right the first time and use care when buying reproduction body panels.

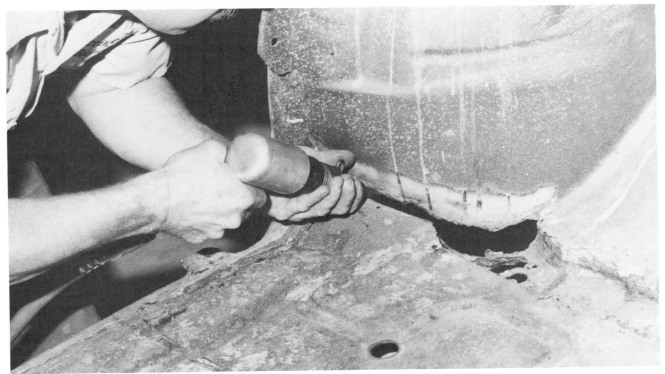

1. There are a variety of different methods to remove damaged or rusted panels: cutting torch, air chisel and cutting disc. Cutting torches are good for removing large areas of metal, badly rusted sections and for fast work.

Air chisels work well on seams. Cutting discs are used when you want straight, precise cuts, especially when you're going to install patch panels.

2. On this trunk floor, both a cutting disc and air chisel were used to remove the rotted metal.

4. If you're fitting new panels, drill and place three or four screws to temporarily hold the panel in place.

3. The quarter panel was removed from this car because the accident damage, which had been hidden by plastic filler, was too extensive for body work. The deck and part of the trunk were rotted, requiring removal and new metal replacement pieces installed. Don't be afraid of body warpage as long as you're removing panels. Cutting out any major body braces, however, could cause the body to twist once they are removed.

5. Spot weld, stitch weld or braze the panel into place. Do not apply too much heat or the panel and surrounding metal may warp.

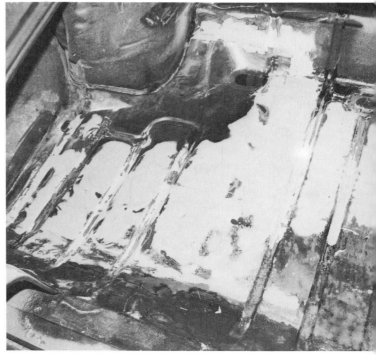

7. Use either lead or All-Metal to fill in the welded seams and any rough spots in the trunk area. Sand the areas smooth.

6. Once the panel is welded into place, grind the weld flash smooth.

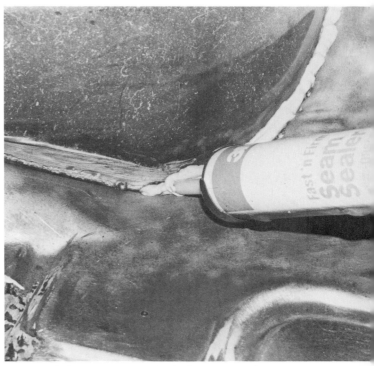

8. Apply 3M seam sealer to all the floor seams. Smooth it with your finger to duplicate the factory appearance. Don't make it look pretty, just give it an assembly line look.

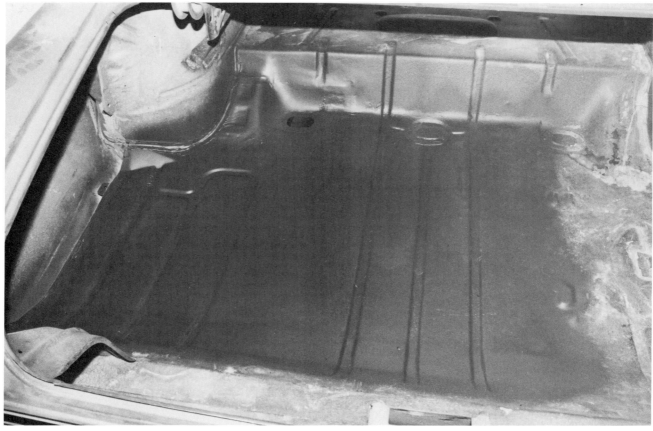

9. Apply dark primer to the repaired area to find any floor imperfections. If you find some, work these areas smooth. Although trunk fleck paint hides a lot of ills, don't do a second-rate finishing job in the trunk.

10. Check the lower quarter for rust. If the area is weak, grind off the rust and patch or repair the metal.

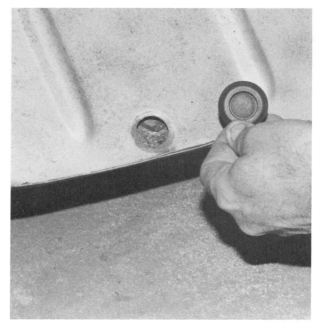

11. Always make sure the rear quarter panel drains are open. Never close this area off because if water gets down into this cavity, it can't drain and rust will reform.

Using lead and plastic filler

Lead and plastic fillers were both used by car makers in the sixties and seventies. Lead was utilized on all exterior seams, and plastic was applied to smooth slight body imperfections. Lead repair requires considerable practice before perfecting the technique, that's why plastic is popular. It's easier to use than lead and is much faster. It's better to use lead on all body seams, just as the assembly plant did. You can also use All-Metal, which is a catalyzed, metal-impregnated product. It's a cross between lead and plastic, easy to use and has some of the characteristics of lead.

Plastic should only be used to smooth out slight body imperfections, and not as a filler. Plastic filler creates heat when it's applied, and too much filler can warp long, flat body panels. Always use as little plastic filler as possible. If you have to use more than a $\frac{1}{16}$ in., then you haven't worked the damaged area out enough.

2. Use either an electric or MIG welder to fill unwanted holes like these nameplate piercings on a replacement panel.

3. After the holes have been filled, use a small grinder to smooth the area out.

1. These small rust holes have been ground and are now being filled on this backglass channel. These can be brazed in if there are small holes. If not, they must be metal patched, and then filled.

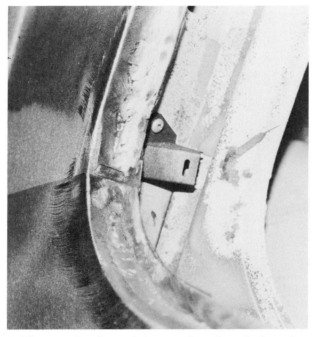

4. The completed repair is smooth and ready for priming and painting.

6. All-Metal is applied to the seam where the replacement rear quarter panel meets the C-pillar.

5. Applying All-Metal to the rear quarter panel; remember to keep the coats of All-Metal as thin as possible.

182

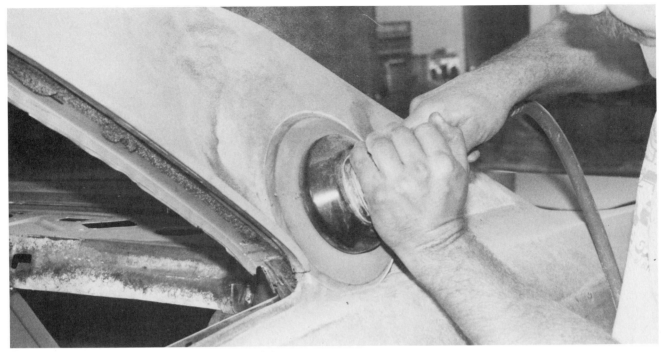

7. Once the All-Metal has set, use a DA to sand the area smooth. Work the area carefully, using your fingers to check the smoothness.

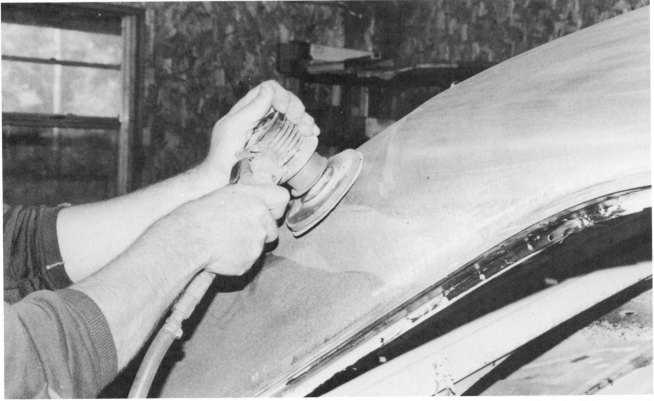

8. This body seam was leaded in and is now being sanded with a DA. Always be careful of the heat generated by the DA. Move the DA around, because keeping it in one spot for too long can cause the metal to warp.

Selecting the right paint

There are three basic types of paint: lacquer, enamel and urethane. Each paint has its own special characteristics. Lacquer is by far the easiest to use because it can be layered to achieve a superior depth of shine. It also involves the most work if you desire a concours-winning shine. To get a quality lacquer paint finish, you must apply three or four coats of paint, let it thoroughly dry and then sand two of the coats off. Continue to do this until you have seven to ten coats of paint that have been sanded. This is why show cars have what is called a "hand-sanded lacquer" paint job. Never apply more than ten finished coats (in other words, you had to apply twenty coats total, with half of them sanded down).

Because lacquer has a tendency to crack when too much paint is applied, remember the more time you take spraying and sanding your finish, the better the final result will be. Clear should only be used with high metallic colors and only as a mixing agent. Your three final recoats should be a mixture of fifty-percent clear and fifty-percent color, then seventy-percent clear and thirty-percent color and then a final coat consisting of ninety-percent clear and ten-percent color. This will eliminate the blotches that seem to appear in metallic paints. It will also eliminate buffing hot spots when you compound buff the finish. Lacquer requires a lot of work to finish. After you have hand-sanded the paint for the last time, you now have to compound buff it out. Use a coarse compound and a buffer that runs in the 2,000 to 2,400 rpm range. After compound buffing, then polish buff it. This is a mild compound with a polish to bring up the depth in the shine. Now orbital wax and finally hand wax the paint.

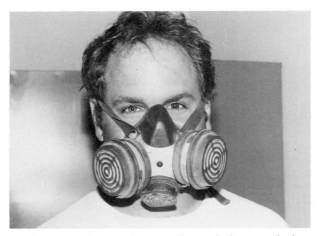

1. Wear a respirator when sanding, priming or painting. Breathing in fumes or dust from body or paint work can cause permanent lung damage. It may look funny and be cumbersome to wear, but the alternative of internal injury is far less pleasant.

Lacquer paint is the easiest to spot or touch up, but it also chips the easiest. Lacquer also requires constant upkeep. Waxing once a month is virtually a necessity. Lacquer is not the paint of choice for the lazy, but the results are worth the extra work.

Enamel is a tried-and-true paint. It has been used for years, although not as long as lacquer. It was developed because it is much easier and faster to get a finished result than lacquer. It is sprayed on in two to five coats and no sanding is required between coats. It takes longer to dry and does not have the depth of shine that lacquer has. It is more durable, but is much harder to color match if repair is necessary. It also has a tendency to "orange peel," instead of having the glass-smooth finish of lacquer. Applying enamel paint requires a dirt- and dust-free environment.

Urethane is the latest development in automotive paint. It has excellent depth of shine and greater durability. It also has the ability to be sanded just like lacquer after it has hardened. If done correctly, urethane will look like a lacquer paint finish. The difficulty is in achieving correct color matches to the factory lacquer or enamel paint used twenty to thirty years ago. It can be mixed approximately the original color, but getting a perfect match is nearly impossible. Touch up or spot work is as with enamel; sometimes whole panels have to painted to match existing areas. Urethane does have superior durability, and is recommended if the car is going to be driven much of the time. It is very chip resistant and requires less upkeep than lacquer. Urethane is the hardest to paint, and should be done by a professional who is experienced in its application.

The right environment and equipment

A quality paint job is only as good as the environment in which it is applied. Dust and floating debris will ruin a carefully-laid paint job. The paint environment must be dust free: That means a clean floor, ceiling and walls and an exhaust fan stationed at a window to remove airborne dust and paint spray.

Make sure you have plenty of light, 50 ft. of ¼ or ⅜ in. air hose, at least a three-horsepower compressor with a filter and water trap and a mixing bench or table. You'll also need plenty of paint strainers, quality stir sticks (don't use a broken yardstick or a screwdriver!), a top-quality spray gun with a pressure regulator, paint masks and head cover.

When painting the body, ground it to eliminate static electricity. Grounding can be done by draping a chain over some point on the body and letting it touch the floor. The bottom line to a good paint finish is this: The cleaner the shop, the better the job.

Priming

How well the car is primed will show in the finished paint job. Remember, the primer is the base for your paint. Always use the same brand of primer as the paint. That also goes for all reducers and thinners. Also make sure the primer is compatible with the paint you're using: Lacquer primer for lacquer paint, enamel for enamel and so on.

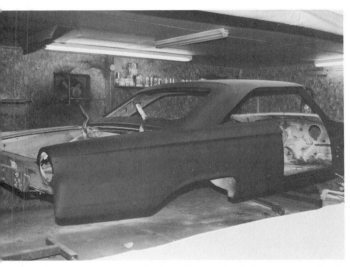

1. Always use a dark primer. By doing so, any body flaws are easier to spot as you sand through the first coat of primer.

3. Continue to sand and prime until the body starts to take on a smooth and even look.

2. The floorpans and firewall should also be primed.

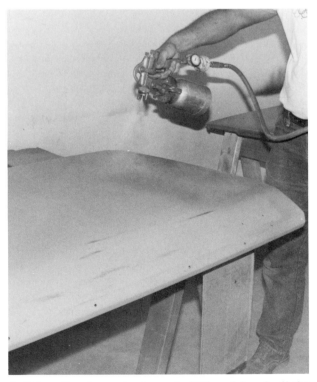

4. Prime the doors, fenders, decklid and hood off the body.

5. After you've primed and sanded the body enough times that you are satisfied it's as smooth as possible, the car is now ready for painting.

6. Priming and block sanding the hood make for a better finish. One time is not enough. Three or four times is more like it. Take the time and extra effort here; the results will be worth it.

Painting

Always mix the paint according to the manufacturer's directions on the can and spray at their recommended pressures. Also check the shop temperature and use the correct thinners or reducers for the temperatures as specified by the

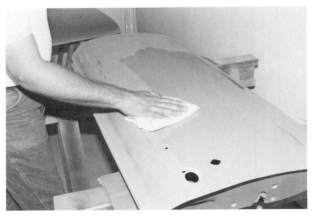

1. After you're sure the shop is clean, use a tack rag to wipe down the surface of the car and all off-body panels to be painted.

manufacturer. If you don't follow these directions, your paint will either dry too fast or too slow. If you are spraying lacquer, avoid painting on days with high humidity, low temperatures or rain (or soon after). Try to spray in temperatures between the high-fifties and the mid-nineties. Also, don't spray urethanes or enamels in low temperatures or rain.

3. As the body is being painted, move over and spray the panels off the car such as the hood and fenders. If you're spraying lacquer, these panels should be sanded at the same time as the body. This ensures these panels will have the same color and depth of shine as the body. Remember to finish the underside of the hood, even if it's going to get an insulator pad (remember that some makes have a thirty-percent gloss black underhood).

Painting the underbody and firewall

2. Test spray your gun by spraying a clean piece of primered scrap metal to check your pressure, pattern and flow. If it is correct, begin painting the body. Start at the center of the roof, and use long, overlapping strokes. Continue from the front of the roof to the rear of the roof. Do one side at a time. After you have finished one side, go over to the other side and spray in the same manner. Spray light, even coats, and don't put too much paint on at one time. You can't paint the whole car in one coat.

After the roof is covered, move to the sides. Just remember you don't want to lean on your fresh paint. Continue to work until the whole car is covered. If you're using lacquer, your first coat will flash dry in about ten minutes. Go back and start again in the same sequence you used on the first coat. If you're using enamel or urethane, spray the first coat medium wet, allow it to flash dry and then follow with a full wet coat. Allow it to flash dry again, and then apply a final wet coat. Follow the paint directions, don't rush and your paint job should turn out the way you want.

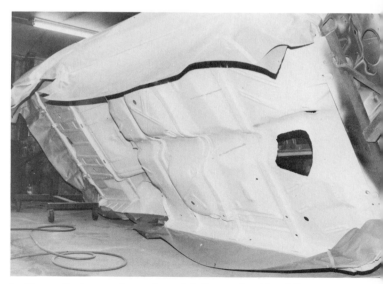

1. Depending on make and model, the underside of the car may be painted body color or thirty-percent gloss black. Regardless of color, make sure the body panels are protected as the underbody is painted. Notice how the paint edge is feathered as the underbody meets the firewall. Paint the entire engine compartment and firewall exterior color on Chrysler products.

2. Prepare the firewall for painting just as you did the body. The better the preparation, the better the end result will be.

4. After the firewall is painted, replace any factory assembly codes or markings. Always replace these in their original positions, even if you'll never see them again. The judges won't see them, but you know they're there.

Applying body schutz

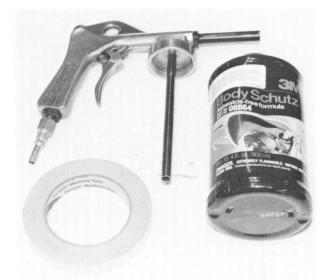

3. Most cars use a thirty-percent gloss black for the firewall finish. Careful use of overspray to reproduce factory painting techniques is acceptable and encouraged for a concours restoration.

1. To spray the body schutz, you'll need a body schutz or undercoat gun, masking tape and a can of 3M Body Schutz.

2. The body schutz is applied after the body has been painted. This is how the trunk inner quarters look before the body schutz application.

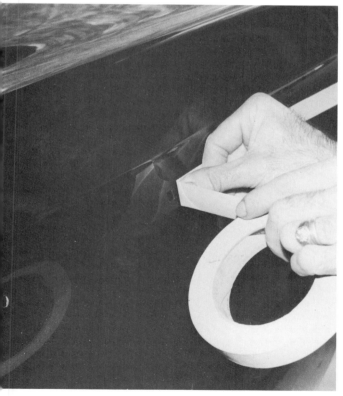

3. Mask off any holes that open into the trunk area.

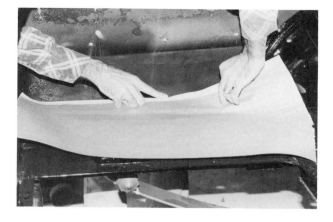

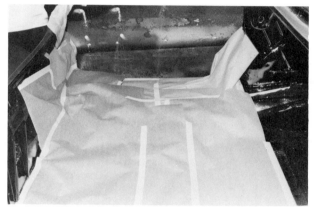

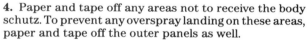

4. Paper and tape off any areas not to receive the body schutz. To prevent any overspray landing on these areas, paper and tape off the outer panels as well.

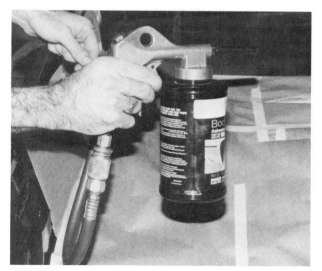

5. Stir or shake the schutz thoroughly and then attach the container directly to the body schutz paint gun. By adjusting the air pressure you can change the schutz spray pattern. With a little experimentation, you can duplicate the original pattern.

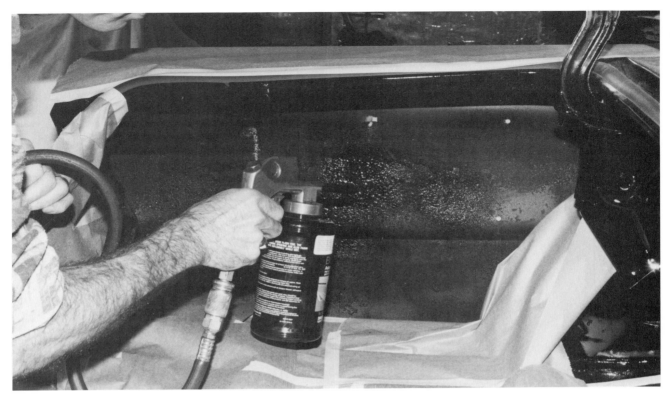

6. Spray about 8 to 10 in. away and overlap your paint strokes.

7. Since it gets a little dark in the trunk corners, use a light in the trunk area to be able to see into all the corners as you are painting. Don't forget to spray down into the well and under the lip of the rear quarter panel.

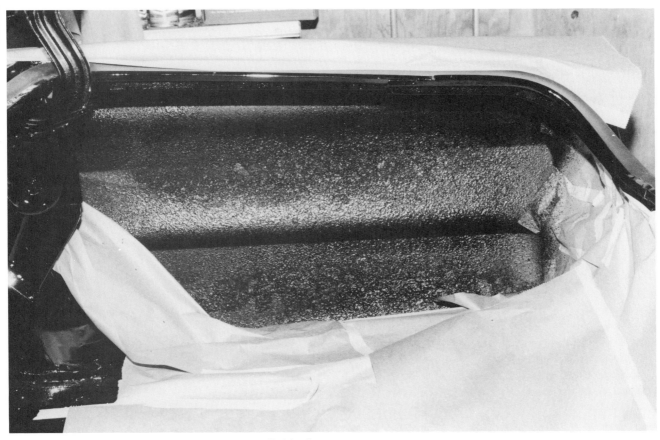

8. This is what it looks like after you have just finished spraying.

9. This product was also used in the doors for sound deadener. Before painting here, use masking tape to tape over any holes and then begin to spray into the doors.

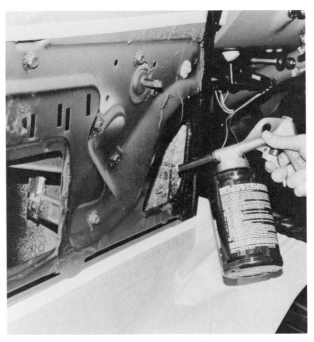

10. Move the spray gun around so that you can get into all the cavities.

11. Also, don't forget to spray in the rear quarter window area. Remember to tape off any holes in the quarter panel before spraying.

13. Now disassemble the spray gun and soak it in lacquer thinner. After it has soaked for about fifteen minutes, clean and dry it off and reassemble.

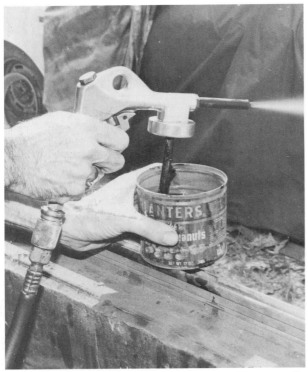

12. After you have finished, clean your spray gun by running lacquer thinner through it.

14. Now go back and carefully remove your tape and paper. Always remember to pull the tape back over itself when you are removing it.

Installing trunk weatherstripping

1. Pre-fit the trunk weatherstrip. This means you see how it will fit and if there is enough length provided. Do not cut off any excess. Use a flat-blade screwdriver to carefully tuck the weatherstrip into place.

2. After you have pre-fit the weatherstripping, remove it and place a small bead of weatherstrip adhesive in the channel.

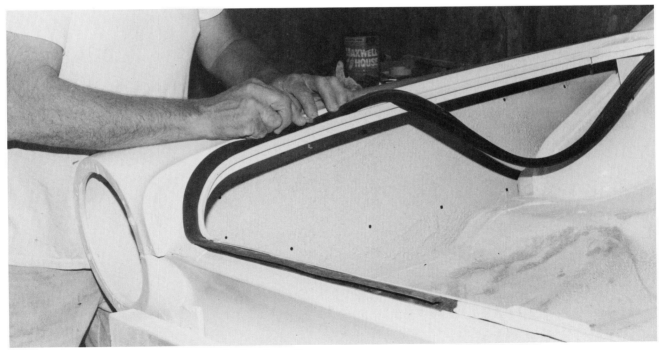

3. Now install the trunk weatherstripping into the channel, tucking it in as you go just as you did during the trial fitting.

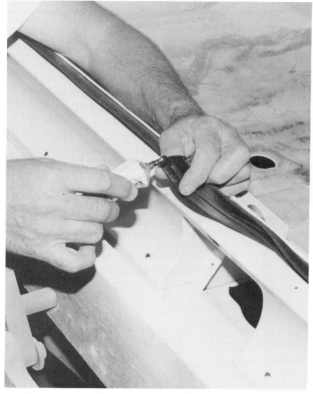

4. Work the weatherstripping all the way around to your starting point. Place the two ends together, and cut the one end about ½ in. longer than is needed. Place a small dab of weatherstrip adhesive or super glue in each end. Take the remaining end and butt it to the other end. Making one end ½ in. longer, causes it to press up against the starting end and provides a tighter joint.

5. The finished trunk weatherstripping should be even and the joint shouldn't be visible.

Spraying trunk fleck paint

1. Most cars built in the sixties and seventies received a "fleck" type paint to finish the trunk floor and sides. Depending on manufacturer, these paints are usually flecked with gray and white, black and gray or various shades of gray and green or green and aqua. You'll need a paint gun and the correct fleck paint to finish the trunk. Trunk fleck paint is also sold in aerosol bottles.

2. Stir the trunk paint thoroughly before use. Do not thin the mixture unless the directions specify to do so.

3. Pour the trunk paint into a one-quart spray cup.

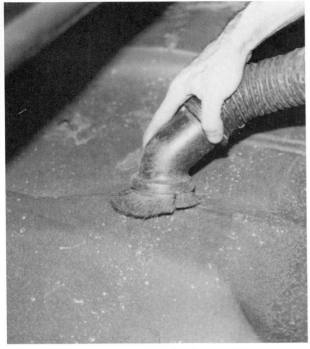

4. Use a brush to loosen any paint dust and then vacuum the trunk floor, lower rear quarter cavities and the rear axle hump. Make sure the trunk floor is clean before any trunk paint is applied.

5. Now you can spray the trunk. The pattern of the fleck paint can be adjusted by increasing or decreasing the air pressure. The higher the pressure, the smaller the flecks. The lower the pressure, the larger the specks.

6. Don't forget to spray in all the corners and crevices. Do the front area behind the seats first. Then cover both wheelwells and the rear quarter cavities. Do the trunk floor last.

Interior painting

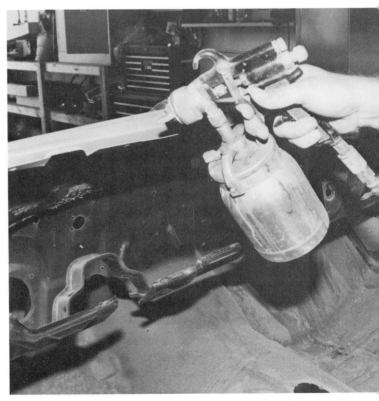

1. The interior is sprayed just as you would the exterior. All interiors are sprayed with a sixty-percent gloss, low-gloss or semi-gloss finish, depending on make and location in the car. The factory parts book usually supplies information on interior paint. Most auto paint stores also have information on how interiors should be finished. Prepare the areas to be painted just as you would the exterior. Here again, sanding and good old elbow grease will pay off in the end. Use thin, overlapping strokes when you paint, just as you did for the exterior.

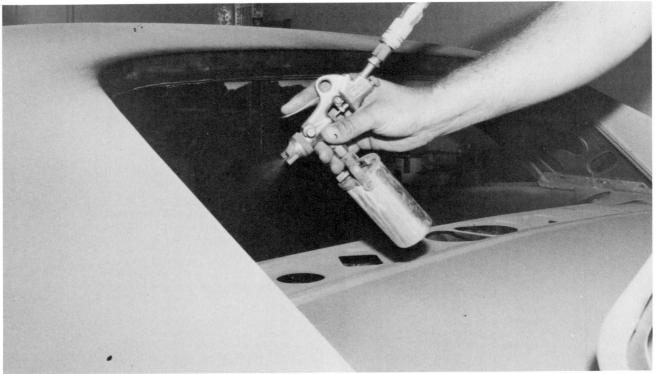

2. Always do the pillar posts, rear package shelf and sail panels. It's much easier to do them now than when the car is finished. Tape off any exterior areas that might receive any paint overspray.

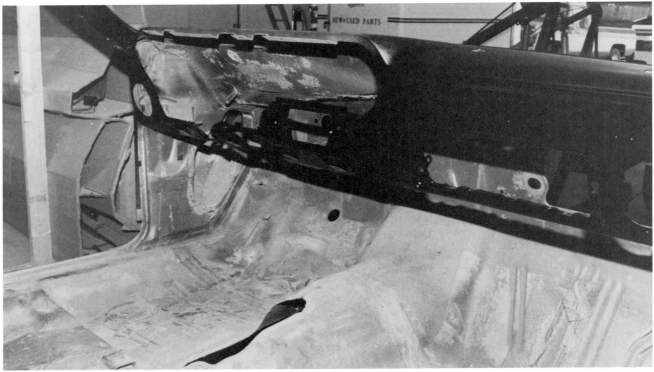

3. If the dash can be removed from the car, it just makes the job of repainting that much easier. If not, you'll have to paint it in the car. Take your time, tape off the exterior paint where overspray might reach and you'll paint the interior with a minimum of problems.

Sanding the finished paint

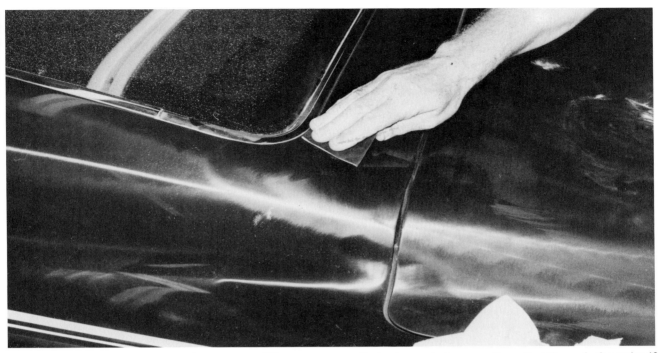

1. Use ultrafine sand paper to sand out any small imperfections in the final finish. Sand any areas wet. This will eliminate most chances of sanding through the paint if you're careful.

2. Always keep the paper wet and flat. Sand up to but never on any edges. It is also a good idea to use a sanding pad (a small, flat rubber pad is available from 3M) when sanding the surface. The pad will distribute your hand pressure evenly upon the painted surface. Now allow the painted body and panels to sit in the sun as long as possible (several weeks is ideal) to allow the paint to cure.

Installing hinges and doors

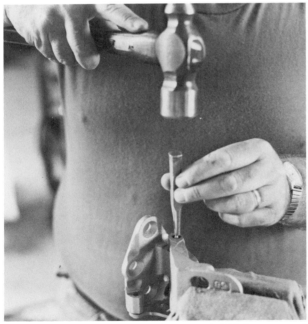

1. After you have removed the hinges from the door, place each one in a vise and use a screwdriver to carefully remove the hinge spring. Use eye protection to avoid personal injury.

2. Take the hinge out of the vise, turn it 180 degrees and reclamp it. Use a punch and hammer to drive the old hinge pin out. Note how the hinge is assembled before you drive the pin out, because if you drop the pin and the hinge comes apart, you could possibly reassemble it improperly. After the pin is removed, use a nylon punch to drive out the brass or nylon pin bushings.

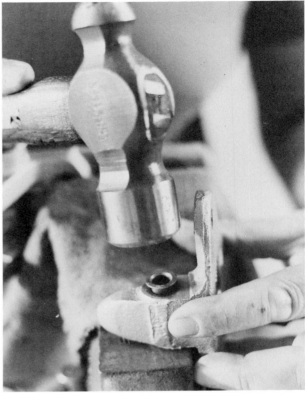

3. Now take the new bushing and install it in the door hinge. Make sure you seat the shoulder of the bushing against the hinge surface. Gently tap the brass bushing into place. Striking the bushing hard will cause it to distort or flatten.

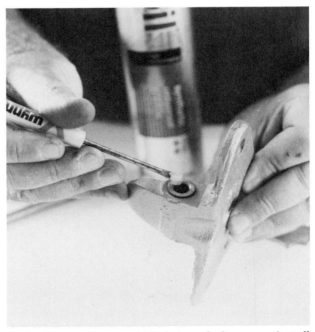

4. Apply a small amount of lubricant before you reinstall the hinge pin. This will ease the pin installation.

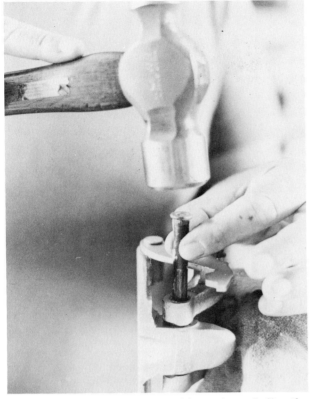

5. Place some lubricant on the hinge pin and align the two halves of the hinge together. Secure the main section of the hinge in a vise (use a towel to protect the hinge). After the hinge halves are aligned, gently tap the hinge pin into place. Be sure to seat the pin against the hinge shoulder so that the splined shank of the pin secures it in place.

6. Reinstall the hinges on the pillar post and torque to the specifications found in the factory service or body repair manual. Then install the door to the hinges. Snug the bolts but don't torque them down. You'll have to align the door for both height and gap by moving the door around on the hinges.

Installing door weatherstripping

1. Trail fit the door weatherstripping to make sure it is the proper length. Once you're satisfied it's correct, apply a thin bead of weatherstrip cement on the door crease. Then place a small bead on the door weatherstrip. Install the weatherstrip, working from the front to the rear of the door.

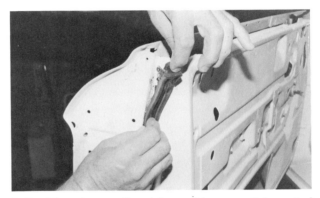

2. Position the weatherstrip, making sure it is seated against the door in the proper location. Press it down to get a good adhesive seal.

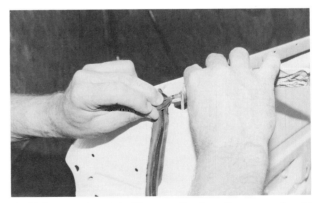

3. If the weatherstrip fits over the door lip, remember to place a small amount of weatherstrip adhesive there, and then press the weatherstrip into place.

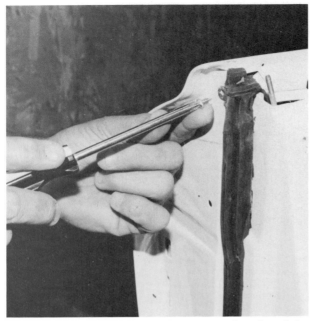

4. If a mounting screw is used to secure the edge of the weatherstrip, align the hole in the door with the one in the weatherstrip and install the screw.

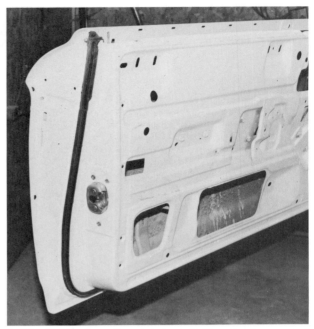

5. The finished weatherstrip installation. Apply a coat of protectorant to the rubber at this time. Now that the weatherstrip is installed, finish aligning the door. Once it is properly aligned, torque the door hinge bolts to the specifications found in the factory service or body manual.

Body-to-frame installation

1. There are a variety of ways to lower a composite body back on a frame. The body can be picked up by six helpers, lifted off the stands and then the frame is rolled into position under the body. When picking up the body by hand, wear work gloves or place rags under the body because metal edges can be sharp and could cause injury to hands. Once the body is properly located over the frame, lower it into place.

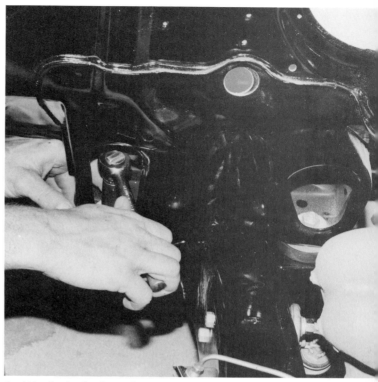

2. If you are using a set of body stands, roll the chassis under the body. Position floorjacks under the body and release the body stands. Lower the front of the body onto the frame and then carefully lower the rear of the body into place.

4. Attach the body-to-frame bolts at the firewall first, then work toward the rear. Snug the bolts but do not torque them down.

3. Use new body-to-frame bolts and bushings. Avoid polyurethane bushings, as they will creak, cause undue body shake and make for an uncomfortable ride.

5. After the front bolts are installed, attach the floorpan bolts next. Snug them down but don't torque them yet.

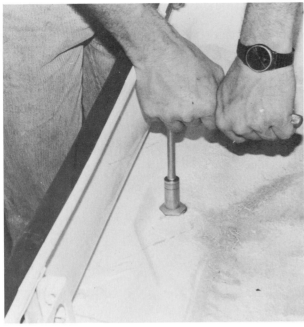

6. Continue to work toward the rear and finish up at the trunk pan. Check your body height, making sure the body is sitting evenly. Once you are sure the body is correctly positioned, tighten *all* the bolts to factory specifications.

8. Thread the body-to-frame bolt through the frame rail. You'll probably have to jockey the subframe around until the bolt slips into place.

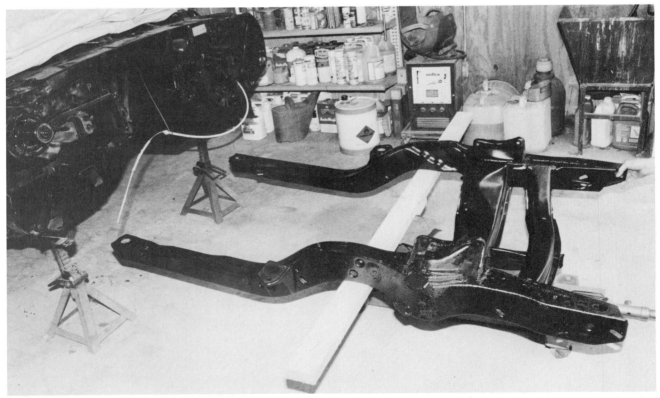

7. On unibody cars, position a floorjack under the front cross-member. A 2x4 supported by wood blocks will steady the assembly until you are ready to install the subframe. With a helper, remove the 2x4 and blocks, pick up the rear rails and position the rear of the subframe under the body as the helper works the floorjack.

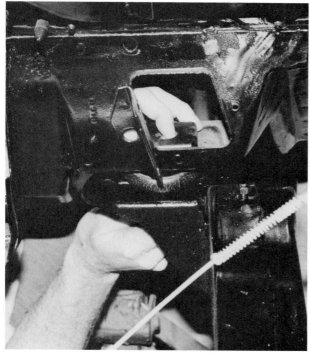

9. Now place the rubber bushing into place and install the nut. Snug the bolt and make sure the subframe assembly is correctly aligned. Once you are satisfied it is in position, torque the body-to-frame bolts to the manufacturer's specifications.

10. With the subframe now secured, place jackstands under the front frame rails to make sure the car is balanced.

Installing the fuel tank

1. Place the rubber seal or anti-squeak pads on the top of the fuel tank. Place the fuel tank on a padded floorjack and roll it under the trunk pan. Lift the tank with the floorjack and slip the rear of the new tank straps into the slots in the trunk pan. Pull the straps around the tank and position the front of the straps in the retaining brackets. In some cases, anti-squeak pads may be used between the straps and the tank.

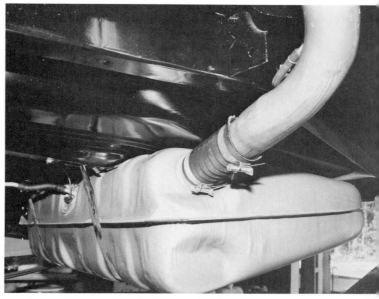

Thread the carriage bolts securing the straps to the body into place and loosely tighten the nuts. On cars with rear-mounted filler necks, the end of the neck should be correctly aligned in the fuel filler door cavity. On side-mounted filler necks, install the neck, the rubber coupler and clamps. Make sure everything is aligned properly and then torque the carriage bolts and the clamps.

7

Reassembly

Now that the body is back on the completed chassis (or the subframe, rear suspension and drivetrain are installed on unibody cars), you can begin reattaching components under the hood and to the body.

As you progressed through the drivetrain, chassis and body, you've learned how critical the factor of quality craftsmanship can be. With the exception of the bodywork, most of your efforts will be hidden from view, obscured by other components or by the body itself. Chances are, the only ones to scrutinize this work will be show judges, and if they're competent, they won't miss a trick.

Nearly all of the work to be done now will be clearly visible to the casual observer. The craftsmanship you've developed will be invaluable as you move through the underhood and exterior of your musclecar. There's always the temptation to rush things here. As the car takes form and gets closer to completion, many restorers get ahead of themselves. Don't fall into the trap of the "let's just put this thing on to see how it will look" syndrome. This will only cause you to rush other things to get to this point. Take your time refinishing and reinstalling components. Step back occasionally and admire your work. And give yourself a pat on the back—a lot of first-time restorers never get this far.

Underhood refinishing chart

This underhood refinishing chart will assist you in restoring the numerous small components located on the engine or in the engine compartment. If you are restoring a musclecar for concours showing in a particular marque club, it's recommended you research the judging standards for that club. Requirements for restoration vary from club to club.

Component	GM	Ford	Mopar	AMC
Inner fenders	30% GB	30% GB	Body color	Body color
Fender-to-inner fender bolts	NBO	NBO	Body color	Body color
Shock tower brackets	—	30% GB	—	30% GB
Shock tower braces	—	30% GB	—	—
Cooling system components				
Core support	GB	GB	Body color*	—
Radiator	GB	GB	GB	GB
Core support bolts	NBO	NBO	N/Body color	N/Body color
Core support-to-fender braces	30% GB	—	—	—
Fan shield	30% GB	GB	30% GB	30% GB
Brake and steering components				
Master cylinder	CI	CI	GB or CI	GB or CI
Master cylinder cap	GC	GC/C/CH	GC/B	GC/N
Power brake booster	GC	B	B	B
Steering box	N	N	N	N
Power steering pump	30% GB	**	GB	GB
Engine components				
Distributor	N	N	N	N
Coil	60% GB	***	GB	GB
Generator	N/GB	N/GB	N/GB	N/GB
Alternator	N	N	N	N
Voltage regulator	B w/script	B w/script	B w/script	B w/script
Fuel and brake lines	N	N	N	N
Throttle linkage	N	N	N	N

Component Accessories	GM	Ford	Mopar	AMC
Wiper motor	30% GB/N	30% GB/N	N or GC	N or GC
Heater motor cover	GB	GB	N or 30% GB	GB
A/C evaporation unit	GB	GB	GB	GB
Horns	GB	GB	GB‡	GB
Hood components				
Hood hinges	B or GO	B or N	Body color	Body color
Hood hinge springs	GO	N	Body color	Body color
Hood catch and latch	N	N	N	N
Ram Air boxes	30% GB	30% GB	‡‡	30% GB

Legend

GB .... Gloss black
CI .... Cast iron
N .... Natural steel or aluminum
BO .... Black oxide
GC .... Gold chromate
NBO .... Natural black oxide
C .... Copper
CH .... Chrome
B .... Black
GO .... Gray oxide

*It has been discovered that some Mopar core supports were body color on the engine side and semi-gloss black on the grille side.

**Natural and gloss black for early production; blue metal for late production.

***Semi-gloss black with mustard-color top.

‡The Road Runner's horn was light purple with a decal applied to horn.

‡‡On some Mopar products, Ram Air boxes are painted different colors. Check to find what color combinations are correct for your car.

Master cylinder and booster refinishing

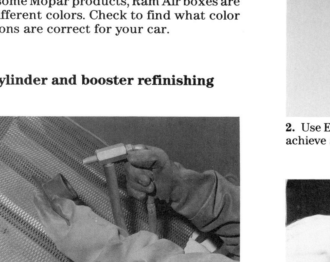

1. Whether you chose to refinish the master cylinder yourself or use a replacement, it will have to be glass-bead blasted to remove surface rust. It's a good idea to refinish the original, as replacement units may not have the bleed valve in the proper location.

2. Use Eastwood's Spray Gray or Seymour's Cast Iron to achieve a correct appearance on the master cylinder.

3. Before spraying the master cylinder, stuff a rag down into the cylinder bowl to protect it from the Spray Gray. Suspend the cylinder and hold the can 6–8 in. away from the surface. Apply several light coats, allowing five to ten minutes drying time between coats.

4. The master cylinder cap and bale must also be refinished. Depending on manufacturer, the cap and bale are painted black or plated in chromate. If you want to refinish these yourself, refer to chapter five on refinishing small parts to achieve a dulled chromate appearance on the cap. Also remember to clean the rubber reservoir diaphragm and replace it if it's torn.

6. If the car is equipped with power assisted brakes, the booster will have to be refinished. The booster can be painted to match the dulled zinc-chromate plating process, or you can elect to disassemble the booster and have it replated. The brake line junction block is natural brass in appearance. The brake lines should be made from new stock and bent to match the old lines.

Wiper motor and linkage refinishing

5. Once it's completed, place the master cylinder into position on the firewall. The attaching bolts should be black or natural. Install the pedal rod and tighten the master cylinder to the firewall.

1. Install the wiper motor mounting plate on the firewall or under the cowl, depending on manufacturer. Remember to apply some strip caulk around this plate to insulate against water leaks.

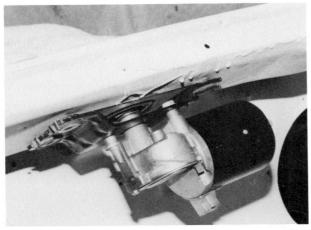

2. Install the wiper motor, carefully lining up the rubber insulator washers and threading the mounting bolts. Tighten down the bolts.

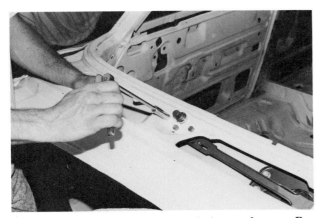

3. Now install the wiper transmission and arms. Remember the arms are marked left and right for correct installation. During the underhood work, place a cover over the engine to keep it clean and protected.

4. Each arm receives a retainer and bezel. Install the retainer and carefully tighten down the bezel, avoiding damage to the bezel and the paint.

5. This pivot clip retains the arms to the transmission and should be installed last.

6. On GM cars, the wiper and washer assemblies are an integral unit and are installed on the firewall. The wiper transmission and links are installed as outlined above. For Mopar and Ford, the wiper motor is bolted on the firewall or cowl and the wiper transmission is attached with a clip on Fords or a bolt on Mopars.

207

Engine wiring harness

When it comes to the engine wiring harness, the restorer has two choices. If the original engine and front end harnesses haven't been spliced, burnt or mangled, they can be refinished and reused. If the harness is beyond restoration, companies like M&H Electric Fabricators offer reproductions of virtually any harness necessary with the correct color codes and connectors.

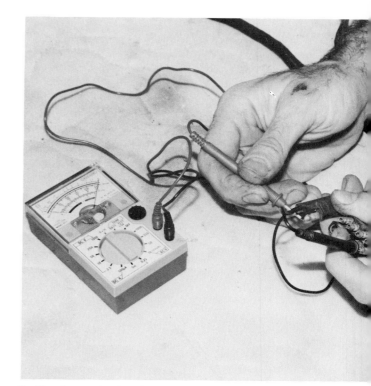

3. Check continuity through each wire using an ohm meter. Now is the time to repair any broken or frayed wires.

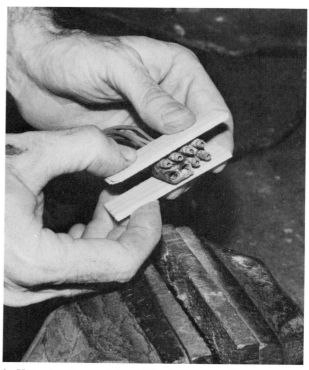

1. If the original can be refinished, use a quality paint stripper like Tal-Strip to clean the wiring harnesses. It's better than lacquer thinner because it doesn't fade the wire colors and leaves the wiring more flexible.

2. Because the stripper is highly caustic, wear rubber gloves while working with the paint stripper. Brush the paint stripper onto the wiring harness. Allow the stripper to work on the harness for approximately fifteen minutes. Then wash the stripper off with water.

4. Use a broken paint paddle to protect the gang plug. Put the plug into a vise to hold it in place and then stretch out the harness.

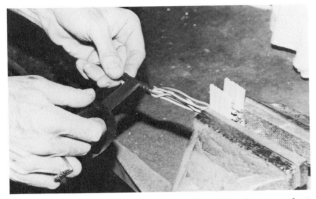

5. To rewrap the harness, use electrician's tape that matches the sheen of the original harness wrap. As you retape the harness, use tight, overlapping wraps.

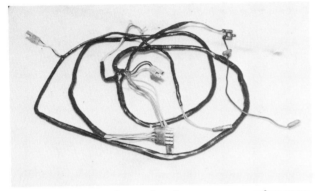

6. Continue wrapping and make sure you overlap carefully, paying particular attention to those areas on the harness where bundles branch off.

Inner fender installation

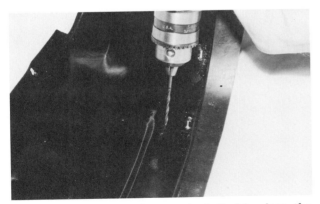

1. Before the inner fenders can be bolted in place, the upper control arm rubber shields must be installed. To install the shields, first line up the rubber shield with metal inner fender and use a $3/32$ in. drill bit to drive the staple mounting holes. Drill through the old mounting holes and into the new rubber shield.

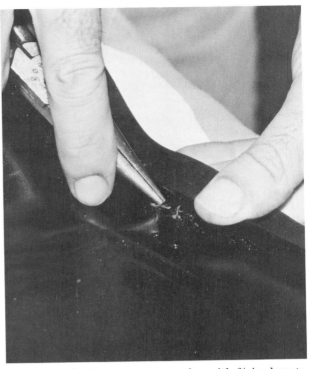

2. Use standard staple gun staples with ⅜ in. legs to duplicate the factory-installed staples. Push the staples through the rubber and metal and bend the legs over with needle-nose pliers.

3. With the rubber shields now installed, set the inner fenders into place on the frame rails.

209

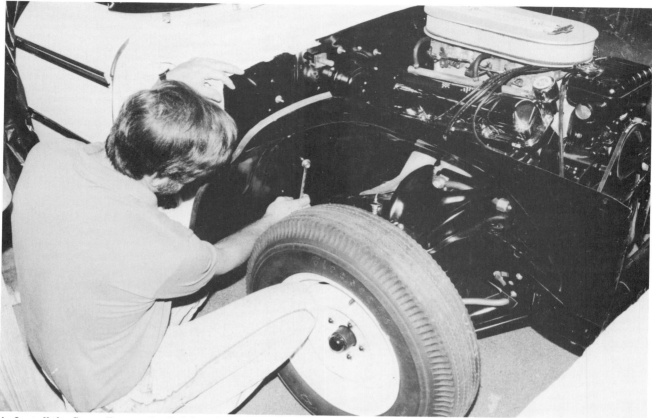

4. Install the firewall mounting bolt but don't tighten the bolt yet.

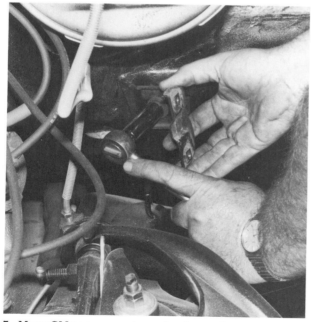

5. Many GM cars use an inner fender-to-firewall bracket. This bracket is finished in semi-gloss black to match the inner fender. Install the bracket now, but don't tighten the bolt down yet.

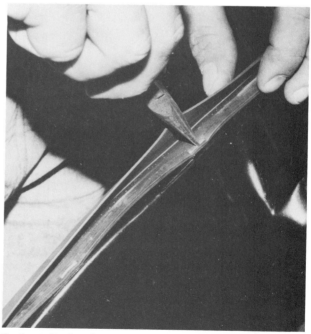

6. Install the fender apron-to-firewall seals if so equipped. The seals were originally retained by staples. You'll have to install staples to make it look correct.

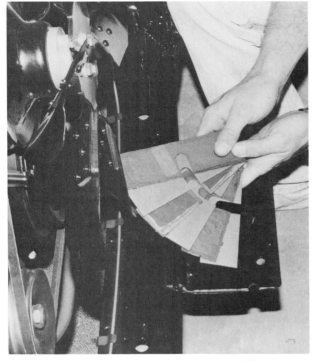

7. Some cars require core support shims. These shims were removed when you disassembled the car. If so equipped, lay out the shims and set them on the core support mount.

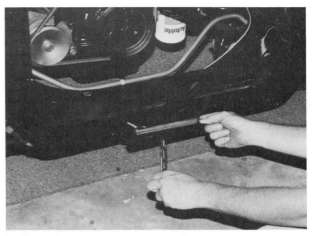

9. Snug the core support mounting nut.

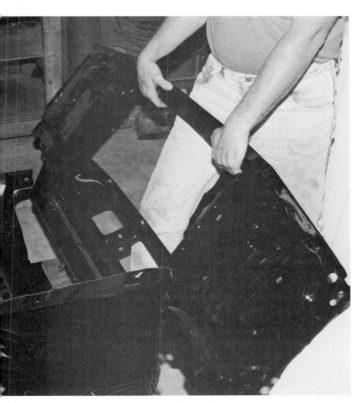

8. Set the core support into place.

10. On GM cars, the core support mounts to the frame rails and is cushioned by bushings. Install the bushings and washers, thread the bolt through the assembly and snug the nut.

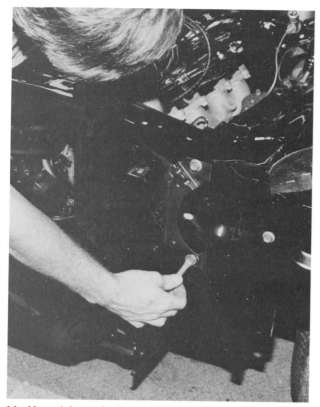

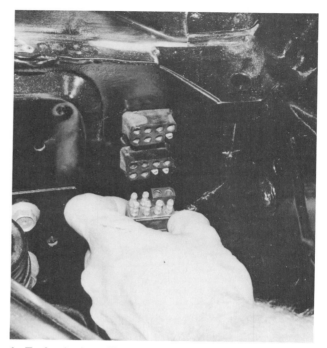

11. Now tighten the inner fender-to-core support bolts. Don't torque them down; just snug them.

1. To begin installing the engine and front end harnesses, line up each engine harness with the matching firewall plug.

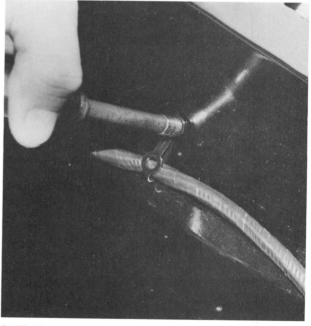

12. With the core support and inner fenders mounted, you can now begin installing the other engine compartment components such as harnesses, hoses and ground straps.

2. The harnesses are routed through clips or straps that are installed on the inner fender and retained either by a screw or popped into predrilled holes. Route the harness on the inner fender and clip the harness strap into place. Using a $5/16$ in. nutdriver to snap the strap lock into the place makes the installation easier.

3. Remember to route the harness through the core support as it was originally done by the factory. While it would have been easier to route this harness on the outside of the core support, this is how the assembly plant did it.

4. Remember to attach all the headlight harness ground straps.

5. Grommets were used whereever the harness routes through the sheetmetal to prevent the insulation from fraying and shorting out. If the originals are in excellent condition, you can glass-bead blast them and soak them with protectorant or use Plastic Dip to recoat them.

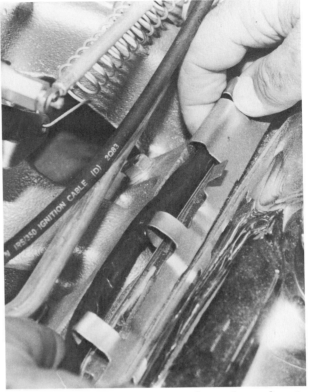

6. Lay the engine harness out on the engine and route the bundles. Some cars use a retainer to protect the harness from oil and hot engine parts.

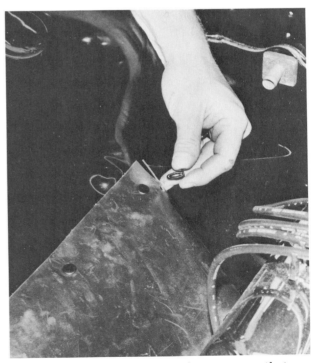

7. Some cars use upper control arm covers that are retained by clips or studs to the inner fenders.

213

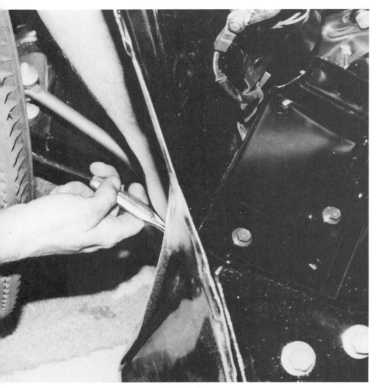

8. Install the battery tray and tighten the attaching bolts to the inner fender or core support.

9. The engine compartment harness is routed along the firewall and retained by straps that clip or screw to the firewall. Make sure the male and female plugs are securely mated.

10. Install the solenoid on the inner fender (if so equipped), voltage regulator, horns, horn relay, underhood lamp (if so equipped) and any other components. Now connect the harness to these components as well as the heater blower motor and then install the battery cables.

11. Route and install the correctly coded heater hose and clamps. Some cars retain the hoses with a strap on the inner fender while others utilize a bracket that's mounted to the engine.

12. On cars equipped with air conditioning, install the necessary valves, vacuum lines and hoses to the engine.

13. Install the engine-to-firewall ground strap. On some cars, there may also be engine-to-frame ground straps as well.

Radiator, shroud and hoses installation

1. Once the core support is in place and all components have been installed, you can now drop the radiator into place. The radiator is retained by rubber-cushioned cradles in the bottom of the core support or bolted directly to the core support.

2. If the car is equipped with air conditioning, install the condenser first.

3. Air conditioned cars also use metal and rubber baffles attached to the core support to aid in airflow, reducing engine temperature. These should be installed now.

4. Because radiators are date coded, it's important to retain the original tanks when you take it to a radiator shop for repair. Paint the radiator gloss black and make sure the fins are straight and the overflow tube clips are in place prior to installation.

5. Center the radiator in the core support and carefully lower it into the rubber cradles. You'll probably have to jockey the radiator around several times to get it in the exact location.

6. Most cars use a bracket or shield to secure the radiator at the top of the core support.

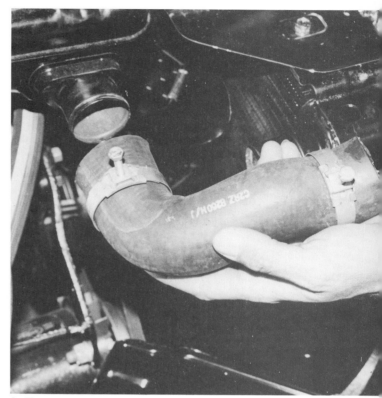

8. Tower-style screw clamps were also used.

7. Once the radiator is in place, the upper and lower hoses can be installed. No manufacturer ever installed flex hoses or worm-style hose clamps. The upper and lower hoses should be molded, and the proper clamps installed. Most manufacturers used Corbin spring clips, as shown here.

9. Use the correct radiator cap. Stant, RobertShaw or any other aftermarket brand (upper and lower right) were never original equipment. Factory caps are shown at upper and lower left and top.

10. As you detail the engine compartment, make sure all the hoses and wires are routed neatly and correctly. Old magazine road test articles usually include underhood pictures. You can study these photographs to determine how everything should be positioned. Current magazines like *Musclecar Review* publish spreads on restored musclecars that can also provide you with good information on underhood appearance. Chrysler products like this 1969 Charger 500 with 440 engine had a black crinkle finish air cleaner with the engine displacement decal on the painted air cleaner lid (often referred to as the "pie tin").

11. Musclecars of the early seventies, like this 1974 455 Super Duty Trans Am, are more difficult to restore properly because of the emissions equipment and optional accessories. Notice the special decal on the valve cover and the "SD-455" decal on the shaker hood. Notice the hood hinges are natural finish rather than the replacement black finish.

12. This 1969 428 Talladega has decals on the air cleaner. These decals are available from Jim Osborn Reproductions (101 Ridgecrest Drive, Lawrenceville, GA 30245). Also note the chrome top of the air cleaner. Many musclecars used air cleaners that were either all chromed or had chrome tops and painted bottoms. Most Ford high-performance engines had chrome tops and the bottoms were painted Engine Blue.

Window glass installation

New front and rear window glass is an essential part of a musclecar restoration. Don't plan on reusing your old glass unless it is perfect with no deep scratches or chips. Chances are it will be damaged or broken during removal.

All original equipment window glass is date coded, and replacement glass can be stenciled with the same information as appeared on the OE glass. Companies like OEM Glass (PO Box 362, Hwy. 9 East, Bloomington, IL 61702) reproduce exact replacements and can date code all the window glass for your restoration.

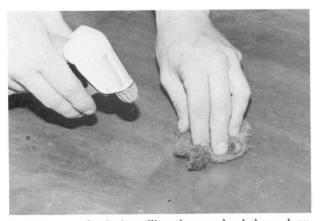

1. Before you begin installing the new backglass, clean the surface and edges thoroughly, using a high-quality glass cleaner. Clean the edges of the glass with glass cleaner and 000 steel wool. You may also need to use a razor blade on the edges.

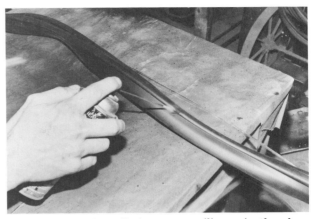

2. To facilitate installation, spray silicone in the glass channel of the new weatherstripping.

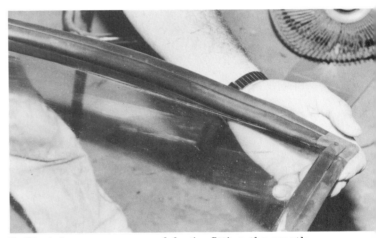

3. Start in one corner and begin fitting the weatherstripping to the glass. After you have installed the weatherstripping all around the window glass, make sure it's fitted tightly with no bulges or gaps.

4. Now fit the molding to the weatherstripping (if so equipped). Carefully slide the molding onto the weatherstripping. Spray some silicone into the molding groove to ease the installation.

5. Check to ensure that all joints are well fitted and the moldings line up properly. Take your time and inspect your work as you go along.

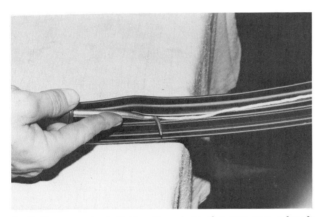

6. Before you install the glass into the car, use a hook tool and place heavy string or cord into the weatherstripping-to-body channel. Use enough cord to go around the glass twice. You will be pulling hard on this cord to seat the weatherstripping, so make sure it's strong enough.

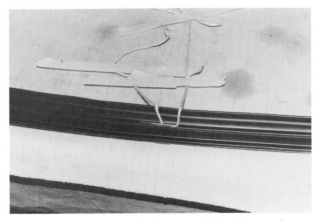

7. You should start at the bottom of the glass and continue around twice. When you've finished, tape the string to the glass.

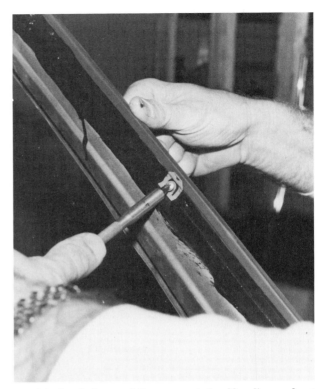

8. If the backglass moldings are retained by clips and not the weatherstripping, now is the time to install the clips.

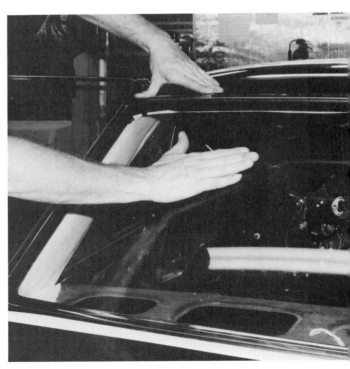

9. Carefully center and set the glass into the opening and work it towards the bottom of the channel. Take the palm of your hand and hit the glass firmly toward the bottom of the channel to help it seat.

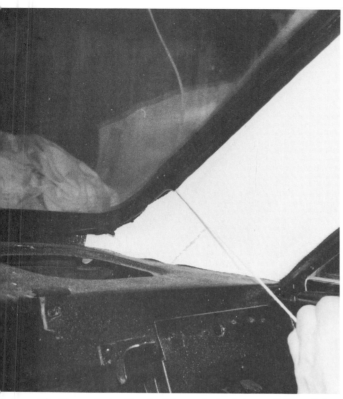

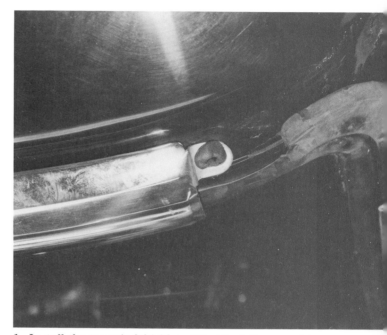

Reveal molding installation

10. Now, go to the inside and start to pull the string towards one side of the glass. Go about halfway on one side and then pull the cord on the other side the same length. Have a helper tap the glass with the palm of their hand right above where the string is being pulled. That will help the glass to seat easier. Pull the string out carefully, and the window glass will be installed.

1. Install the top windshield molding first. Some moldings clip into place, while others clip and use screws at both ends. If it is attached by screws at the end of the molding, remember to put some strip caulk into the screw holes to prevent any leaks.

11. Install the front glass exactly the same way using the same procedures and sequence.

2. Install the top corner and pillar molding next. If the car has a driprail molding, this will have to be installed also. Most driprail moldings are incorporated into the top windshield corner molding.

221

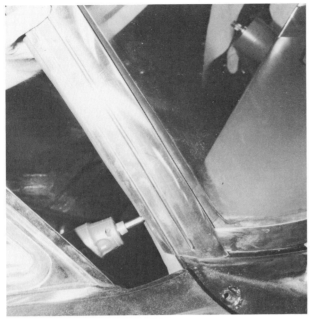

3. After you have fit the pillar molding into place, finish the installation by tightening the mounting screws.

Doorhandle installation

2. Begin the reassembly by installing the O-ring and spring onto the pushbutton assembly.

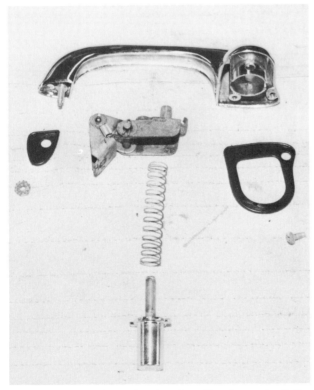

1. Prior to installing the doorhandles, lay out all the necessary parts. New O-rings and gaskets should be purchased.

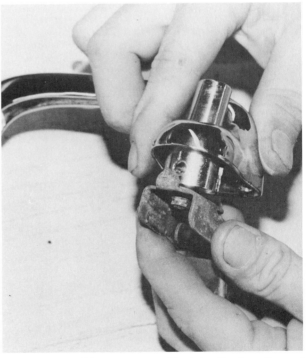

3. Set the pushbutton assembly into the handle and then install the opening mechanism. Tighten the retaining screws. Lubricate the button mechanism with spray lithium white grease or liquid graphite to ensure smooth operation.

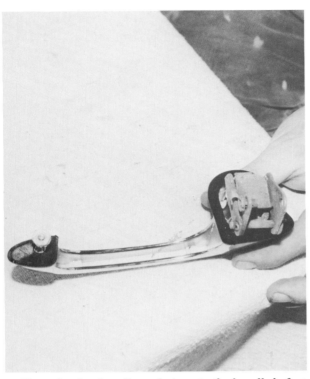

4. Place the doorhandle gaskets onto the handle before installing the assembly on the door.

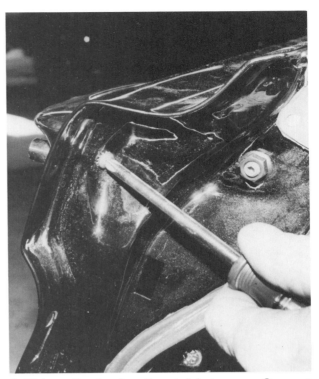

6. Tighten the doorhandle retaining screws. On some cars, the screws are accessible as shown; on others, it will be necessary to reach through the door bracing to tighten the screws. Once the handles are secured, attach the door latch mechanism rods to the doorhandle.

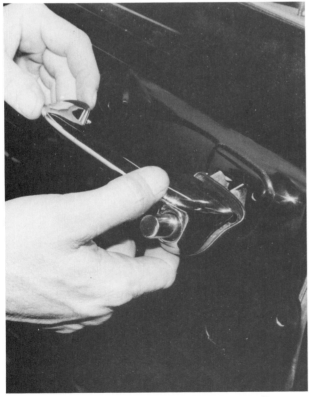

5. Carefully place the doorhandle into the handle opening, making sure you don't nick or scratch the paint.

7. Lubricate the door lock mechanism with spray white grease or graphite and install in the door lock openings.

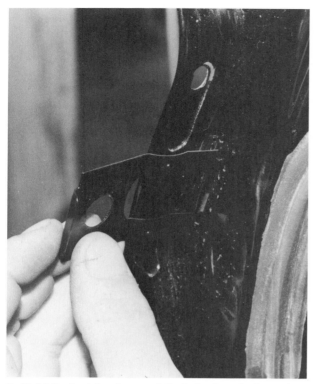

8. Hold the lock in place and feed the door lock retainer through the door slot and onto the door lock cylinder. Push the retainer until it is flush with the doorjamb.

Trunk reassembly

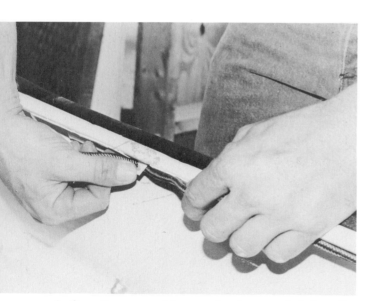

1. Once the rear end harness has been routed along the floorpan and past the rear seat bulkhead, place it along the trunk lip. There are tabs that hold the harness in place. Make sure you feed it behind the trunk latch mechanism.

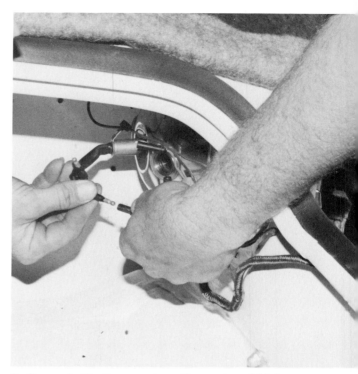

2. Connect all butt connecters, if so equipped. Make sure you check the color codes to ensure you are connecting the right wires together.

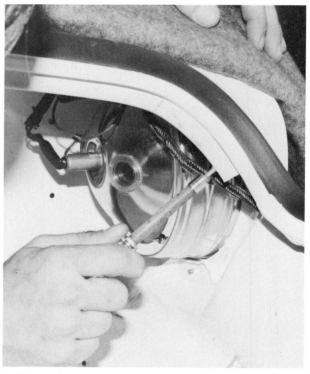

3. Remember to connect all ground terminals to the body of the car. These are usually retained by ¼ or ⁵⁄₁₆ in. screws.

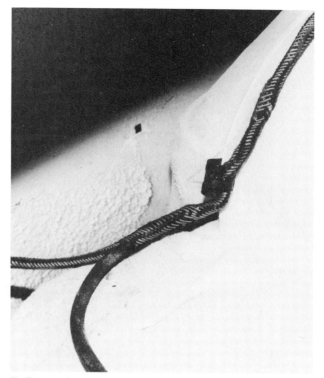

4. Feed the fuel tank sending unit wire through the trunk and connect it to the sending unit. The tag lamp wire will also be fed through a rubber grommet in the trunkpan.

5. Remember to use the correct wiring harness clips to hold the harness in place, both in the trunk and as it runs along the floorpan.

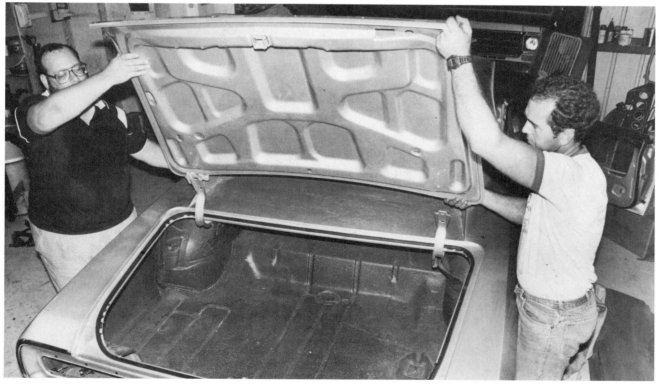

6. Install the deck lid and snug up the attaching bolts. Don't tighten them down yet.

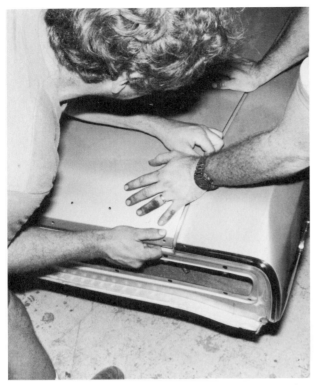

7. Close the deck lid and check your gaps on the sides and at the rear of the lid.

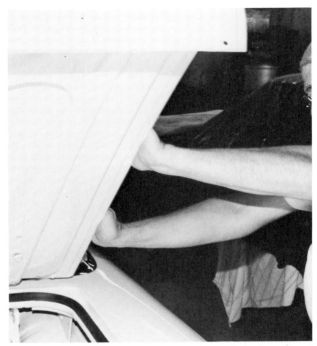

9. Sometimes you may have to gently push on the side of the deck lid to obtain the correct side gap. Make sure the bolts are tight and then push the deck lid toward the side with the largest gap. Don't use too much force. A quick, firm push is usually all that's needed.

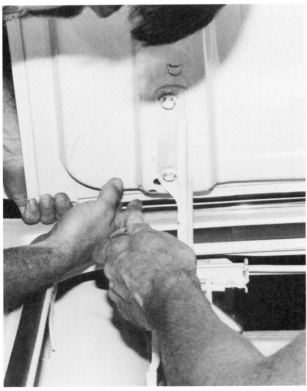

8. To adjust the decklid for proper fit, loosen the hinge bolts and move the deck lid to obtain the proper gap.

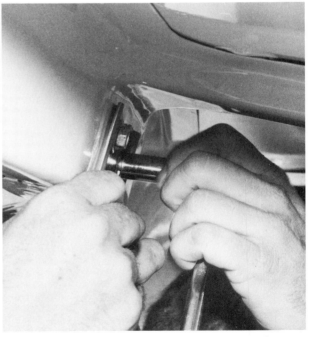

10. Now install the deck lid latch. Check to make sure the lock mechanism will open with the key, and then close the deck lid. Make sure it opens and closes easily. You can also adjust the height of the deck lid by raising or lowering the latch assembly.

Front unibody sheetmetal installation cars

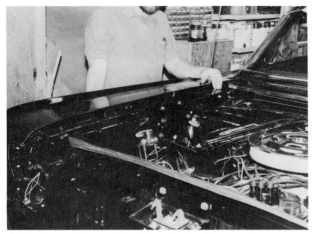

1. Before you start installing the fenders, make sure you tap all the mounting holes. Carefully set the fender into place. If the car is equipped with a drop-in fender-mount radio antenna, this is the time to install the antenna. Also, check that your fender moldings or emblems can be installed after the fender is attached. If not, install them now. Use strip caulk in each hole to prevent paint nicks and water leakage.

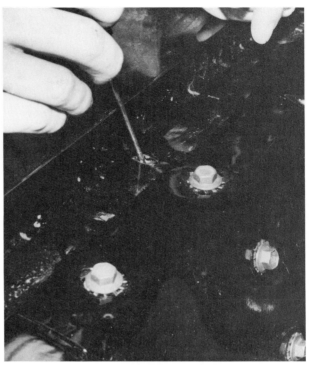

3. It may be necessary to align some of the J-clips as you install the attaching bolts. Make sure they are centered in each opening.

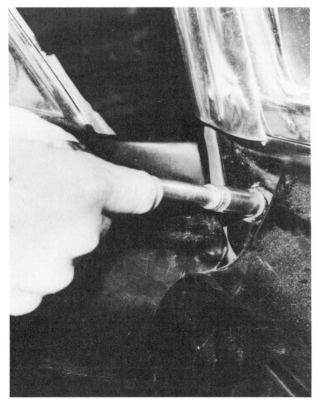

2. Install the bolts attaching the fender to the body. Start from the rear and work forward. Do not tighten the bolts, just snug them down.

4. Remember that most fenders have a mounting bolt mounted behind the kick panel as well. Once the upper attaching bolts have been installed, thread in the lower fender bolt and tighten.

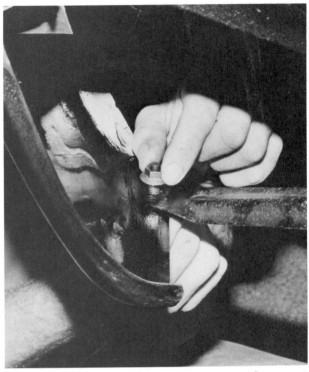

5. Now install the front lower corner support brace nut and bolt. Install and tighten the fender-to-core-support bolts.

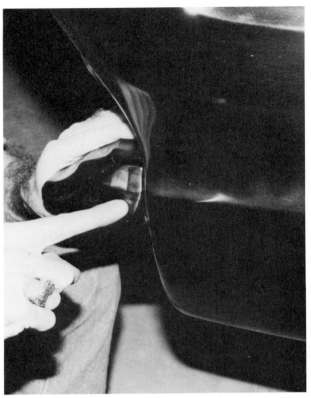

7. It's a good idea to polish the lower valance before you install it. Remember to align the valance to the fenders before you tighten the attaching bolts.

6. Install the hood catch and grille center support.

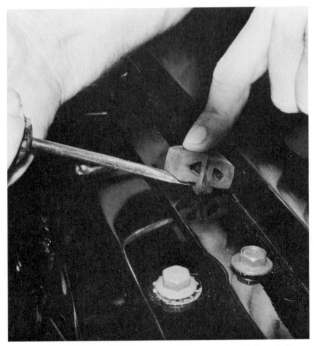

8. Install the hood bumpers, using care not to nick or damage the paint as you install them. A little silicone spray will help slip the bumpers into place.

9. Install the hood hinges. Snug the bolts but don't tighten them yet.

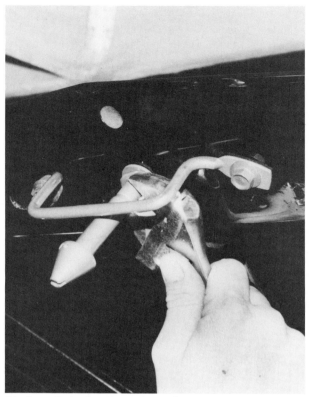

11. Install the hood catch mechanism and dowel pin.

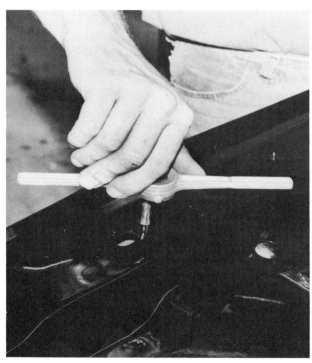

10. Before you install the hood, tap the hood hinge-to-hood bolt holes. This will ease the threading of the bolts while you and an assistant are holding the hood up.

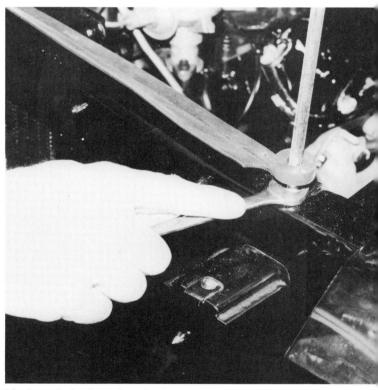

12. Install the front hood adjustment bumpers. Screw these all the way down.

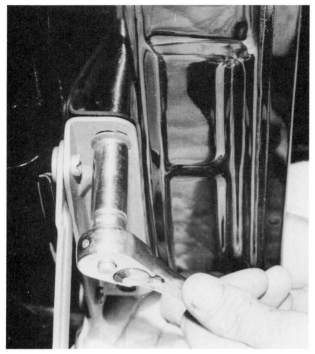

13. Carefully set the hood onto the hinges and snug the bolts. Gently close the hood and check the gaps and heights. Use a straight edge to check the heights from fender to hood and hood to cowl.

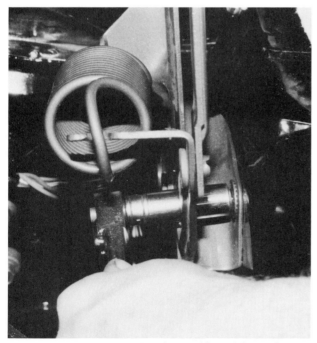

14. The hood height can be changed by raising or lowering the hood hinges at the fender and by raising or lowering the front hood adjustment and dowel pin. The gap is checked by moving the hood on the hood hinges and also by adjusting the catch mechanism on the front.

230

Front sheet metal installation

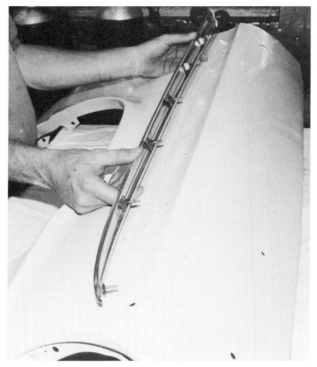

1. Before installing the fenders on a composite body-frame car, place any moldings or emblems on the fender, attach and tighten the retaining nuts. If the car has a front fender antenna, install it now and remember to feed the antenna lead through the doorjamb.

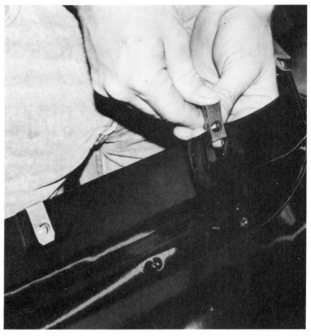

2. Install the inner fender-to-fender mounting clips.

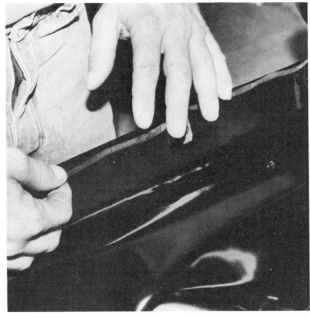

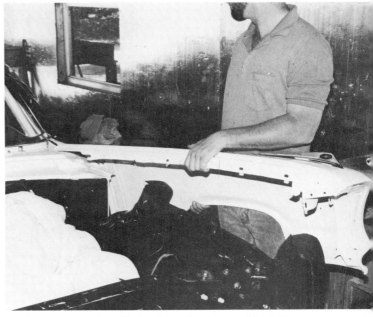

3. Lay a bead of strip caulk along the mounting edge of the inner fender. This will prevent rattling and water leaks. Also remember that many cars use a strip of rubber to insulate the fender from the cowl to prevent rattles. Install any hidden mounting clips and pads onto the fender.

4. You can now install the front fenders and bolt them into place. Body shims were installed at the factory to help place the fenders in alignment with the doors. If necessary, install the shims you removed from the car during disassembly. Also install the inner fender-to-outer fender bolts and snug them down.

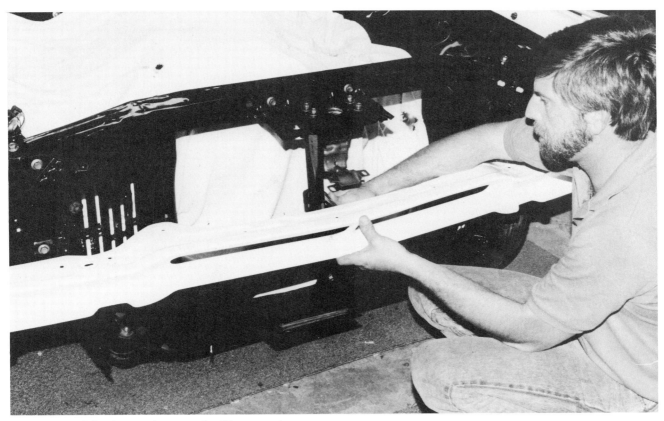

5. Now install the front valance and grille support.

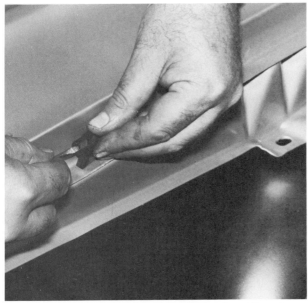

6. Install the hood bumpers into the fenders. If you have to use a small screwdriver to install them, be careful not to damage the paint. Some silicone spray will ease the installation.

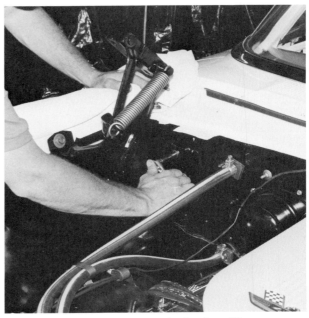

8. Install the hood hinges to the fenders. Place a rag on the fender to protect the paint while you're installing the hinges.

7. Prior to installing the hood, measure the distance from fender to fender at the rear and the front. Now measure the hood at the same locations. Make any necessary adjustments to the fenders now to ensure no paint damage will occur to the fenders or the hood once it's installed.

9. Place the hood on the car and bolt it to the hinges. Carefully raise and lower the hood as assistants check clearances at the fenders. Make any final fender adjustments now.

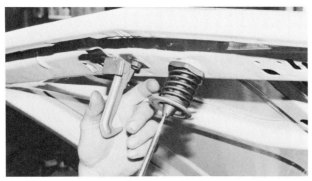

10. Once you are satisfied everything is aligned properly, install the hood latch components to the hood and the core support.

11. Tighten all of the fender, inner fender and core support bolts that you snugged before. By leaving them loose until now, you can adjust any of the inner fenders or core support to help line up and install the front fenders.

Aligning sheetmetal

Alignment of the front sheetmetal and doors requires patience. It also requires the factory service or body manual. Follow the factory specifications for alignment of doors, fenders and cowl.

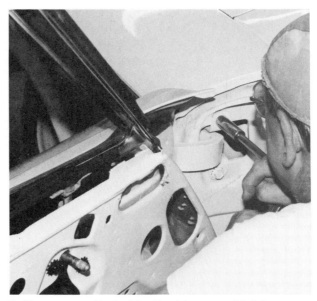

1. Doors are adjusted by the hinges and latch assemblies. To adjust the in-and-out movement of the door at the front fender, loosen the front hinge-to-door bolts and push, pull or twist the door to obtain the correct fit at the fender.

2. Sometimes you may have to adjust the fender to meet the door. This is usually done by adjusting the two rear fender-to-cowl bolts. If you need to move the edge of the fender up or to bring the fender line out to match the door, add body shims.

233

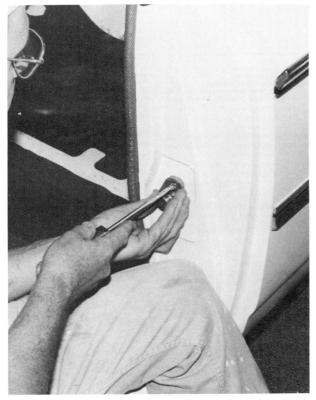

3. The striker is also used to adjust the latching of the door and the rear fit. Loosen the striker and tap it with the butt of the screwdriver handle to adjust it until the door latches tightly and evenly with the quarter panel. Then retighten the striker.

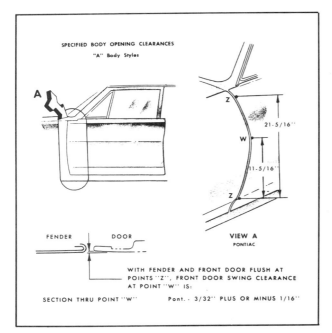

SPECIFIED BODY OPENING CLEARANCES
"A" Body Styles

21-5/16"

11-5/16"

FENDER   DOOR

VIEW A
PONTIAC

WITH FENDER AND FRONT DOOR FLUSH AT POINTS "Z", FRONT DOOR SWING CLEARANCE AT POINT "W" IS:

SECTION THRU POINT "W"   Pont. - 3/32" PLUS OR MINUS 1/16"

GM factory body manual for this 1966 A body car lists sheet-metal clearances.

Convertible top installation

Like upholstery, a convertible top installation can be a complete disaster for the novice restorer. We recommend having a professional install your convertible top. Even professionals don't get it right the first time. We've seen them have to redo an installation several times before it was correct. It's not a job for the amateur.

Here are some steps you should follow for having your convertible top replaced:

1. Always purchase the best-quality top material available.

2. Always replace the top pads and straps.

3. Always replace the back window. Some cars were equipped with clear plastic, some with glass. Use the one that is correct for your car.

4. Replace all of the top weatherstripping.

5. Check the operation of the top mechanism before the new top is installed. Make sure all of the bows, header, pump, lift cylinders and lines are functioning properly. Also inspect the cables, and replace any worn or frayed cables or stops. Replace whatever is necessary. It's also a good idea to replace all of the lines. All concours-restored convertibles have brand-new lift cylinders and pumps.

6. Make sure you paint the convertible top frame completely before a new top is installed and replate any plated parts at this time.

7. When the top is installed, make sure it fits on the frame evenly. One side should not be lower than the other. It should fit evenly across the windshield header. There should not be any gap between the top of the side glass and the roofrail weatherstripping. Also, there shouldn't be any wrinkles or stretch marks. The top should fit evenly around the top well and back seat. The side rails bead should also be even and not have any waves in it.

8. After it's installed, it's a good idea to let the top sit in the hot sun and shrink. This will usually take out any slight wrinkles.

Vinyl top installation

Back in the late seventies, before the musclecar hobby became sophisticated, vinyl tops on musclecars were generally considered a nuisance and peeled off when the car was repainted. With musclecar restorations now done more accurately, vinyl tops are being reinstalled when appropriate. As in the case of convertible tops, unless you've installed one before, it's advised you have a professional shop install a vinyl top for you. Follow these tips and you shouldn't have any problem getting a vinyl top installed properly.

1. Always find the correct grain pattern. Make sure the top is seamed in the correct places. Some tops were seamed on each side, while others were seamed down the middle.

2. Make sure all of the moldings that the top must fit under have been removed.

3. Make sure the top is tucked down into the windshield and back glass channels.

4. All air bubbles must be worked out of the top.

5. Check that the seams are even from front to back.

6. Make sure the top is tucked under all of the moldings when they are reinstalled.

Front end trim installation

1. Begin assembling the headlamp components by installing both headlamp bucket assemblies.

A well-installed vinyl top with the fabric tucked into the glass channels.

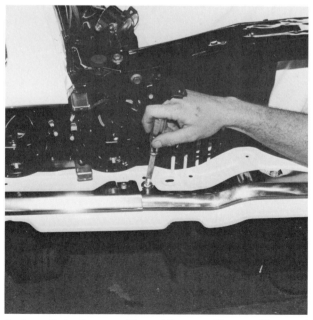

2. Install the lower grille moldings, radiator grille panel (if so equipped) and grille or grilles.

A trim, smooth vinyl top installation that looks sharp even at the edges where the fabric is tucked under the moldings.

3. Install the headlamps by first plugging the harness socket into the lamps and then placing the lamps in the buckets. Then install the retaining rings and attaching hardware. Follow the procedures as outlined in the factory service manual.

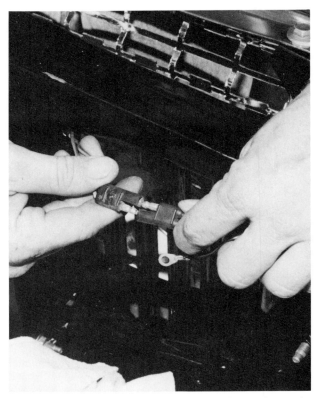

5. Connect the headlamp harness leads to the main front end harness. Now screw the ground lead to the body.

4. The headlamps should be the correct script or embossed type for your car. A Ford headlamp is shown.

6. If the car has a separate radiator grille panel, such as this GTO, now install the grilles. If the parking lamp assembly is installed in the grille, route the harness to the grille and plug it in before aligning the grilles and bolting them into place.

7. Install the parking lamp socket, bulb, lens and trim bezel (if so equipped).

8. Install the headlamp trim bezel or cover, using new chrome screws and reinforcement nuts.

Bumper preparation and installation

Many restorers search for NOS bumpers, nicely wrapped in the original paper and sporting a part number. Buying an NOS bumper can be a waste of money, because the factory chrome is usually inferior to quality rechroming.

Unless the original bumpers are badly rusted, it's wiser and cheaper in the long run to send the original bumpers to the rechrome shop. Minor nicks and dents can be repaired by a competent shop, and the cost of repair and rechroming can be equal to or less than the cost of an NOS bumper. In most cases, an NOS bumper will need to be rechromed for concours showing, putting an additional dent in your restoration budget.

One final note about rechromed bumpers. We recommend you avoid bargain-priced rechromed bumpers that can be found at swap meets. You're better off finding a local shop that specializes in bumper repair and rechroming. They can usually do as good a job as some of the nationally advertised shops and at less cost. If possible, inspect some of their work. Look for sanding scratches and grinding marks. If these are present, find another bumper shop.

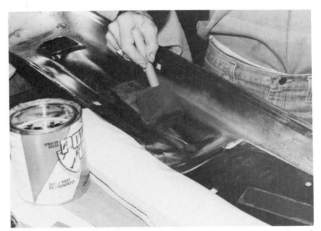

1. Before installation, lay the bumpers on a soft pad and paint the backs of the bumpers with POR 15. Once the POR 15 has dried, apply several coats of dull aluminum or stainless steel paint for a factory-finished look. Remember to tape all the bumper bolt holes before painting the inside of the bumpers.

2. Beadblast and paint the bumper-to-frame mounting brakets semi-gloss black. Some cars use a reinforcement bar that is mounted against the bumper and secured by the mounting brackets. Once they are dry, install the brackets. Do not overtighten the bumper bolts. These only need to be snugged. If you over-tighten them, the bolt will dimple the outside of the bumper and probably crack the chrome.

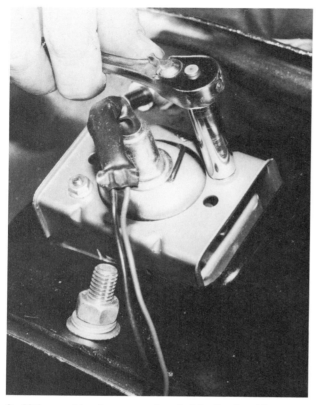

3. If the parking lamps are located in the front bumper, install the lamp assembly prior to installing the bumper on the car.

4. Once the front bumper is assembled, place it on a floorjack and position the bumper at the front of the car.

5. With the bumper on the jack, carefully align the bracket mounting holes at the frame. Install the bolts and snug them down.

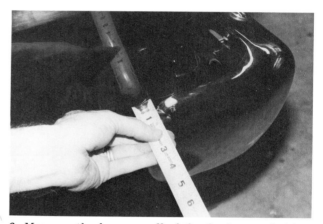

6. Measure the bumper off of the fenders and either headlamp doors or grille; align the bumper to achieve equal measurements at both places at both sides.

7. You may have to adjust both the braces and the bumper brackets to achieve the correct fit. Remember that nothing is more noticeable than a crooked or uneven bumper.

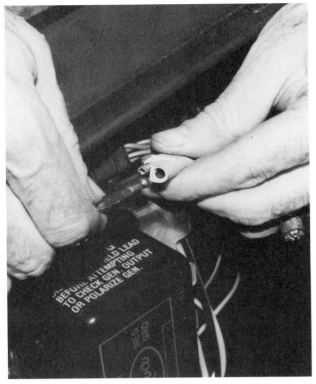

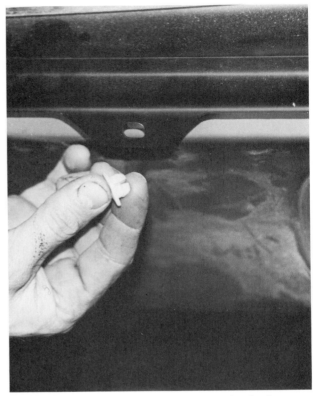

8. If the parking lamp assembly is located in the bumper, install it now. Once the bumper is securely in place, hook up the parking lamp harness to the front end harness.

9. Install new tag mounting grommets in the bumper. These grommets snap into the bumper.

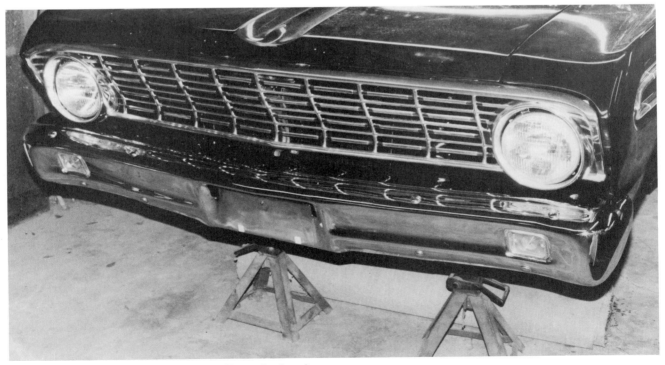

10. The front end is now completed. Clean the headlamps and polish the chrome and trim to remove any grease or fingerprints.

Rear trim installation

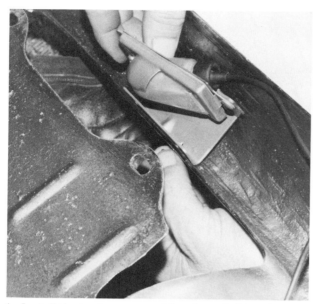

1. Install the tag lamp assembly prior to bolting the rear bumper to the car. Route the wire lead so it will not become pinched once the bumper is installed. If the fuel filler door and tag bracket assembly is located on the bumper, install it now.

2. Carefully raise and install the rear bumper—this requires a helper. Put the bolts in and snug them. Stand back, look at the bumper and determine if the bumper is straight. Now align it with the taillamp housings, trying to get the same distance from the bumper to the housings on both sides. When you achieve this, tighten the bumper and torque to manufacturer's specifications. Please note that some cars are designed to have the rear trim installed before the bumper can be installed.

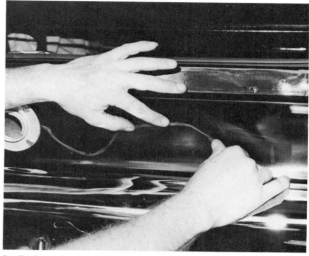

3. Before you install the rear trim panels, place a strip of 3M Strip Caulk behind the trim. This will eliminate any panel rattling.

4. Carefully install the rear trim panel.

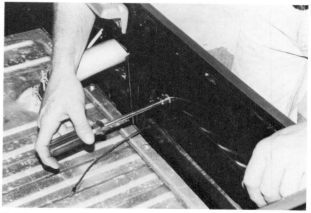

5. Place some strip caulk around any studs that come through the body, attach the retaining nuts and snug them down. Remember to hook up the tag bracket lamp lead.

6. Now install any finishing screws that may be used to retain the taillamp molding.

8. Prior to installation, spray the inside of the taillamp housing with Nybco chrome paint. This paint will provide better reflective quality.

7. Install the gas filler door and the new gas cap. Remember to insert new filler door bumpers.

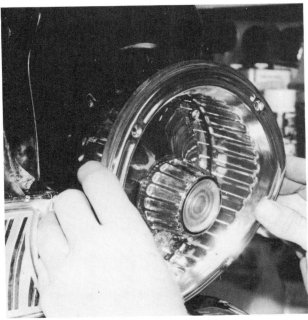

9. Install the taillamp housings, lenses and new gaskets.

10. Always use the correctly coded taillamp lenses. The taillamp on this 1966 Nova SS has Guide numbers in the red lens and the white back-up lamp lens that are coded for 1966 use.

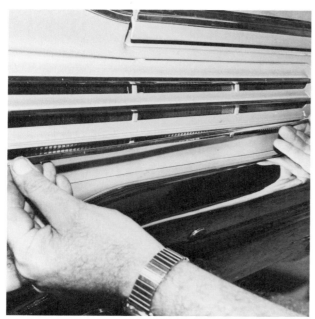

11. Install any rear end moldings and deck lid moldings. Some cars use letters that spell out the nameplate or have emblems ornamenting the taillamp panel; others have decorative trim over the taillamps. Install all of these components if applicable. The rear of the car should now be complete.

Side trim installation

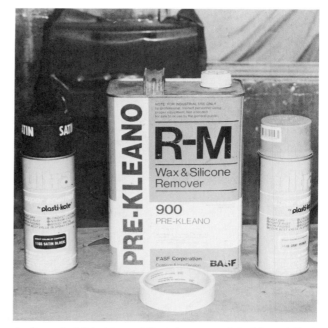

1. Some bright side moldings have a painted insert that will need to be restriped. For the restriping process, you'll need the following materials: masking tape, primer and spray paint. Remember to check for the correct stripe color. Even black can be different glosses—flat, semi-gloss or gloss. In most cases, black molding strips are semi-gloss or satin black.

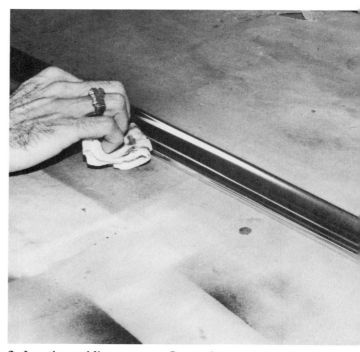

2. Lay the molding out on a flat surface and clean the stripe area thoroughly with Pre-Kleano.

5. Apply light coats of the color. Allow each coat to tack, then spray the next coat. Usually four or six light coats work best.

3. After it is dry, mask off the molding, leaving only the area to be painted. Don't touch this area with your fingers. If you do, rewipe it with Pre-Kleano. Also make sure you have pressed down the edges of the tape. This will give you a clean, sharp edge. Also try to use one continuous piece of tape. This will assure you of a perfect edge.

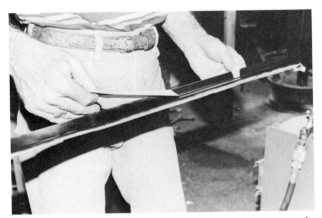

6. After you have applied the last coat, let it start to tack, then carefully remove the tape. *Do not* allow the paint to dry. If you do, the paint will usually chip off at the tape line when the tape is removed. The paint is still flexible when it is still tacky and will allow you to remove the tape without chipping the paint. Also, remember to pull the tape off the back over itself. Never pull tape at any other angle.

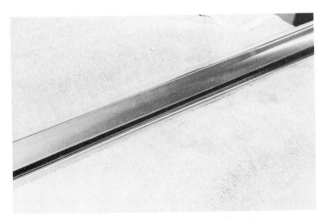

4. Remember to cover all of the molding that doesn't get painted as paint overspray will go everywhere. Apply a light primer coat first. This will give better paint adhesion.

7. Once the paint has dried, the molding is now completed and ready to be installed on the car.

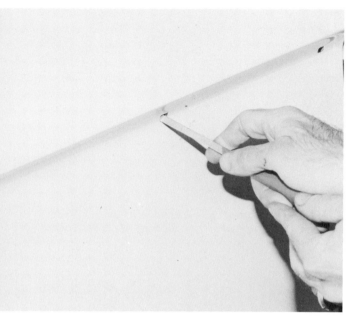

8. Before installing any side moldings, make sure the mounting holes are clean and open. Carefully clean the piercing, using either a round file or flat file, depending on the hole.

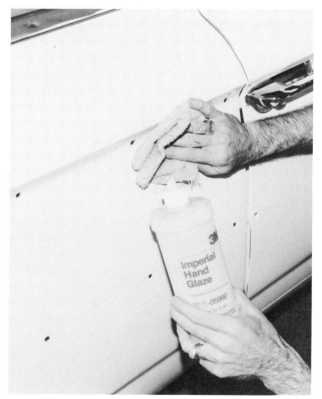

9. Clean and polish over all the mounting holes before installation. Unless you remove the moldings again, this is the only time you'll be able to wax and protect the paint.

244

10. Before you start, check to make sure which clips fit which moldings and how they will install. This way you will be able to install the clips correctly.

Rocker panel moldings

Many cars use bright moldings to cover the rocker panels. These moldings are usually retained by crimp clips and screws. The moldings then snap onto the clips and, once aligned, are screwed into grommets installed into the sheet metal, or into the metal itself.

Remember to put a bead of strip caulk around the pinch clip area to stop water leaks from entering the rocker panel through the clip hole.

11. Always put a bead of strip caulking around any mounting studs before installation. This stops leaks and squeaks.

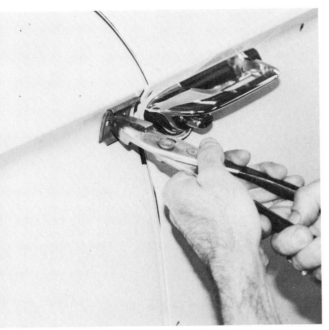

12. Crimp clips are used to retain moldings on some cars. If so equipped, place the clips in the holes and crimp into place.

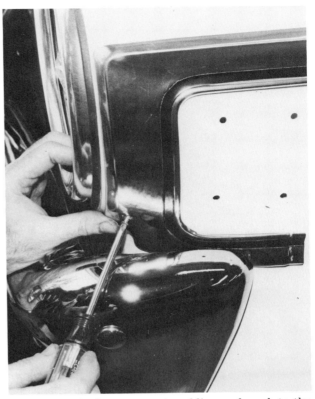

14. Start with the rear-most molding and work to the front. Since you'll be adjusting the moldings, for now just snug the nuts.

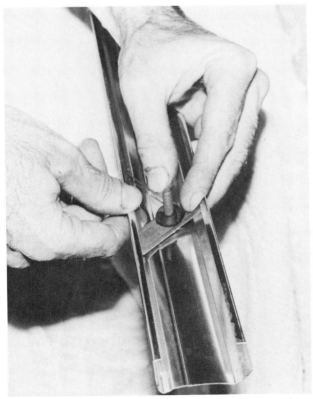

13. If the clips install in the molding, put them in place and then check their fit. Remember to put some strip caulk around any stud that goes into the body. This will help eliminate leaks and possible rust-out.

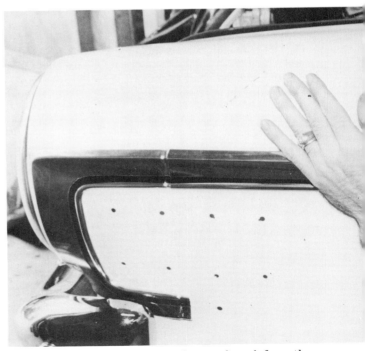

15. Set the next molding into place and work from the front to the rear. Butt the moldings carefully so the paint finish isn't damaged.

245

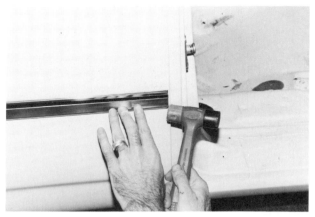

16. Line up the moldings at any joints. You may have to use a rubber hammer to tap the molding back to make sure the moldings line up correctly.

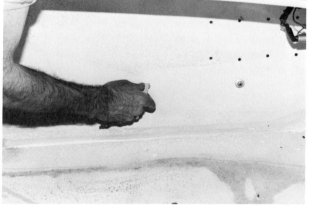

17. Once the moldings are lined up properly, tighten the speed nuts retaining the moldings. Do not overtighten as this can damage the molding and the paint.

18. Always pre-fit any ornaments or emblems before installation. This ornament is retained with speed nuts. Be sure when you install a molding or ornament using these clips that it is positioned correctly, because the nuts are extremely difficult to remove.

19. When the molding is in place, push the speed nut down over the stud. It is made to go on only one way. Make sure you line these clips up all the same way to achieve a symmetrical appearance on the inside of the sheet metal.

20. If you take your time and carefully line up the moldings as they are installed, the quarter-panel bright side trim will be correctly aligned with no damage to the paint finish.

Door molding installation

1. Door moldings usually have studs or bolts at either end so they can be adjusted. Trial-fit the clips before installing the same way you did on the quarter panel.

246

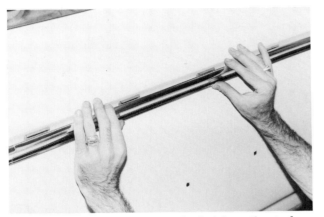

2. Install the door molding but don't tighten the studs or even snug them yet.

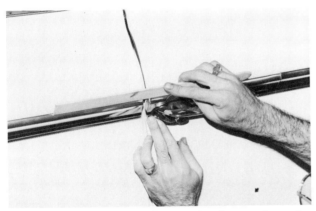

3. Use a straight edge to line up the door and quarter moldings. Adjust the door panel molding until it lines up with the quarter molding. Once they are aligned properly, tighten the bolt or nut. Repeat the process for the lower door molding, if so equipped.

4. The quarter-panel and door moldings are now aligned and installed. The front fender moldings (if so equipped) were installed on the front fender prior to installing the fender on the body.

Driprail molding installation

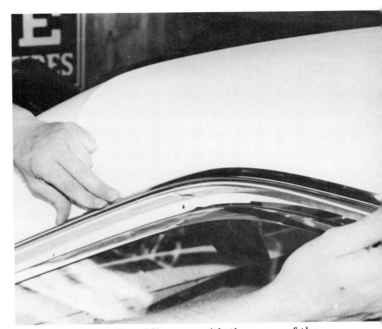

1. Line the driprail moldings up with the curve of the roof. Clip the molding to the top of the driprail, and with the palm of your hand, snap it over the lower edge of the driprail. Start at the rear and work towards the front. It's a good idea to have someone help you install this molding to keep it from scratching the roof as it is installed.

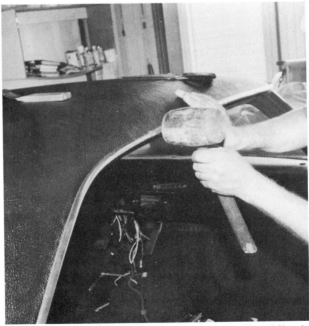

2. On cars equipped with vinyl tops, a driprail molding is installed, followed by a scalp molding that secures the molding to the fabric top. The scalp molding is delicate and requires care when installing.

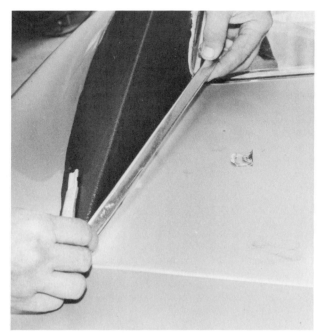

3. Pillar moldings are used on cars with contrasting painted or fabric-covered tops. These moldings are installed with clips or have studs that are retained by speed nuts accessible from inside the trunk area. Convertible tops have pinch weld moldings that are installed with either clips or speed nuts.

Emblem and mirror installation

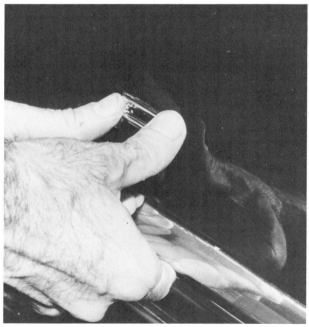

1. When installing hood or trunk letters, always install new barrel clips and use pressure on both sides of the letter to evenly press the letters into place.

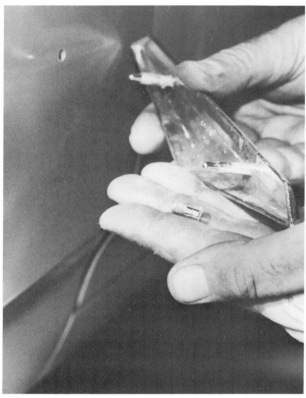

2. Many restorers will use barrel clips on emblems that are usually retained by speed nuts that are not accessible once the fenders are installed. These barrel clips allow the restorer to remove the emblem for cleaning and to wax the paint behind the emblem. The only problem with doing this is that the emblem will tend to work itself away from the sheet metal as the car is driven. You will have to push it back into place from time to time.

3. The fuel filler cap is sometimes located on the side of the car. Some models use a door to cover the cap, while on others the cap is painted body color, as shown here.

248

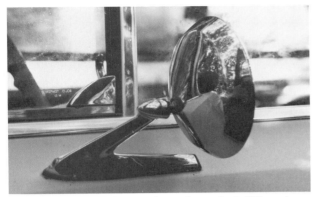

4. Install the outside rearview mirrors last. If the mirror is cable-controlled from inside, route the cable through the hole and lay it inside the door for the time being. Sport mirrors on later-model musclecars were sometimes painted body color. These mirrors should have been painted simultaneously with the body so they color match.

Applying tape stripes

1. Wipe the area where the stripe will be applied with Pre-Kleano so the tape will stick cleanly to the paint. Tar and wax remover also works well.

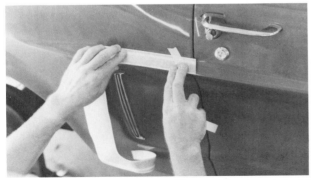

2. Lay out the stripe on the car. Use masking tape to hold it in place. This way you will see how it lays out and how it will have to be applied.

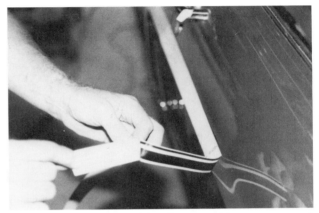

3. With the stripe taped in place, start in one area and loosen the masking tape. Remove a section of the stripe backing and carefully lay the stripe in place. Gently press it into place, working out any bubbles. A rubber pad (such as a sanding pad) sometimes makes it easier to remove air bubbles.

4. Always line up the stripes on any area where they cross an open seam. After the stripe is in place and you have removed any bubbles, carefully remove the stripe covering. Remember to pull it back over itself—never at an angle.

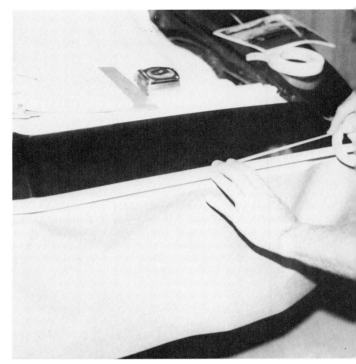

5. On large decals, it is sometimes easier to first apply mild soapy water to the area where the decal is to be placed. This way you can move the decal around before it sticks to the surface. After the decal is correctly positioned, use a rubber squeegee or pad to squeeze out the water from beneath the decal. This will also remove any air bubbles at the same time. Once all the water is removed, the decal will stick in place.

2. After the area has been buffed, start to lay out your stripe by using ⅛, ¼ or ½ in. 3M Fine Line tape. Fine Line tape is much easier to use and gives a sharper edge than regular masking tape.

Painting stripes without stencils

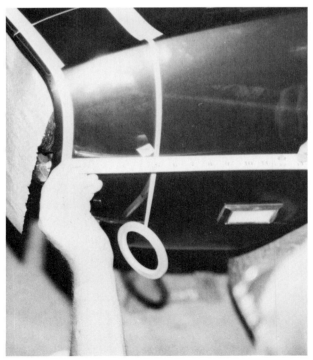

1. Begin by buffing the area to be striped, using a good grade of quick-cutting buffing compound.

3. Use a tape measure to be sure to keep a consistent width to the stripe. This is a critical part of the operation, so do this carefully.

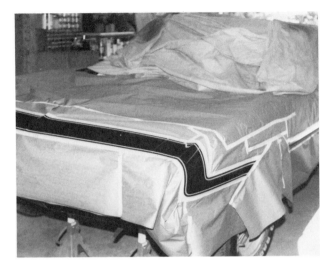

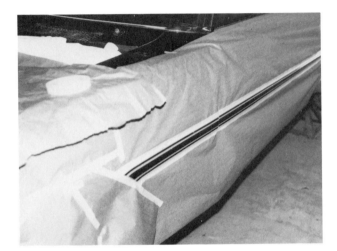

4. Once the tape stripe is laid out, check the dimensions again to be sure it is correctly applied.

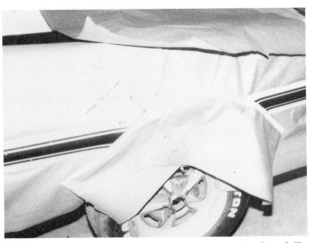

5. Anywhere that the tape lays over a seam, cut the tape and then press it into place on both sides of the seam. After you have done this, put another piece of tape over the seam to continue the stripe. By cutting the tape over the seam and pressing it into place, the painted stripe will be sharp across the seam.

6. Now place paper over the paint to protect it. Carefully position the 3M tape along the paper and the outer edge of the stripe. Pay attention as you go along to ensure an even tape job. Don't forget to cover the wheels from any overspray.

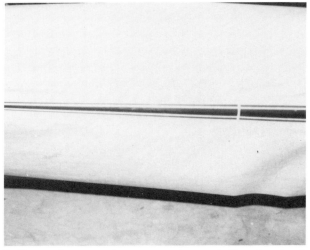

7. Remember to place some tape at the doorjamb opening.

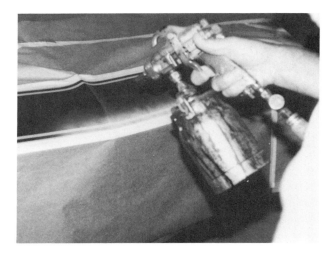

8. Apply the paint using thin layers. Use even strokes and don't apply the paint too heavily. This white stripe is being applied over a dark blue finish.

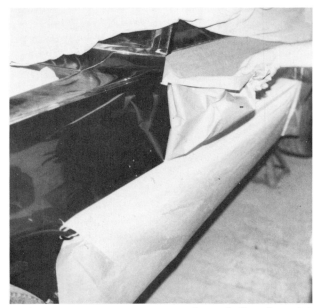

9. Start to remove your paper and tape before the paint has thoroughly dried. By doing this you will have a sharp edge and avoid paint chipping and breaking when the tape is pulled off.

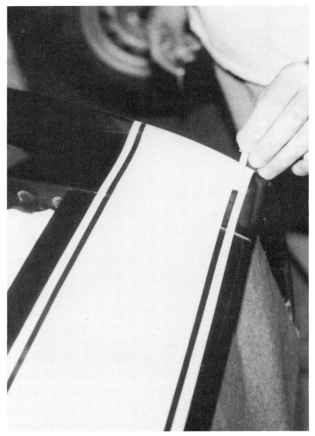

10. Always remember to pull the tape back over itself. Never pull it at an angle to itself.

11. Always make sure you stop the stripe before the wheelwells. Don't carry the stripe over the edge and into the wheelwell area.

8

Interior Restoration

Restoration involves a series of steps that are orchestrated to move the reconstruction of a car along in a logical and systematic process. If you've followed the restoration sequence of this book, the last major hurdle to completion is the interior.

The interior consists of several different elements, all of which are integrated to comprise the passenger compartment. Gauges, seats, headliners, consoles, door panels and other interior components become subassemblies. The interior is completed by restoring all the subassemblies that make up the passenger compartment and then installing them in a logical sequence. Using this sequence of refinishing and installation will move you through the interior restoration process with a minimum of problems, and will prevent you from accidentally damaging one component while installing another.

It is probably hardest to work with soft trim, such as upholstery, door panels and package shelves. They are also the easiest things to damage because they are soft. Use care not to tear, bend or

damage these pieces; replacing new parts because you incorrectly cut or bent something costs money and will slow down the completion of your restoration.

2. Most musclecar instrument panel housings were trimmed with brightwork. Although it looks like chrome, it's actually vaporized aluminum applied using a process known as vacuum metalizing. This "chrome" was applied to the entire panel and the panel was then painted or covered with an insert. This is the same procedure you'll use to restore your panel. There are a variety of companies that replate plastic and advertise in *Hemmings Motor News* and magazines like *Musclecar Review*. One of the best is Gary's Plastic Chrome Plating (39312 Dillingham, Westland, MI 48135). Once you have received the panel back from the platers, use glass cleaner to remove any dust and oils from fingerprints.

Restoring the instrument panel

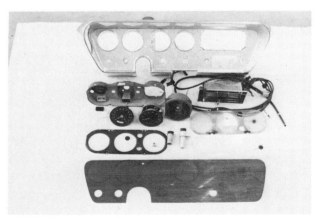

1. You disassembled the instrument panel after it was removed from the car. Now, before you begin refinishing the instrument panel, make sure you have all the parts necessary. Lay them out and inspect each component, noting what has to be done to restore and refinish them.

3. Since only areas like instrument bezels, turn signal indicators, surround trim and other raised areas will remain chromed, they must be covered before the painting process. Use 3M 6300 ⅛ in. fine line stripe tape for narrow trim like the instrument bezels. 3M masking tape for the larger areas like the surround trim works best. Cheap masking tape can possibly remove the chrome plating from the plastic. 3M tape has less tack, reducing the chances of chrome damage. Before you start to tape the area, press a piece of tape onto an inconspicuous spot, such as the back of the panel. Press it firmly and let it stand for a while and then remove it. If it doesn't remove the chrome plating, then you can be reasonably sure it won't damage other areas. Once you're satisfied, begin taping the areas to be painted. Press the tape down firmly, ensuring a sharp paint edge.

5. Paint the instrument panel housing the appropriate color. Depending on manufacturer, the panel is either semi-flat black, semi-gloss black or color keyed in semi-flat or semi-gloss to match the instrument panel and dash. Your factory parts book should provide the correct refinishing information. Spray three or four coats, making sure all edges and surfaces are covered. Now turn the panel upside down and check for runs and unpainted surfaces. Apply other coats if necessary.

4. On those areas that are impossible to tape, such as turn signal bezels, apply some Vaseline to the surface with a Q-tip. Once all the areas on the panel are taped, clean the remainder of the panel housing with Pre-Kleano.

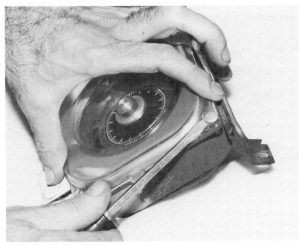

6. Now that the instrument panel is painted, put it aside to dry and begin on the instruments. The first step is to remove the lens from the instruments. Many instruments have date codes stamped on the back or stickers applied. Use care when handling gauges, as they are delicate and can be damaged.

255

7. Use an ohm meter to check gauge integrity. To check gauge operation, voltage must be applied to the gauge. Use several low-voltage DC batteries like Duracell 1.5 volt cells. Ground the negative end of the batteries and touch the positive to the gauge and observe the needle's movement. Remove any gauge that doesn't function and repair or replace it. If you can't repair it yourself, there are a number of companies that can rebuild gauges.

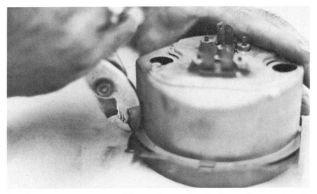

8. Gauges are covered by a clear plastic lens. Some gauge pods must be disassembled to access the lens. Carefully bend back the pod case to remove the lens.

9. Clean the gauge faces as needed. Before you do any thorough cleaning, test your cleaner in an inconspicuous spot to make sure it won't damage the instrument face. Gently wipe the gauge face clean.

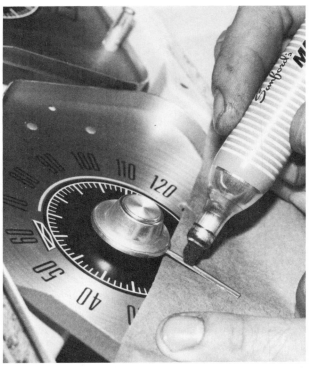

10. Recolor any needles using a marker. Paint will weigh down the needle and affect instrument calibration.

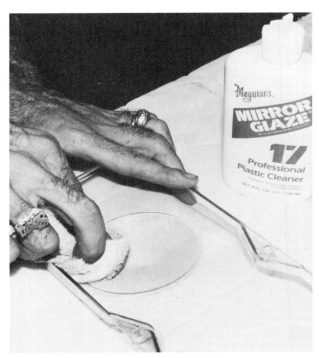

11. Before cleaning and polishing the lens, remove any pointers or other parts attached to the lens. Use Meguiar's Plastic Cleaner and Plastic Polish to clean the lenses. Use the cleaner first. Wipe on and then wipe off, followed by the polish. This process will remove all dirt, dust and most scratches.

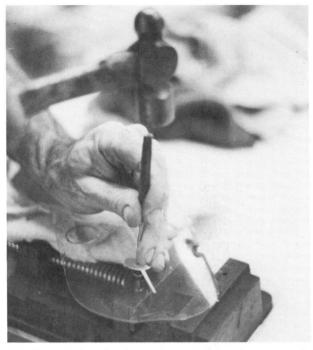

12. Once the lens has been cleaned, the tachometer red-line pointer can be reinstalled by lining the pointer base up with the mounting hole and tapping it into place with a punch.

13. To insulate the gauges from vibration and prevent rattles, replace the flaking factory foam with new self-adhesive household foam weatherstripping on the back side of the gauge cluster.

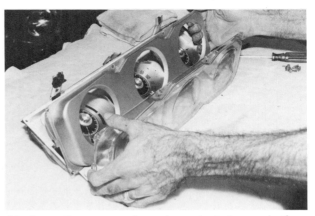

14. Once the gauges have been tested, repaired or replaced if necessary and the lens polished, reassemble the front of the cluster. Be careful not to get fingerprints all over the inside or the outside of the clean assembly.

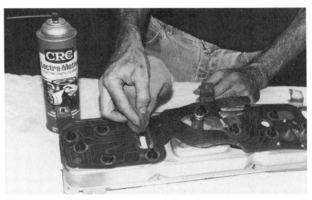

15. Many cars built after 1967 use a printed circuit board in place of a wire harness for the gauge cluster. Check the printed circuit paths for continuity with an ohm meter and clean the plug connections with alcohol or CRC Lectra-Motive parts cleaner to ensure a good electrical contact with the harness plug.

16. Install the circuit board to the rear of the gauge cluster using the ¼ in. screws. Replace all the bulbs; it's much easier to do that now than when everything is reinstalled in the dash.

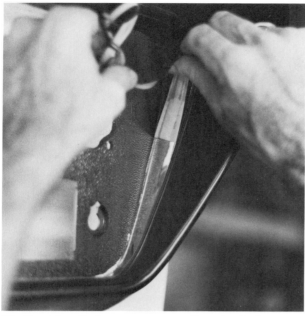

17. Now that the instrument panel housing is dry, carefully remove the masking tape that covers the unpainted chrome sections. Pull the tape back over itself so it won't damage the chrome underneath. Use a small paintbrush to apply paint if touchup is necessary.

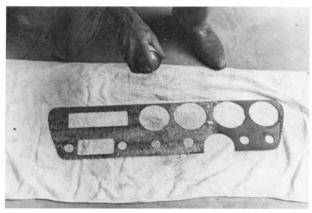

18. If an insert or applique is used, apply 3M General Trim Adhesive to both surfaces after preparing the surfaces with Pre-Kleano. Spray the adhesive on the back of the insert or applique, making sure not to get any on the applique face. Apply the adhesive to the housing using a brush. Once the adhesive has been applied carefully lay the insert or applique on the housing, starting at the top of the housing. Make sure you place it right the first time, because once the surfaces mate, there's no way the insert or applique can be removed or realigned. Work from the top to the bottom, pressing on the applique to make sure the adhesive is thoroughly bonded. You may need to trim the insert or applique in places for a perfect fit. To prevent adhesive from getting on your fingers and messing up the insert or applique and the housing, remove any excess from exposed edges with some Pre-Kleano or Prep-Sol.

19. If the heater control panel is part of the housing, check the operation of cables, switches and controls. Clean, lubricate and repair as necessary. If the control panel is also covered with a separate insert or applique, install it using the same procedures as outlined above for the main housing.

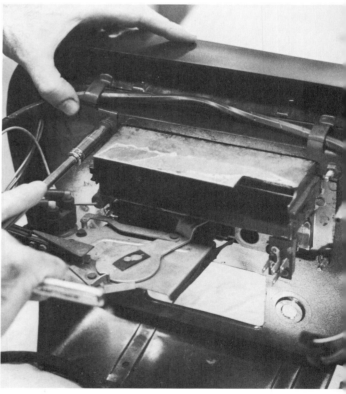

20. Install the heater control panel in the housing. Also route the wiring harness for the control panel and the heater control cables at this time. Do not install the gauge and switch harness, as it will interfere with the installation of the gauge cluster.

21. To prevent the cluster from rattling against the housing, install strip caulk at the attaching points before installation.

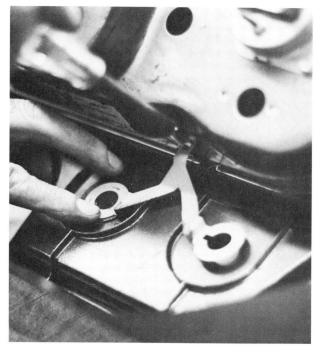

23. Install the ground straps for the switches and controls (if so equipped), then install the wiper, cigar lighter (if so equipped), ignition switch and headlamp switch.

22. Once the housing and the cluster have been refinished, you may now install the cluster. Place the housing on a padded surface and carefully align the mounting points. Secure the cluster, using the attaching screws or nuts. Don't overtighten as you could crack or distort the assembly.

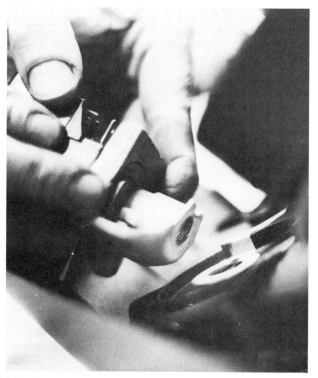

24. Once the headlamp switch is installed and the locking bezel is threaded on to the outside of the housing and tightened, insert the headlamp control shaft into the switch.

25. The headlamp switch will click once the shaft is seated in place.

26. A lock nut is used on some controls. Use a pair of snap-ring pliers or a bezel socket to tighten these down.

27. Install any brackets that support and secure the instrument housing to the dash panel.

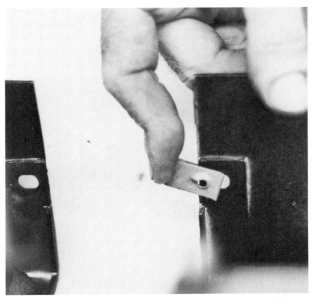

28. Install any J-nuts for attachment of steering column cover plates and other components that attach to the housing. Also install any accessory switches at this time.

29. Install the cluster wiring harness, carefully routing the wiring as shown in the factory service manual. It's much easier to install the harness now before the housing is bolted into the instrument panel.

Dashpad restoration

Many cars of the early sixties used some type of dashpad. Thanks to federal safety regulations, by the late sixties they became mandatory in all cars. These padded dashes have a tendency to split or crack due to extreme heat and cold, and few pads escaped some type of damage.

It is possible to have a damaged dashpad refinished. Check the Services Offered section of *Hemmings Motor News* for companies that can repair damaged pads. If your pad is in good condition, soak it thoroughly in Armor All to restore pliability before you handle or install it.

1. Most dashpads become sun faded. To restore the original color and luster to a faded pad, clean the pad thoroughly first and brush or spray on the interior dye. Allow the dye to dry and then repeat the process. Two coats is usually enough.

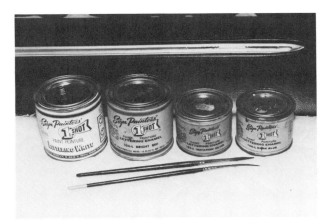

2. To touch up plastic painted trim, use Sign Painter's 1 Shot Lettering Enamel paint and thin-line detail brushes.

Radio repair

It's not unusual for your musclecar's original radio to require some bench time to sound its best. There are three basic ailments afflicting old car radios, and chances are you can repair them yourself. First, bench test the radio by hooking a 12 DC power supply to the power plug on the radio. Plug in an antenna and hook an 8–10 ohm speaker to the speaker plug. Try tuning in stations. If the radio works, the volume control may be scratchy. The symptoms are crackling and noise when you adjust the volume control. The volume may actually drop or cut out as you turn the control.

Sometimes the sound is there, and then sometimes it's gone. This intermittent problem manifests itself when the car goes over a bump in the road. You can duplicate this by gently pressing on the printed circuit board with the wooden end of a small paint brush. The third problem is the unit is plain dead, with no noise or sound coming out of the speaker when the radio is turned on.

You can repair these problems yourself with a few hand tools and a trip to your local electronic parts store. Pick up a low-wattage soldering pencil, solder and a can of contact cleaner/lubricant.

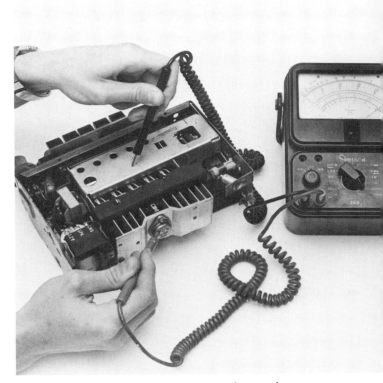

1. If you've eliminated the antenna or the speaker as a problem, when you turn the radio on, do you hear a "thump" before the audio? If you don't, the output transistor could be dead. If the fuse blew when the radio was turned on, it's a good bet the output transistor is shorted. Generally, the output transistor is located on a heatsink on the side or the rear of the radio housing. If you have an ohm meter, set it on the 1K ohms scale and with the negative probe on the radio case and the positive probe on the transistor, watch the meter needle. If it swings all the way to zero when you switch probe polarity, the transistor is shorted.

2. Write down all the numbers on the transistor as well as the model number of the radio, which should be on the case. Any electronic parts house (find them in the Yellow Pages) can cross-reference the number and provide you with a replacement. While you're there, pick up a small tube of heatsink compound.

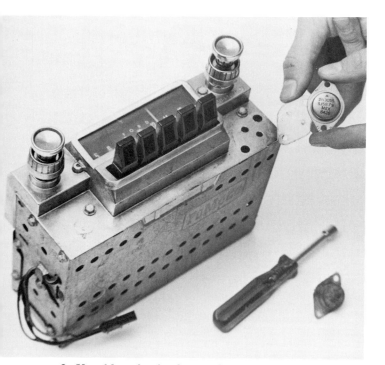

3. Unsolder the leads on the transistor (note their placement—it's *very* important), dab a little of the compound on both sides of the plastic wafer provided with the new transistor and reinstall. On some radios, the output fits into a socket and screws into place, and no soldering is required. Use the ohm meter and again check the transistor case to ground to make sure it's above ground.

4. Sometimes broken solder joints on the printed circuit board inside the radio will cause the sound to cut out when jolted, such as going over bumps. Use a quarter-inch nut driver and remove the radio covers. A magnifying glass will aid in examining each solder connection on the printed circuit boards. A cracked or "cold" solder joint is an intermittent connection and it could be causing your problem.

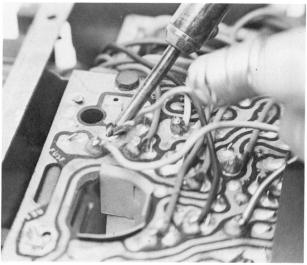

5. Use a small amount of solder to repair the defective joint. Heat the joint with the soldering pencil, allow the solder to melt and flow over the joint, and then remove the soldering pencil.

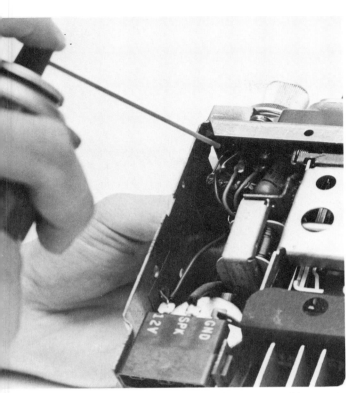

6. A scratchy or intermittent volume control is easy to fix with a can of contact cleaner/lubricant. Never use WD40 or other products like silicone lubricant. With the covers off the radio, you can locate the small opening in the back of the volume control. On Delco radios, there may be a tape dust cover to remove. The contact cleaner has a wand that fits into the spray nozzle so you can spray directly into the control. A few applications may be needed, depending on the condition of the control. Turn the control as you spray. Remember to put a piece of tape back over the opening to keep dirt and dust out of the control.

Radio restoration

If all else fails, take the radio to a reliable electronics repair facility. Chances are they won't have the schematics (circuit diagrams) for your twenty-year-old radio on the shelf. They should be willing to repair it however, if you have the schematics. You can order schematics from Howard W. Sams (4300 West 62nd Street, Indianapolis, IN 46068). Give them the trade name and the radio model number. Don't give them the year and make of your car, because reference material goes by radio number. What you'll receive is a photocopy of the schematics and an invoice. Charges are less than $5 for a complete radio schematic.

There are also a number of companies that advertise in *Hemmings Motor News* that can repair your radio. Vintage AM/FM radios are extremely expensive today, so it's worth the repair costs to get the old box back in shape.

Heater plenum restoration

1. Many restorers overlook the heater plenum during the course of a restoration. Disassembling the plenum and replacing the heater core should always be done for two reasons. First, the assembly requires refinishing, and second, a twenty-year-old heater core is bound to spring a leak once it's pressed into service. Removing and replacing it after the car is completed is not the smartest approach. Now is the time to restore the plenum and components, beginning with the removal of the heater core cover.

2. Carefully remove the heater core anti-rattle clips, then pull the heater core and anti-rattle insulation out from the plenum.

3. Remove the insulation from the heater core.

4. Here's one of the reasons you need to disassemble and restore the plenum assembly. Leaves and other debris can usually be found in a twenty-year-old heater plenum.

6. Unscrew and remove the heater blower motor. Remember to feed the blower motor wiring through any brackets so you don't damage the wiring. Make a diagram of how the wires are routed.

5. Remove any air vent covers. These covers were constructed of metal in the early sixties and plastic in later years. They should be repainted semi-gloss black.

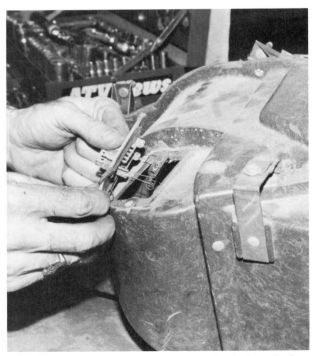

7. Carefully remove the heater control switch and relay. Also remove any remaining cables. Make a note of how the cables are routed and how they are attached to the switch and relay.

8. On most plenum chambers, the side facing the firewall is natural metal in appearance. This color can be obtained by using a cast iron spray or a stainless steel spray and then covering with a coat of dry clear. Even though this area is never seen, it should be refinished. Plenum chambers are either black, gray, gray-white flecked or color-keyed to the interior. Its appearance depends on the make and model. Refinish as required and don't forget the date code. All plenum chambers are date coded prior to the car's date of assembly.

10. Remember to use an anti-rattle rubber kit on your new heater core. If you don't, you'll have a rattle and you could damage the heater core if it moves around within the heater plenum.

11. Insert the new heater core and reinstall the reconditioned heater core retaining clips. Install the refinished heater core cover plate.

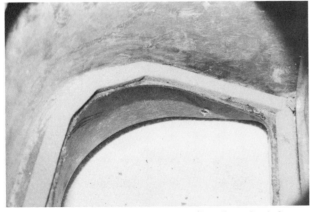

9. When reassembling the plenum chamber, don't forget to insulate and seal all of the doors. If you don't, air leaks and rattles will result. To seal the doors, use any type of open-celled rubber foam with an adhesive back, such as household door seal if a reproduction seal kit is not available.

12. Use strip caulk around the heater motor cover base. This will eliminate air and water leaks.

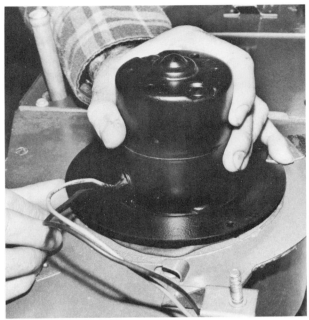

13. Before installing the heater blower motor, test the motor's operation and repair or replace the motor if necessary. You don't want to tear the entire assembly apart again because the blower motor doesn't work! Route the heater motor wiring and install the heater blower motor.

15. Carefully reinstall the heater switch and relay assembly. Again, make sure every component is functional before it goes back in.

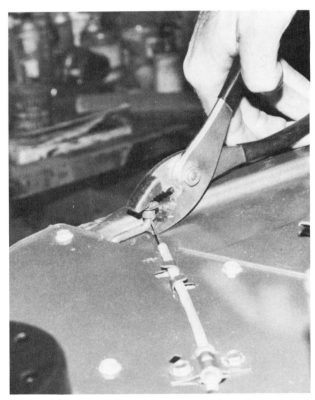

14. Install any cables and recrimp if necessary as you attach them to the control levers.

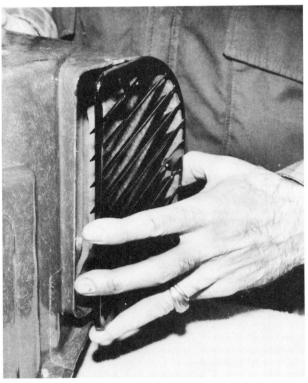

16. Install the refinished air vent. Depending on manufacturer, this vent may be at the center or the end of the plenum.

17. The plenum assembly is now ready to be installed in the car. Notice the date codes duplicated on the plenum chamber and the motor.

Refinishing pedals and steering column

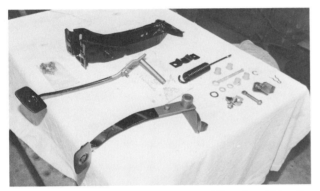

1. The clutch and brake pedal assemblies should be disassembled, bead blasted and painted. The pedals should be painted semi-gloss black along with any brackets and springs.

2. Once the pedals and attaching parts are refinished, install new bushings in the swing pedal bracket and pedal assemblies.

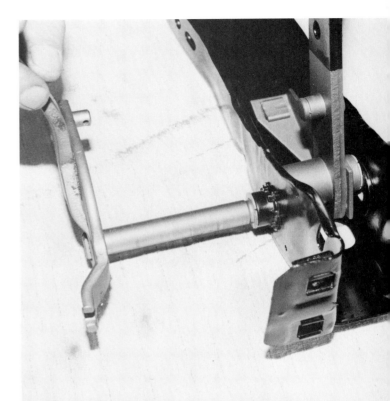

3. Install the brake pedal into the bracket and slide the clutch pedal and shaft through both the bracket and the brake pedal.

4. Install the retaining washer and spring clip.

267

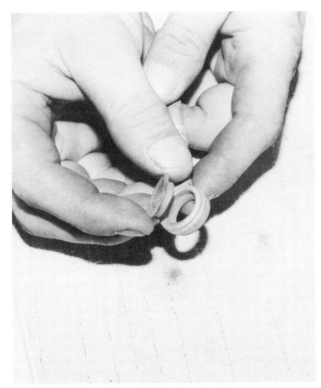

5. Install the master cylinder push rod bushing on the push rod.

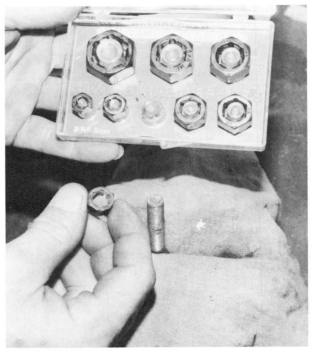

7. Use thread cleaners to chase the threads on the clutch assist spring adjusting bolt. By cleaning the threads, adjustment will be much easier later on.

6. Install the rod onto the stud on the brake pedal and hold it in place with an E-clip.

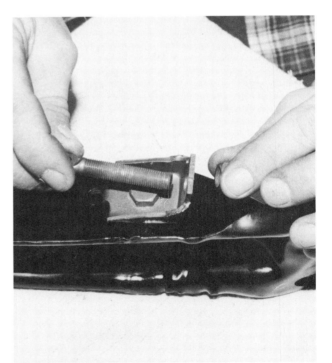

8. Install the clutch assist spring adjusting bracket and adjusting bolt. Parts like the bracket and bolt should have been sprayed with Spray Gray or Stainless Steel paint prior to installation to achieve a natural metal appearance.

9. Install the clutch pedal rubber stop bracket and bumper. Don't tighten the bracket yet.

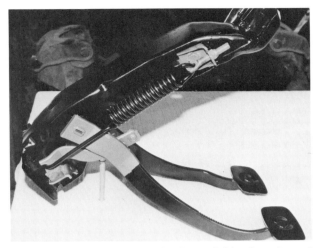

10. Line up the clutch and brake pedal in the released position. They should be even. Now tighten the clutch pedal stop.

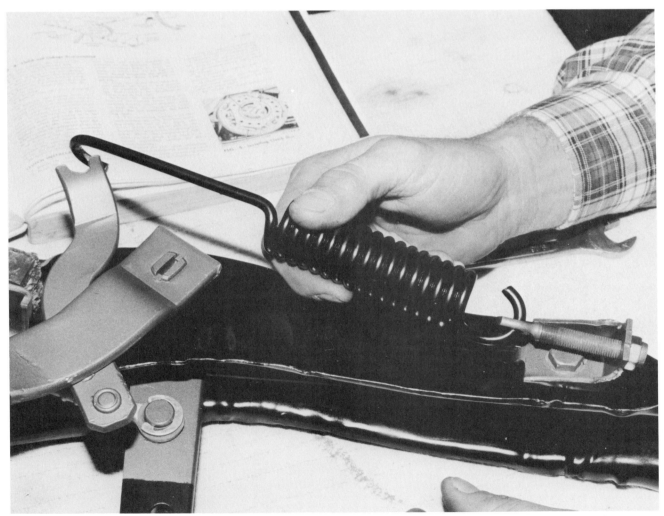

11. Install the clutch assist spring to the clutch pedal and bracket and adjust it according to the specifications found in the factory service manual. The pedals are now ready for installation.

Steering column restoration

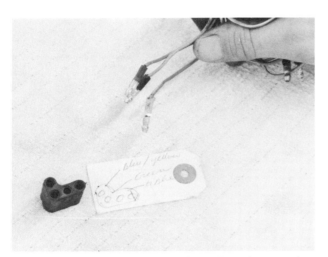

1. Begin disassembly of the steering column by removing the steering wheel. You now have access to the turn signal switch connector. Make a diagram if necessary, noting the wire color codes and their location.

2. Remove the turn signal lever. Remove the canceling cam and the turn signal switch retaining screws.

Restoring steering wheels

Restoring steering wheels is a difficult and time-consuming process. And, like other particularly difficult tasks, you should consider farming it out to a specialist. Painted plastic wheels and wood-grained plastic wheels can be refinished by companies that advertise in *Hemmings Motor News*. Padded wheels can't be redone. Your best bet here is to find an excellent used or NOS padded wheel.

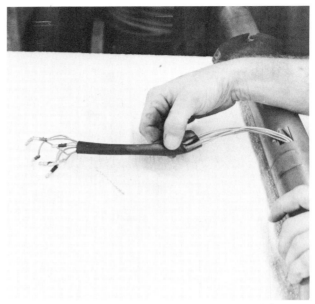

3. Carefully slide the column wiring shield off of the turn signal switch wiring.

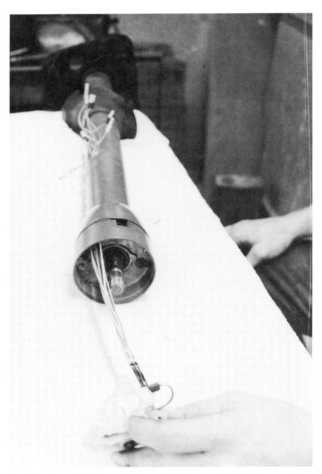

4. Gently pull the switch and wiring out of the top of the steering column.

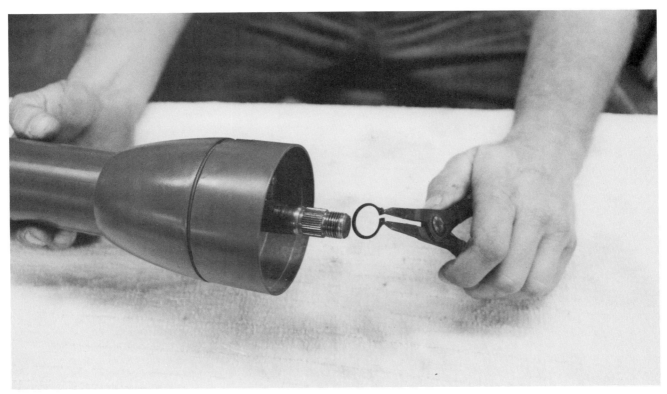

5. Remove the upper bearing snap ring retainer.

6. Remove the upper steering column collar. The collar is usually retained by Phillips-head screws.

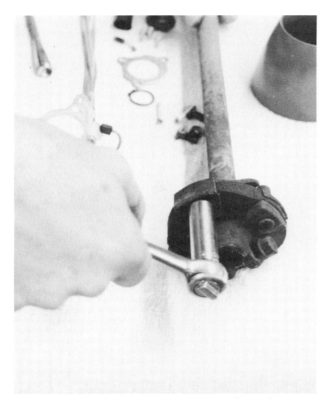

7. Remove the steering column coupler from the steering shaft.

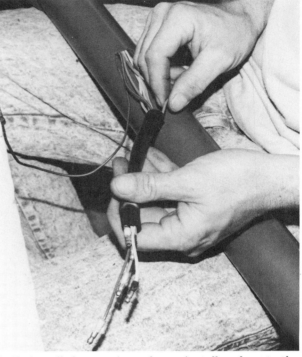

9. To install the steering column, install and route the turn signal switch harness in the column and secure the switch to the column collar plate with the Phillips-head screws.

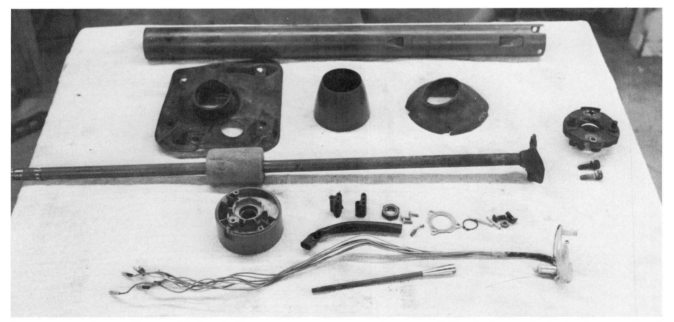

8. The column is now disassembled and all components are ready for refinishing. The column sleeve and collar should be painted to match the instrument panel color. The shaft should be beadblasted and finished with Eastwood's Spray Gray. The internal parts should be cleaned and all moving surfaces lubricated as per the factory service manual. Check the continuity in the turn signal switch harness with an ohm meter and repair any breaks or shorts. The base plate should be painted semi-gloss black. Once all the components have been refinished, reassemble the column by reversing the disassembly process.

272

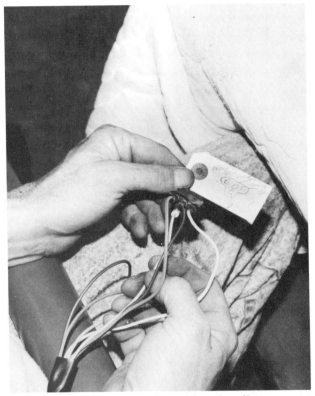

10. Reinstall the connections. Use the diagram you made when the column was taken apart.

11. Slide the lower column floorpan cover plate onto the steering column. If the old rubber insulator for the cover plate is damaged, make a new one using a sheet of closed-cell rubber. Use the old insulator as a pattern and trace an outline. Also trace any holes. Cut the pattern out with scissors. To cut out large holes, fold the rubber in half and cut on the traced lines. Small holes can be cut with a sharp utility knife.

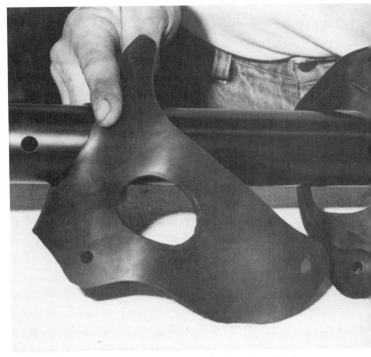

12. The new insulator is now ready for installation. Clean off any chalk marks and trim off any excess.

13. Install the flexible coupler on the steering box. Now slide the column into place and mate the steering column flange to the steering box coupler.

273

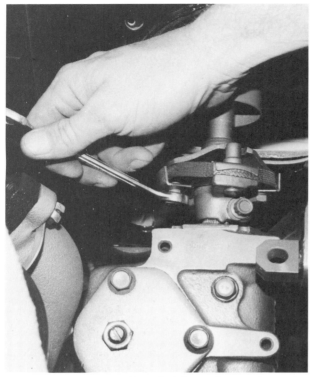

14. Once the two are aligned, tighten the coupler to the steering shaft.

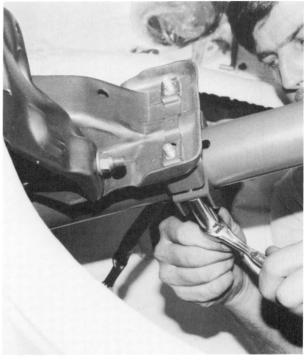

16. You may have to slide the column back and forth to align it properly. Once it's located correctly, torque the bolts.

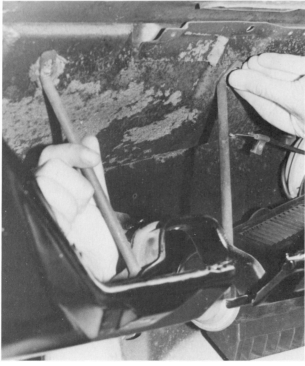

15. Install the steering column-to-cowl support brackets, lift the column up and attach the steering column support bracket.

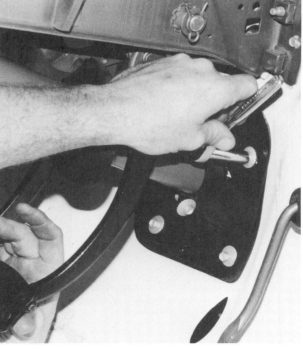

17. Complete the installation by threading in and tightening the lower steering column cover plate bolts and intalling the brake and clutch (if so equipped) pedal assembly.

Firewall pad installation

1. Chances are the original firewall pad will be torn and shredded, so a new one will have to be installed. Start by laying out your old pad; if the old pad is not available, make a pattern of the firewall out of brown kraft paper. Lay the old pad onto a sheet of ½ or 1 in. insulation. Using chalk, outline the pattern onto the insulation and cut the new pattern out. Remember to mark all the mounting holes and openings.

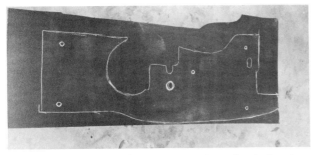

2. Lay the new insulation pattern onto a sheet of waterproof panel board. Again, using chalk, outline the pattern, and remember to mark all the mounting holes and openings.

3. Use a gasket punch to cleanly mark the mounting holes.

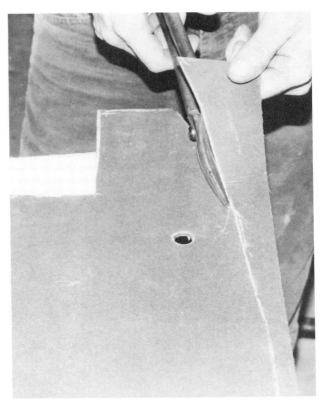

4. With a pair of shears, cut out your pad outline.

5. Spray both the back side of the new firewall pad and the matching side of the insulation with spray adhesive. Now line them up and glue them together.

275

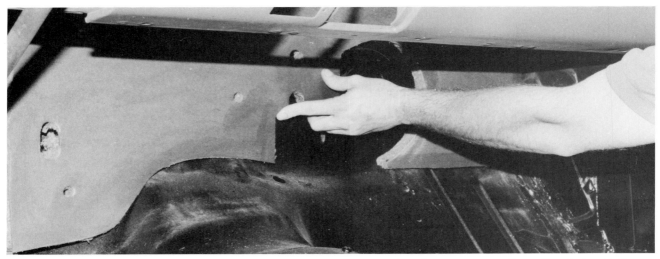

6. If you've followed your pattern faithfully and accurately cut the pad and punched the holes out in the proper locations, your new firewall pad should fit perfectly. After checking the fit of the pad, take it down.

8. To keep the new firewall pad secure, use new retaining clips whenever possible. Install the new firewall pad, using the correct mounting clips or screws.

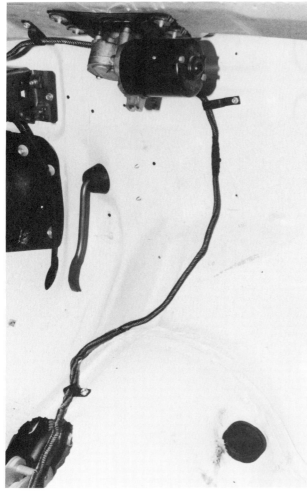

7. Install any wiring that has to go behind the firewall pad, such as the rear taillamp or console wiring harnesses now.

9. Once all the clips are in place and the firewall pad is secured, make sure that all cables, wires and harnesses that aren't located behind the pad are accessible.

Wiring harnesses installation

When you removed the harness, you made diagrams and referenced the factory service manual. You may have also used small hang tags to mark and identify which way the harness routed and what it connected to. That extra time and work invested months ago will now pay off in large dividends as you install the main wiring harness.

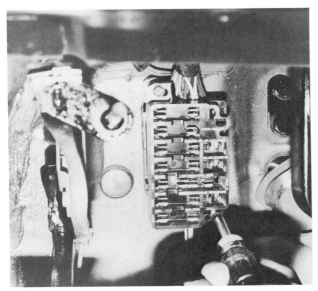

1. The easiest way to install the underdash harness is to start at the fuse block. Position the block into the firewall and snug the attaching bolts.

2. On the other side of the fuse block are the engine and front end harness plugs. Check the position of the plugs. If they are centered properly, go back under the dash and tighten the fuse block attaching bolts.

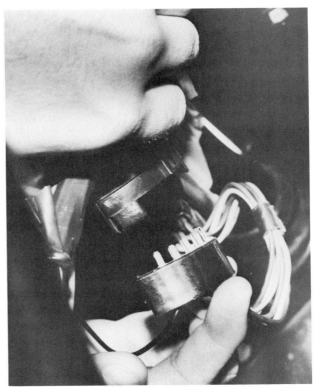

3. Install the turn signal harness to the steering column.

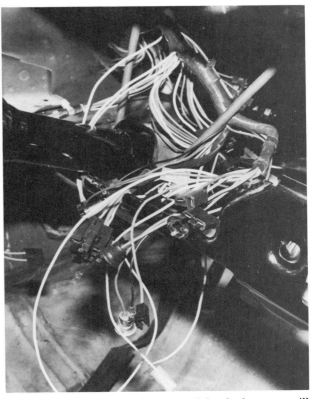

4. Lay the harness over the edge of the dash so you will be able to install the cluster harness connections.

277

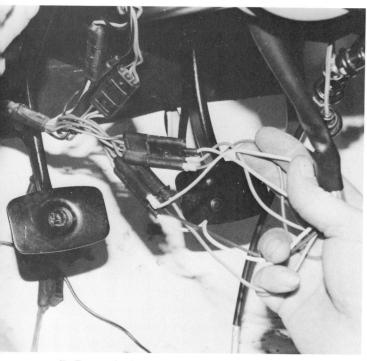

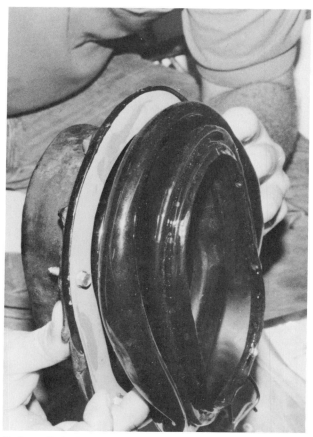

5. Route the harness connectors to any accessory wires and connect them. It looks like a tangled mess, but once you start connecting all the leads, it will be less confusing. Don't forget to reference the factory service manual and study the wiring color codes and what they hook to. With the harness in place, this is the time to install the emergency brake assembly and the left air vent duct (if so equipped).

6. Install the heater air inlet duct and connect it to the fresh air inlet.

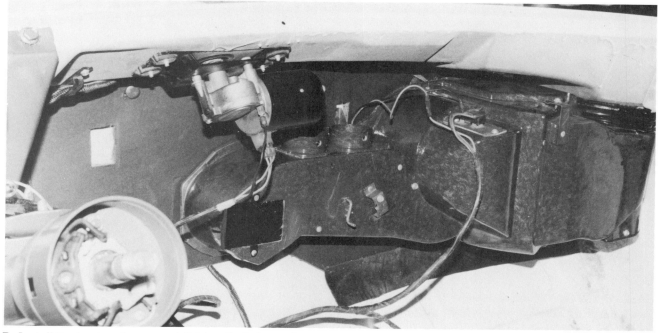

7. Install the heater plenum and tighten the bolts at the firewall securing it in place.

278

8. Install the heater blower motor cover and attach the power supply wire that was routed along the firewall if so equipped.

Instrument panel installation

When the instrument panel was disassembled, all the parts were placed in labeled bags for identification. Before the instrument panel and its components can be reinstalled, make sure all the parts have been cleaned, repaired, refinished or replaced. You'll be connecting the harnesses to the gauges, switches and accessories during this process, and here's when your factory service manual, exploded drawings in the parts book or factory assembly manual will become invaluable. The factory books will illustrate how the wires are routed and connected to the gauges, switches and accessories. By following your diagrams and the factory books, that "bundle of snakes" won't be so bad after all.

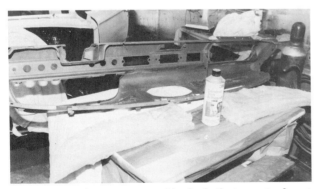

1. Some cars have a removable dash that you took out during disassembly, cleaned, prepped and refinished. Others have a fixed dash that is welded to the body. Either way, the dash has been painted and is ready to have new insulation and soundproofing glued back in as originally done by the factory. Use 3M General Trim Adhesive to glue the insulation into place.

2. If the dash was removed, install it to the cowl. With the dash installed, make sure the harnesses are accessible for cluster installation. Some dashes have a pad that bolts or screws to the panel. You'll install this last.

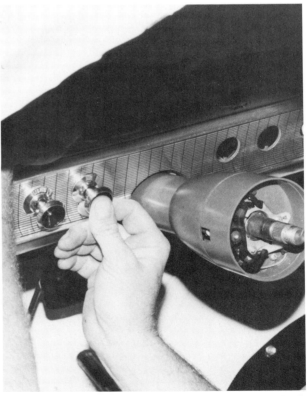

3. If the controls and switches install through the dash and not the instrument cluster housing, put them in now. Also install any knobs, cables and control panels at this time.

4. The radio speaker will either install from the top or up from beneath the dash. Connect the wire harness that will go to the radio to the speaker. If the car is equipped with an accessory rear seat speaker, power antenna or convertible top or reverberation unit, install the switch and plug the harness in.

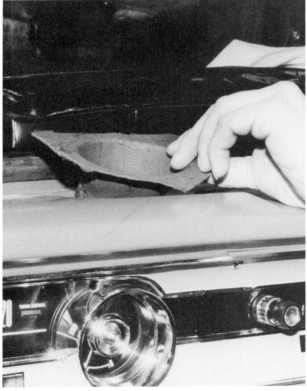

5. The defroster ducts will install either from beneath the dash or from the top. Clip or screw them securely into place.

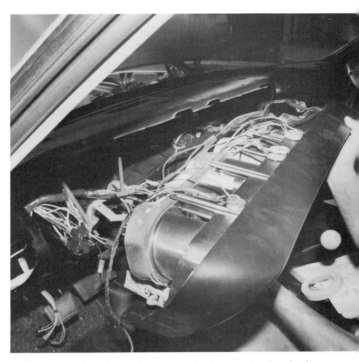

6. Now position the instrument cluster up to the dash and install all the cluster harnesses and wires, following the factory assembly information. By not installing it first, it allowed you easier access to the back of the dash during assembly.

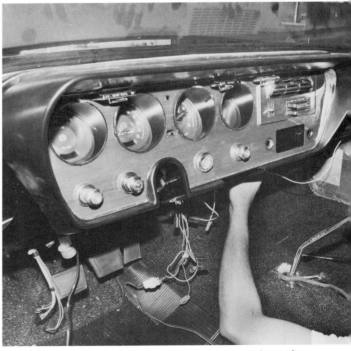

7. Carefully set the cluster housing up against the instrument panel, checking the wiring connections to make sure no plugs or connectors have been separated.

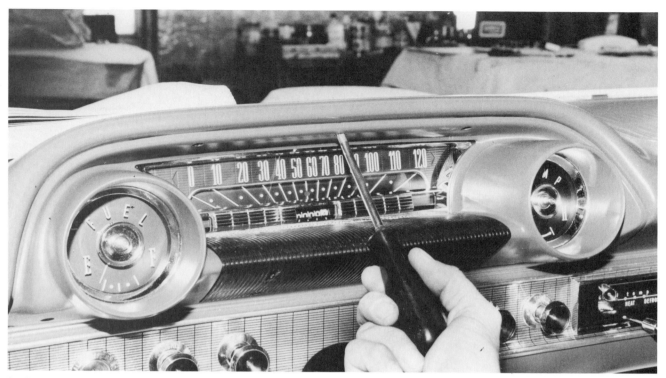

8. Once you are satisfied that everything is intact, install the screws securing the gauge cluster to the instrument panel. At this point, all harness and wires should be routed and connected.

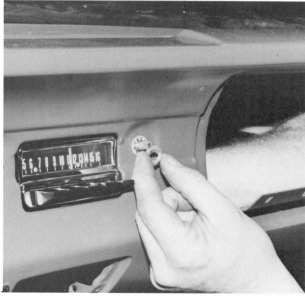

9. Install the speaker cover, using a stub screwdriver. Slide the radio up under the dash and position the face and shafts through the holes. Once you are satisfied the radio is in properly, install the washers and lock nuts on the shafts and tighten them down. Most radios have a support bracket for the rear of the unit. Some radios attach to a face plate that is then screwed to the instrument panel. Once the radio is in place, install the power and speaker leads and plug in the antenna.

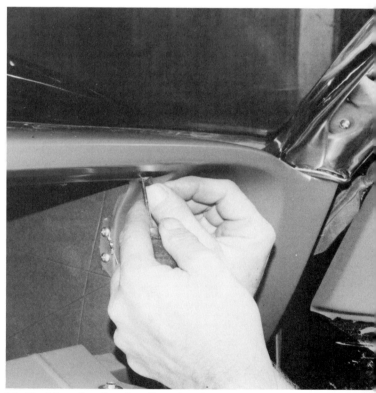

10. Position the glovebox liner in place and install the glovebox door bumpers.

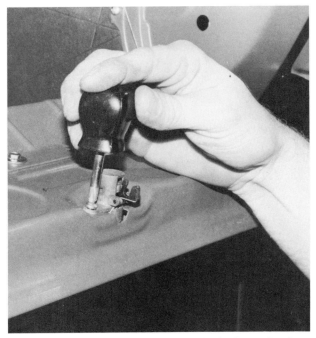

11. Install the glovebox door and the lock mechanism. Also install the catch at the top center of the glovebox. On some cars, there is an emblem on the glovebox door that is either glued or screwed on. Install it now.

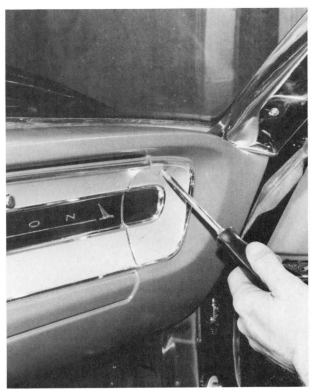

13. Install the glovebox and dash end finish plates.

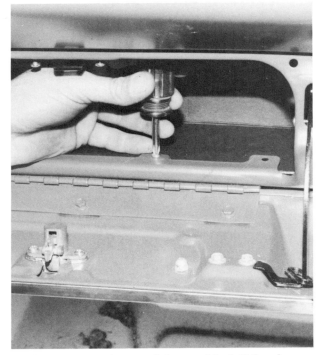

12. Now use a stub screwdriver and install the chrome Phillips-head screws used to secure the glovebox liner to the instrument panel. Close and open the glovebox door. Make sure the latch mechanism works smoothly. Adjust the lock and latch until it does.

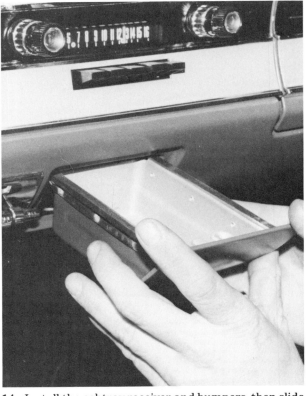

14. Install the ashtray receiver and bumpers, then slide the ashtray on the tracks into the dash board.

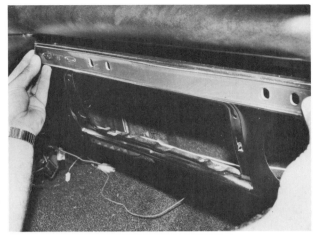

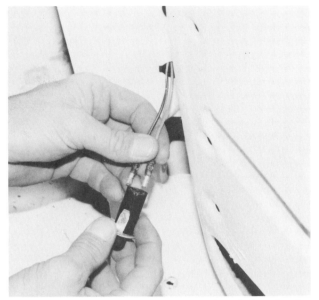

15. Install any other ornaments or nameplates. The last step is to install the dashpad. The pad is retained by screws and clips. Check the factory service or assembly manual for information on installing the dashpad on your particular car. The pad is the last item installed on the instrument panel. This is done to prevent any damage to the pad while the other components are being installed.

16. Connect the leads to the doorjamb switches for the courtesy lamps and install the switches in the door pillar posts.

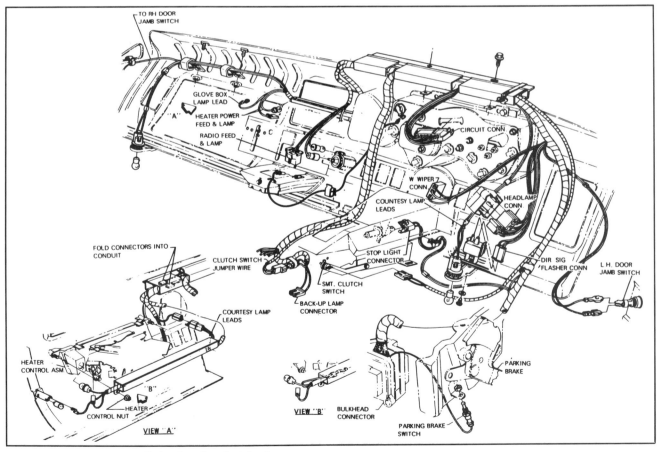

Factory diagrams show all the details of wiring harness installation.

17. Some cars, such as this 1968 Yenko Camaro, had aftermarket tachometers installed. Make sure you research the correct mounting location for tachs and underdash gauges. Don't just put it where you think it should be. Check old magazine road tests, advertisements and brochures to verify the mounting location.

Installing roofrail weatherstripping

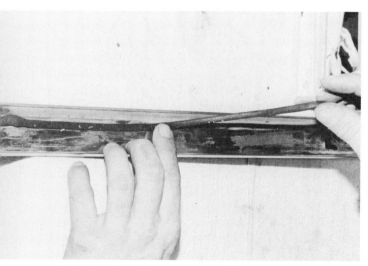

1. Before installing the roofrail channel, place a bead of strip caulk on the back of the channel. This will seal it to the roof.

2. Place the channel up at the roofrail and install the retaining screws.

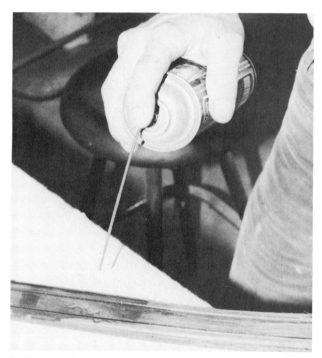

3. Spray silicone on the roofrail weatherstripping. Most roofrail weatherstripping has to be compressed to fit in the roofrail channel. By spraying silicone on the weatherstripping, it is easier to push it up into the channel and will allow a slight amount of back-and-forth movement. This allows you to align the weatherstripping to the window and door transition.

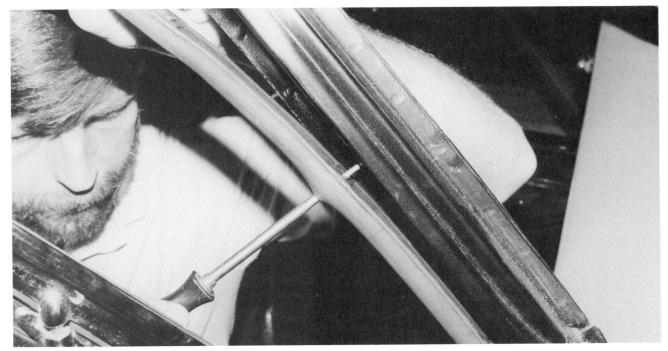

4. Start at the front of the roof and position the weatherstripping in place. Attach the screws retaining the weatherstripping to the channel.

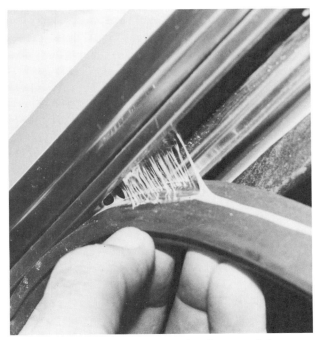

5. Some cars don't use screws. On those models, run a bead of adhesive on the weatherstripping and press it on the channel. Now peel the weatherstripping back. This causes the adhesive to bond to both surfaces, providing a better seal. Now press the weatherstripping into place. Work the weatherstripping into the channel along the roof. Use a tucking tool to ease the installation.

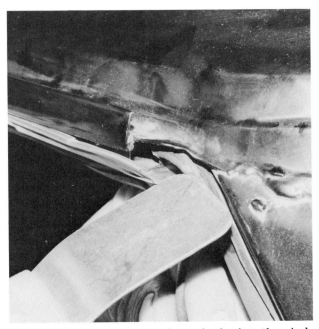

6. Make sure to tuck the weatherstripping into the windshield pillar corner. Also add some strip caulk to fill any gaps in this area. After you have installed the weatherstripping and the window glass, roll up the windows into the roofrail weatherstripping to stretch and seat the rubber and to make sure you have the weatherstripping transition in the right place, allowing the door to be opened with the window up.

Installing vent windows and side glass

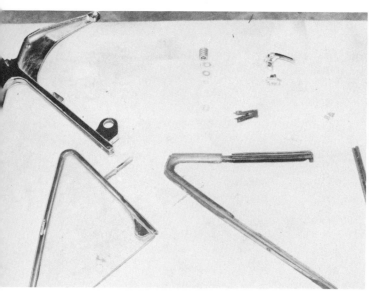

1. After you have rechromed and polished all the bright trim and installed new rubber weatherstripping, lay out all the parts to begin reassembly of the vent window.

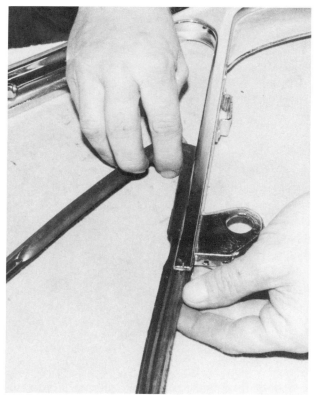

2. Spray silicone on the rubber weatherstripping and slide it into place in the vent frame. After the weatherstripping is in place, screw, pop rivet or brad the metal insert edge to the vent frame assembly.

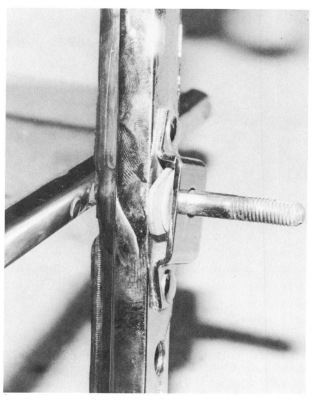

3. Place the vent glass and frame pivot down through the weatherstripping. Install the vent frame stops onto the shaft as you push it through the pivot opening. Put the vent frame pivot into the frame assembly.

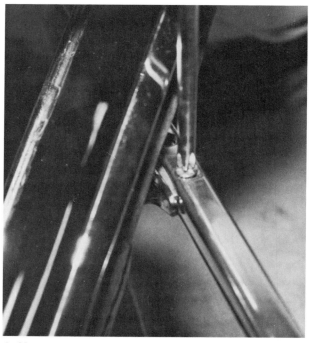

4. Now place the pivot onto the vent glass and frame. Line up the mounting holes and install the screws.

5. Now install the pivot washers, spring, retaining nut and lock.

7. Put the handle in the correct position. Line up the roll pin hole and use a pair of pipe pliers to squeeze the roll pin into place. Note the correct date code and logo on the glass.

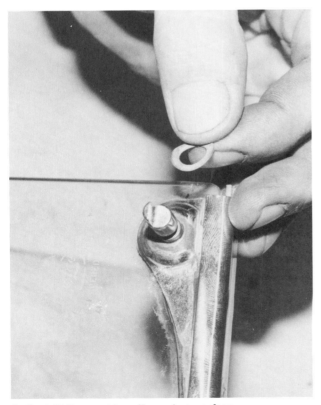

6. Install the vent handle spring washer.

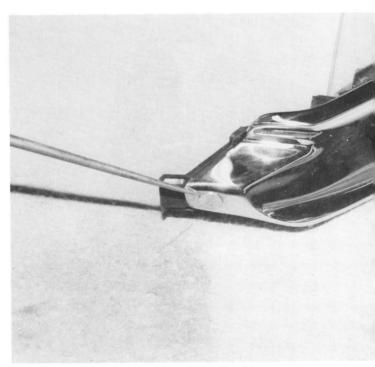

8. Install the upper bumper retaining brad.

287

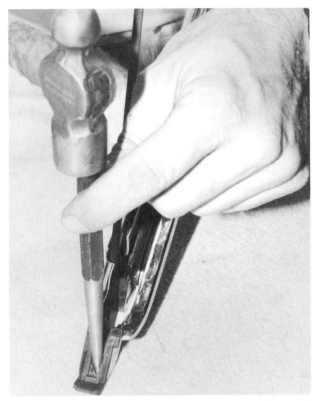

9. Slide the upper rubber bumper in place over the brad and use a drift to flatten the brad.

10. Pop-rivet or brad the division bar rubber weather-stripping to the division bar.

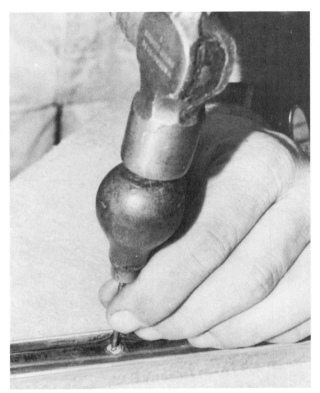

11. Drive the pop rivet mandrel out of the rivet.

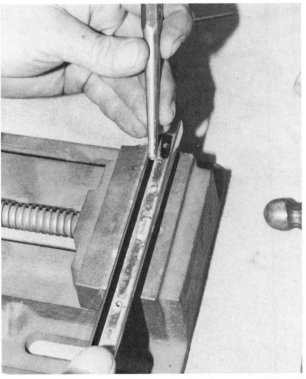

12. Now take a drift to flatten out the rivet case. This will allow the glass run channel to set flush into the division bar retaining channel.

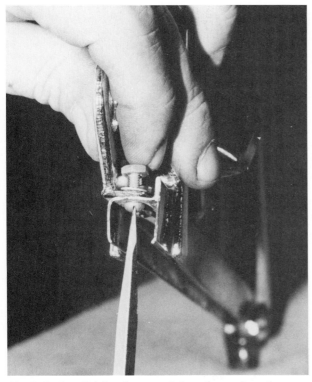

13. Bolt the division bar retaining channel to the vent window assembly.

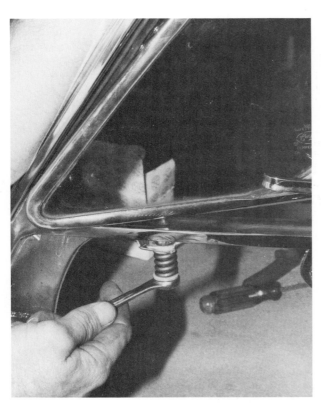

14. Now adjust the vent glass so it opens and closes properly.

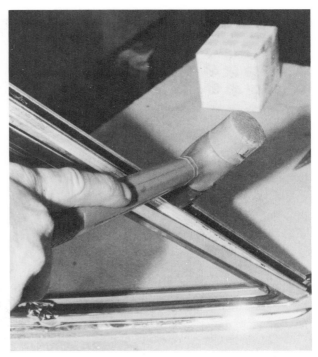

15. Slide the glass run channel into place and use a softblow hammer to tap it flush.

Installing front door glass

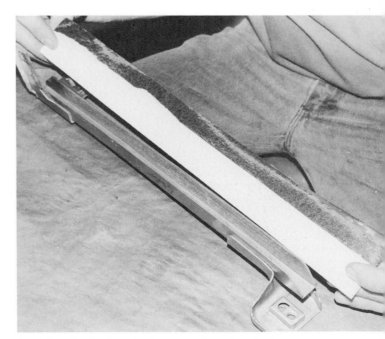

1. Before beginning the door window glass installation, remember to clean the glass, all chrome and bright trim. Reline the rear glass channel by using an adhesive-backed moleskin or mohair. Cut it to fit and place it into the channel. Do one side of the channel at a time.

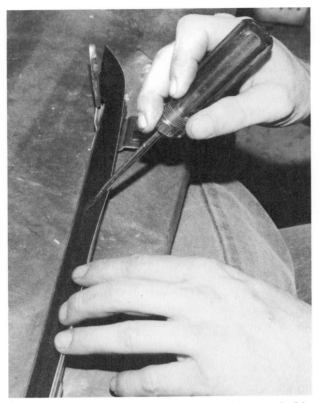

2. Use a wide-blade screwdriver to tuck the moleskin into the corners of the channel.

4. If the channel incorporates a lower stop, it's a good idea to cover this stop with the adhesive moleskin.

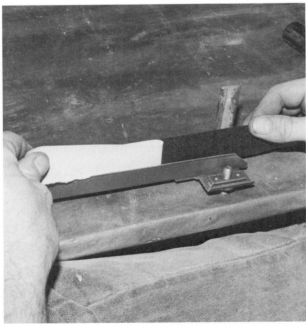

3. Now place the other side of the moleskin down into place and remove the paper backing. Tuck this side down with the screwdriver. The moleskin is now installed in the rear glass channel. Cut off any excess with a pair of shears.

5. Now place the rear glass channel into the door and attach the bolts and nuts on the door edge loosely.

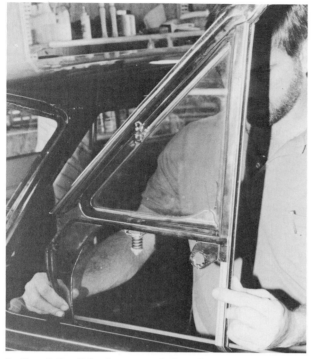

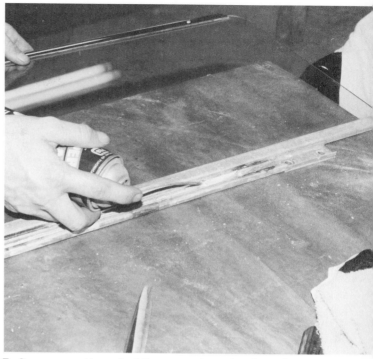

6. Carefully slide the vent window frame and glass run channel into the door. Do not bolt it into place yet.

7. Spray a coating of white grease into the door glass channel so the mechanism will operate smoothly.

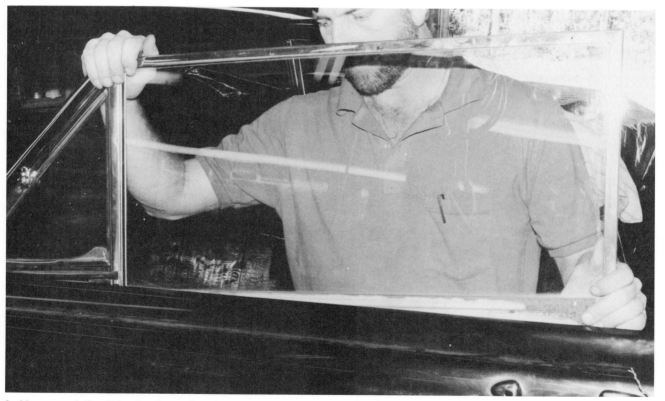

8. Now carefully slide the door glass into place. Make sure it slides easily into the front and rear channels. It will take some jockeying to maneuver the door glass into the channels. Carefully let the window slide down until it stops against the lower door stop bracket.

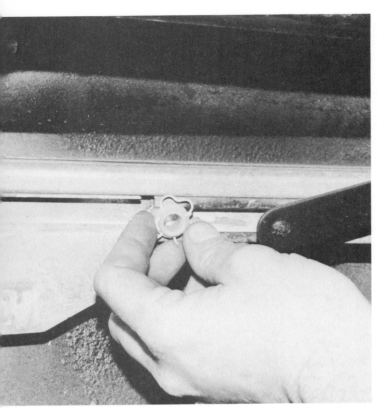

9. Slide the roller assembly into the glass channel.

11. Attach the front and rear stops onto the glass frame.

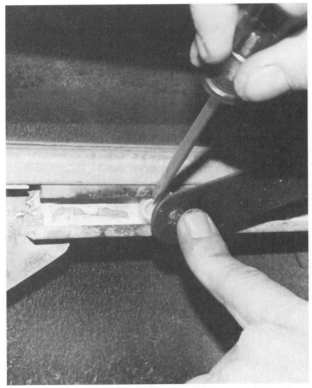

10. Line the regulator arm with the channel and rollers and snap the arm studs into the rollers.

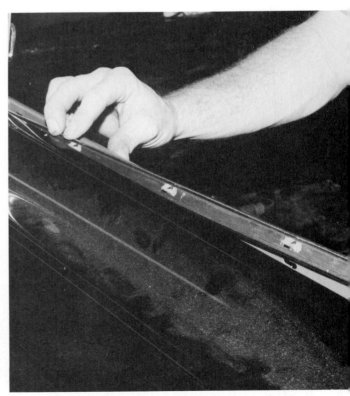

12. Line up the clips to the attaching holes in the door and install the outer beltline weatherstripping.

13. Start to snug up the vent frame and the front and rear glass run channel bolts.

14. Roll the door glass up to the top of the vent frame assembly. Slowly close the door and make sure it lines up with the rear quarter glass. Now tighten the front door glass upper stops.

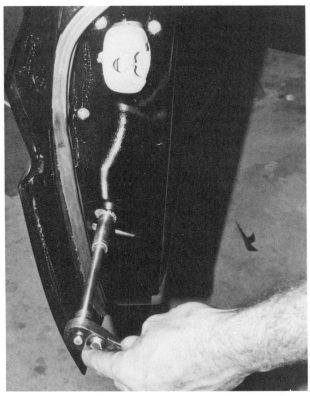

15. Make sure the glass is just touching the outer beltline weatherstrip and is parallel to it. To do this, adjust the vent frame and rear glass channels.

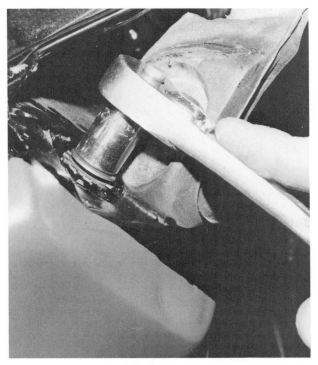

16. Once you are satisfied the glass is aligned properly, tighten all glass channel retaining bolts.

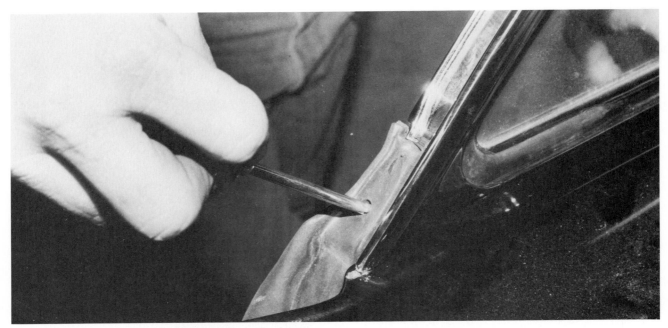

17. Now attach the vent window weatherstripping to the inside of the door and the leading edge of the vent-window assembly with a Phillips-head screw.

Rear quarter glass installation

1. Start by cleaning the glass thoroughly. Also polish any stainless steel or chrome now before installation. Use 000 steel wool and glass cleaner to clean any overspray or heavy dirt off of the glass.

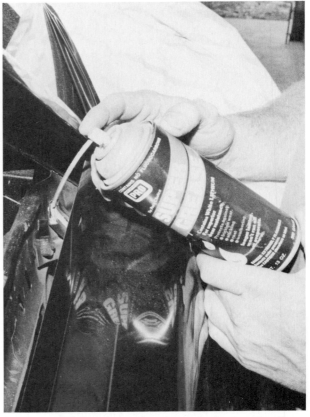

2. If you didn't remove the channels during the disassembly process, you can clean and spray the roller channels with white grease now.

3. Reinstall the front and rear channels. Install the lower stop.

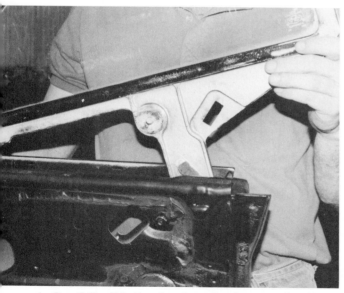

4. Carefully slide the glass into the glass opening, lining up the rollers with the channels. Slide the rollers down into the channels. This process takes time. Be patient and gently "feel" the rollers into position by rocking the window assembly back and forth until it slips into place.

5. The upper glass stop has two bolts that install through the inner sheetmetal.

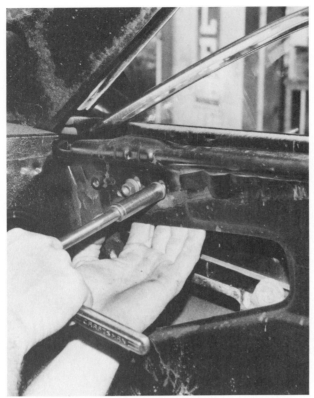

6. Slip the stop into place, install the nuts and tighten.

8. Install the front upper glass stop.

7. Attach the regulator arms and clip to the glass frame.

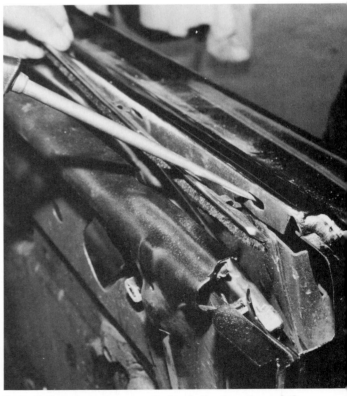

9. Roll the glass down and check the location of the outer beltline weatherstripping attaching holes. Line up the outer beltline attaching clips with the attaching holes and clip the weatherstripping into place.

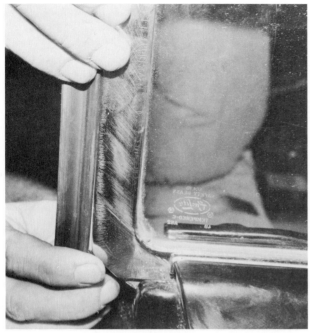

10. Spray silicone on the roll-up window weatherstripping and place one side into the glass channel.

11. Use a putty knife or tucking tool and tuck the back side of the rubber lip into the glass channel. On GM cars, this weatherstripping slips into the trim and locks into place.

12. Place the upper retaining screw back into place and the process is complete.

One-piece headliner dyeing and installation

1. Musclecars built in the early seventies used a one-piece headliner. Replacements will come in black and will have to be dyed. Use a vinyl cleaner, conditioner and quality vinyl dye on the new headliner.

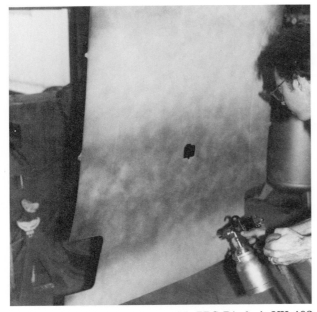

2. Clean the headliner first with PPG Ditzler's UK 403 Vinyl Cleaner. After it dries, apply PPG UK 405 Vinyl Conditioner. Now pour PPG Spray Vinyl Dye into your spray gun jar and start to spray the headliner. This dye is already pre-mixed and will not have to be thinned. Spraying at 35 to 45 psi, use even, overlapping strokes. Allow about ten minutes drying time between coats—longer if the temperature is below 50 degrees Fahrenheit.

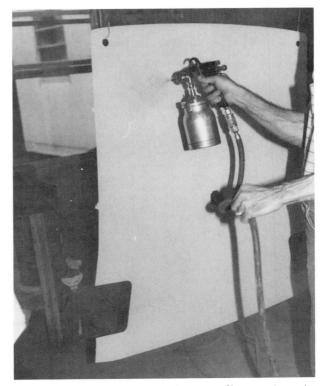

3. Finish out with two or three medium wet coats. Remember to allow adequate time for the dye to dry between each coat. After about one hour, the headliner will be dry and can be handled.

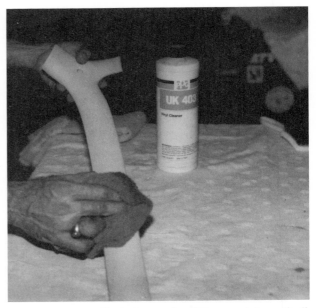

4. This is an excellent time to do all the garnish, roofrail, windshield, backglass, sail and trim panels, shoulder harness covers, coat hooks (unless it's chrome or black) and visors. By dyeing everything at the same time, you're assured all components will color match. Follow the same procedure as dyeing the headliner.

5. Now carefully put the new headliner in place. Start by installing the domelight assembly, visors and roofrail moldings to hold the headliner in place.

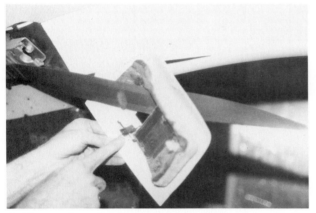

6. If so equipped, slide the shoulder belt cover over the shoulder belts and reinstall the retaining clip to hold the cover in place.

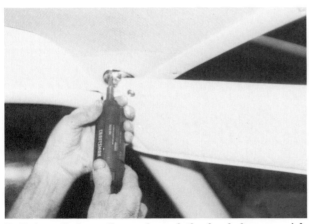

7. Reinstall the sail panels and the backglass garnish molding. Install the redyed rear side trim panel and install the coat hooks. Install the visor mounting brackets and then the sun visors.

Cloth or vinyl headliner dyeing and installation

Whether you order a new headliner or reuse the original, it will have to be redyed. It's possible to reuse the original headliner if it was removed carefully and is in excellent condition. If the headliner is dryrotted or torn, replace it. If it's in good shape and is just stained, it can be redyed and reinstalled in the car.

1. Many of the early musclecars used cloth or vinyl headliners fitted with metal bows. If you are going to reuse your old headliner, it will have to be redyed. Use PPG Ditzler's Spray Vinyl Dye to do this. Also use their Cleaner UK 403 and Vinyl Conditioner UK 405 to obtain the best results. Lay the headliner out flat and use thumbtacks to hold it in place.

2. Now use the Ditzler Cleaner to completely clean the headliner. Clean the headliner at least twice to remove heavy dirt and stains. After it's dry, apply the Ditzler's Vinyl Conditioner to the headliner.

5. 3M Trim Adhesive will be used to bond the insulation and sections of the headliner. The General Trim Adhesive has an adjustable spray nozzle that makes the job easier.

3. Now use Ditzler's Spray Vinyl Dye and redye the headliner, applying two or three even coats to do the job. Let the headliner dry and you're ready to install it.

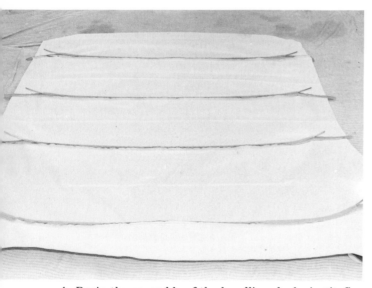

4. Begin the assembly of the headliner by laying it, finished side down, on a clean surface and install the bows in the listings (the pockets sewn in the headliner). Work each bow carefully through the listings a few inches at a time until it's installed. Make sure you install the bows in the same position as when you removed them. If the ends were color coded, make sure they are also in the same place.

6. Most of the insulation came out when the old headliner was removed. Remove any chunks still sticking to the roof and install 40 oz. carpet jute or 1 in. insulation, cutting it to size and bonding it to the roof with 3M Trim Adhesive. Don't forget to reinstall any harnesses for dome, roofrail or rear pillar courtesy lamps. Also place a strip of masking tape on the roof, allowing it to dangle down marking the location of the coat hook.

7. For our installation, we used a commercial-grade adhesive sprayed with air. If you're using an aerosol-delivered adhesive, the procedures are still the same. Apply adhesive to the edges of the roof, masking off any areas not to be covered.

9. Tape off the clips around the roof edges. When the headliner is glued to the roof, this will allow a clean line of adhesion.

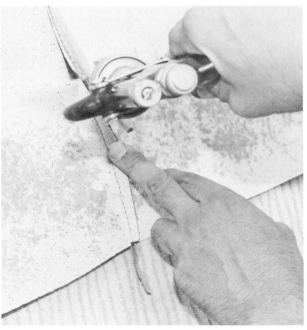

8. Spray a light coat of adhesive on the edges of the headliner. Spray both sides of the listings.

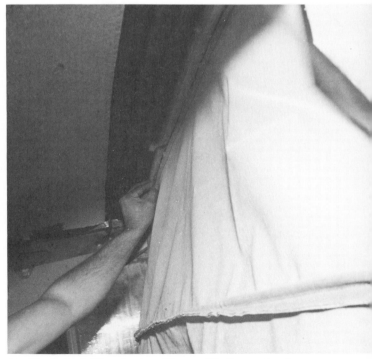

10. Begin installing the headliner with the center bow, inserting both ends in the clips. You'll have to jockey the bow until it slips into place.

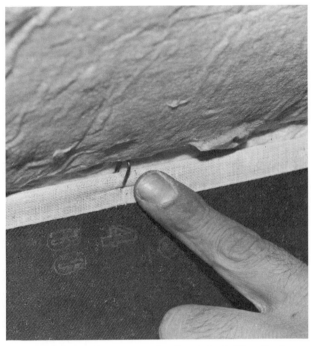

11. Work from the rear to the front, installing the bows in the retaining clips. The rear bows are retained by this wire. It goes through the listing. Don't hook it too deep. If you do, it will pucker the headliner.

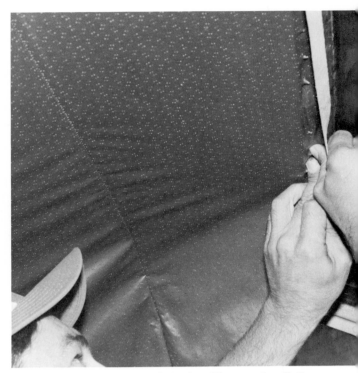

13. Now go to the front of the headliner and pull the headliner forward to tighten it. Hook it to the clips at the center of the windshield. If no clip is used, glue or staple the headliner securely into place.

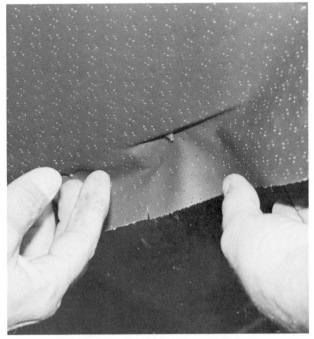

12. Once all the bows have been installed, make sure the headliner is aligned properly. If you are satisfied the headliner is straight, attach the rear of the headliner to the clip located at the center of the rear window. If your car does not have a clip, you will either glue or staple the headliner in place.

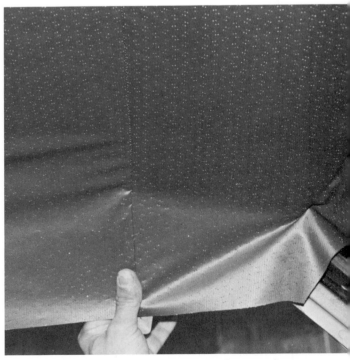

14. With the headliner clipped at the front and rear, work any wrinkles out to the side by running your thumb along the bows.

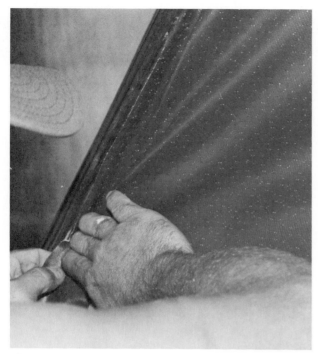

15. Now begin installing the sides of the headliner. Hook the headliner to the clips, pulling and stretching the material as you work towards the back. Take extra care to get any wrinkles out of the material as you can as it's attached to the clips on the roof. If no clip is used, glue or staple the headliner into place.

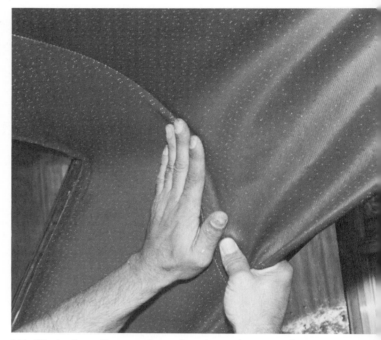

17. Work along the rear bow, drawing out any puckers or wrinkles as you move to the outside. Attach it to the clips at the edge of the roofrail. Use a putty knife to tuck the excess material in. Go to the other side of the car and repeat the procedure, taking care to evenly work the wrinkles out. Continue to work out any excess material and wrinkles by running your fingers on both sides of the bows towards the outside of the headliner. Reglue or restaple if clips are not used to secure the headliner.

16. Once the headliner is attached to the clips, make a relief cut in the headliner so it will lay properly at the package shelf.

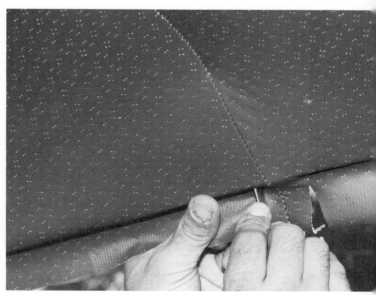

18. Make small relief cuts ½ in. from the bow on each side of the seam, as you continue to stretch the material and attach it to the clips. As you work around the windshield pillars, make small cuts to shape the material to conform to the pillars. Don't cut too deeply or the pillar trim won't hide the cuts.

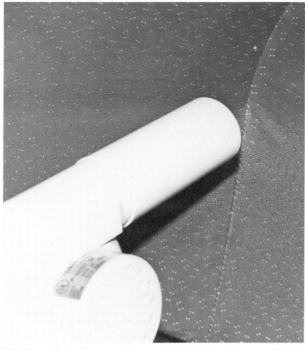

19. Use a hair dryer or heat gun on low setting to shrink any wrinkles. Don't get too close to the material, as it could be damaged from the heat. Work a small section at a time.

21. Locate the coat hook hole, using the masking tape marker as your reference.

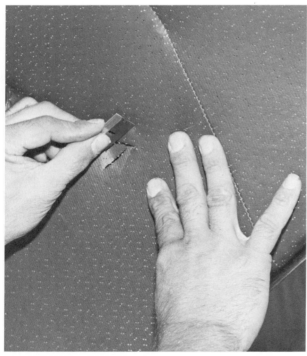

20. Make small incisions in the material to retrieve the lamp harness. Connect the lamp bezel and screw the assembly into the roof supports or pillar. If the material starts to pucker, make the slits slightly longer.

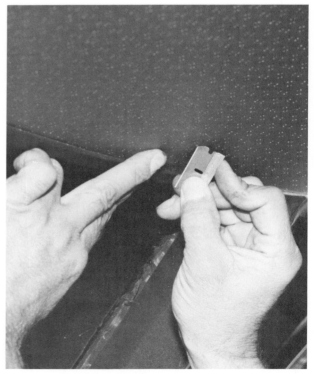

22. Make incisions for the sun visor mounting brackets and install the brackets and visors. With the visors in place, it will be easier to locate the rearview mirror mounting holes.

23. Install the inside pillar moldings and any other trim that covers the edges of the headliner such as the trim around the inside of the rear window.

Carpet dyeing and installation

If the original carpet is in excellent condition, with no frays or worn spots, you can reuse it; however, you'll probably need to redye the carpet. Install the carpet in the car before dyeing, as it could change shape if it's done outside of the car and then installed. Vacuum the carpet thoroughly before you begin redyeing. You will need dye shampoo, such as Auto Magic's, a sponge and a long-bristle nylon brush.

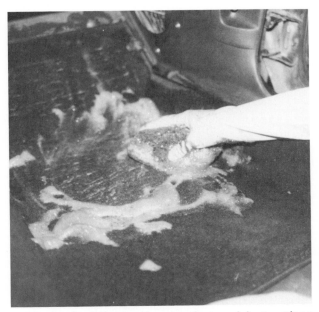

1. Mix the dye following the manufacturer's instructions on the label. Wear rubber gloves because the dye is hard to remove from the skin, and use the sponge to apply the dye. Start in one area, such as the front or rear floor section. Saturate the sponge and then vigorously wipe the dye into the carpet. Keep the sponge wet.

2. After you have applied the dye with the sponge, scrub the dye into the carpet with the nylon brush. Don't worry about getting the dye on any painted surfaces; just wipe off immediately with the wet rag.

3. After you have finished scrubbing with the brush, vacuum the carpet section with a wet-n-dry vacuum. Start without the bristle attachment and vacuum up the suds and excess water. Then use the vacuum's bristle head attachment to bring up the carpet's nap. Move the vacuum against the grain of the carpet, usually from front to rear. Continue to do all of the other sections of the carpet until you are finished. Do not wet the whole carpet and then go back and do each section. Do the carpet just like you would wax a car—a section at a time.

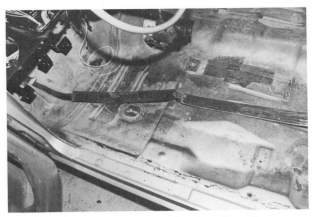

4. Before you lay in new carpeting, install any harnesses that run to the rear of the car. Along with the rear body harness, you'll need to install the necessary power leads for accessories such as rear window defoggers, power antennas, rear seat speakers and others if so equipped.

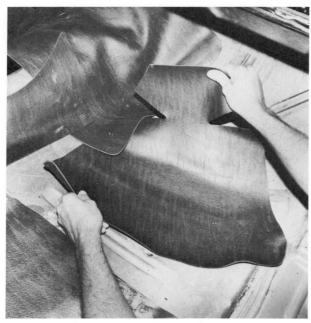

5. Vacuum the floorpan thoroughly, then install new sound deadener, making sure all of the floorpan plugs have been reinstalled. Use strip caulk on the plugs to insure a water-tight seal. The deadener is made of rubber with an adhesive backing that will hold it in place under the carpet. Lay the deadener out and smooth it down so there are no lumps or ridges. With the deadener in place, vacuum the floor again before you start to install the carpet.

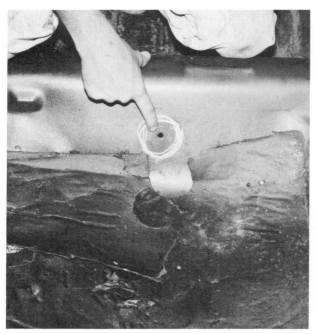

6. Remove the floor shift lever. Check and circle all the seat track and seatbelt mounting holes. Some consoles use a sliding shifter cover like this 1966 Nova SS. This is a two-piece console.

7. Lay the carpet out before starting to install it. Lay the old carpet alongside the new replacement carpet and compare the two. Are they identical in size and shape? Inspect the location of holes and cuts. Do not lay the old carpet on top of the new carpet and start to cut any holes! You must remember that the old carpet has stretched and the jute padding has compressed. If you precut the holes by using the old carpet as a pattern, you'll find the holes won't line up and the carpet won't fit correctly. Cut any holes in the carpet as you need to once you begin laying the new carpet in place.

8. Start in the rear of the car, using a punch to push the carpet into the first mounting hole. If the car is equipped with seatbelts, start at the transmission tunnel mounting hole.

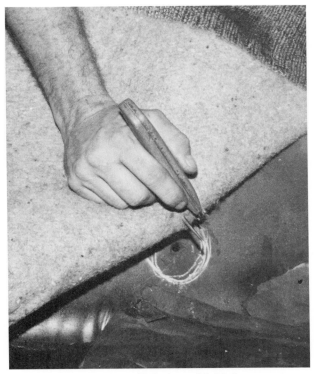

9. Leave the punch in the hole and fold the carpet over by the first hole and start to cut out a small opening using a utility knife.

11. Fold the front section of the carpet in half (side to side) and push it up under the accelerator and brake pedal. Now fold it open and work the ridges out of it, smoothing it toward the outside of the car. Make sure it is up to the firewall pad and smooth it out over the transmission tunnel. If the carpet sags over the tunnel or on the firewall section of the floor, don't worry. Cut some 1 in. fiberglass insulation into 12x12 in. sheets and pad the areas needed. Trim the pads as necessary.

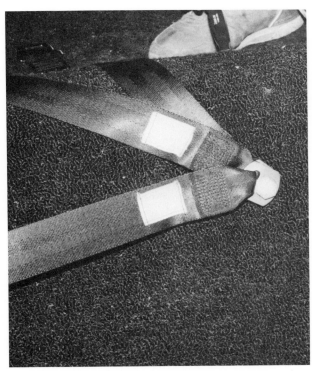

10. After the hole is cut, install the seatbelts, if so equipped. Now, do the other side of the transmission tunnel. Continue to work toward the outside of the car.

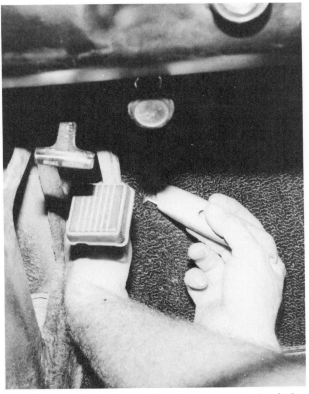

12. Now cut the holes out for the seat mounting bolts, seatbelts and dimmer switch grommet.

307

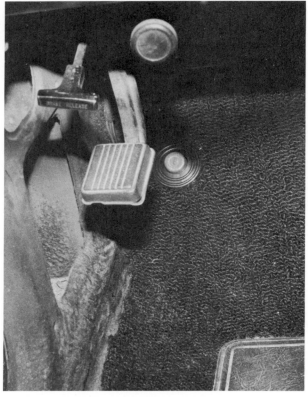

13. Keep the incisions small. It's much easier to lengthen the cut than to overcut and ruin the carpet. Now install the kick panels.

14. Set the sill plate in place and use an awl or pick to line up the mounting holes. Use chromed Phillips-head screws to secure the sill plate to the floor. Gently screw the sill plate down. Do not overtighten the screws. This can cause the sill to distort or pull the screw through the plate.

Shifter installation

1. Start by cutting an x in the carpet over the shifter hole.

2. Keep the cuts short in length until you can place your finger down in the hole and feel the edges of the shifter opening in the floorpan, then cut the carpet back to the shifter hole opening.

3. If your shifter uses a trunnion cap and spring, install them now, and then slip the shifter lever down onto the shift mechanism. If you have a Hurst shifter, and the lever was removed from the shifter, snap the lever back into place.

5. Slide the shift boot and bezel into place and use a pick or awl to locate the mounting holes. The boot and bezel are used whether the car is equipped with a console or not. Snug up the bezel mounting screws, but don't over-tighten them. If you do, it will either distort or crack the bezel.

4. If the shifter is a one-piece assembly, you had to remove it from the shifter mounting plate before install-ing the carpet. With the hole now cut in the carpet, reinstall the shifter to the plate on the transmission tailshaft. If you have an automatic transmission with floor-mounted shifter, make a small cut in the carpet and feed the shift cable through.

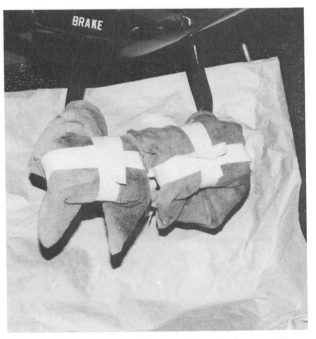

6. To keep the carpet and the pedal pads clean until you are ready to show the car, place kraft paper on the floor and wrap the pedals with clean towels secured with masking tape. When you're ready to show the car, remove the covers and paper to display fresh, clean pedals and carpet.

309

Center console restoration and installation

Most musclecars of the sixties and seventies were equipped with bucket seats and a center console. Depending on the year and make of your car, the console may be a one- or two-piece unit. Virtually all consoles were color-keyed to match the interior. The one-piece units are usually made from plastic and may be padded. The two-piece units usually have a plastic base and a top plate that screws to the base and may be painted and trimmed with chrome. Either way, the console should be redyed.

If the car is equipped with manual transmission, the cup surrounding the shift lever will need to be refinished. Most automatic transmission-equipped cars with consoles use a cover plate that incorporates the gear detents in a clear plastic lens.

Check and repair the console harness. This harness supplies the power for the gearshift pattern illumination, glovebox lamp and console courtesy lamp (if so equipped). If a tachometer or vacuum gauge is located on the console, check the instrument's function and clean it as outlined in the beginning of this chapter.

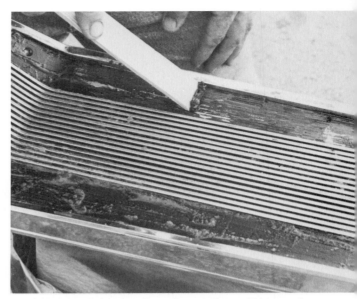

1. If the console is two-piece, the top plate will have to be stripped of any paint and refinished. Use Tal-Strip to remove the old paint. Remember to observe safety for hands and eyes when using paint stripper and work in a ventilated area.

2. Once the paint has been loosened by the Tal-Strip, use a small putty knife to remove the paint. Use 000 steel wool to get any remaining paint off the console top.

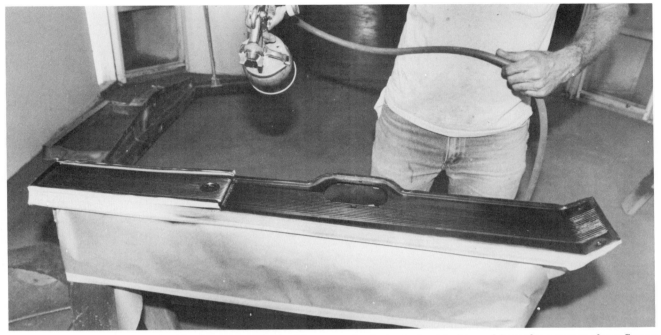

3. If the console is trimmed with chrome, mask it with tape prior to painting. Place the console top on sawhorses for refinishing. If the console is color-keyed to the dash or interior, use the same interior lacquer or enamel that you applied to the dash and garnish moldings. If it was trimmed in black, use a good-quality enamel with a flat-tening agent added to achieve the correct gloss. Spray three medium-wet coats at the paint manufacturer's recommended pressure, usually 35–50 psi. Before the paint is fully dried, carefully remove all of the masking tape.

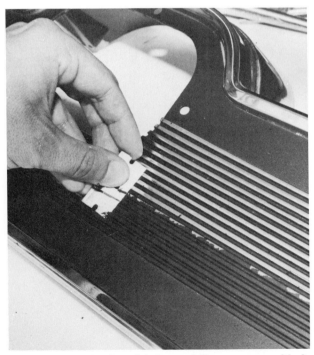

4. Once the paint has dried, carefully use a razor blade to remove any paint overspray on the chrome surfaces. Polish the chrome and, if the console is two-piece, mate it to the console base.

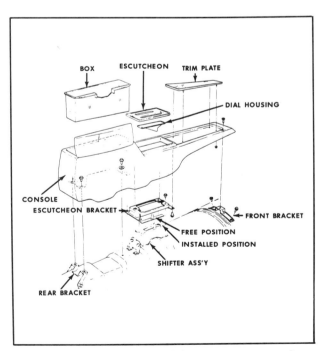

5. Assemble the console and its components such as glovebox, courtesy lamp, console-mounted instruments, trim plate and harness. Locate the console mounting bracket holes under the carpet and install the mounting brackets.

311

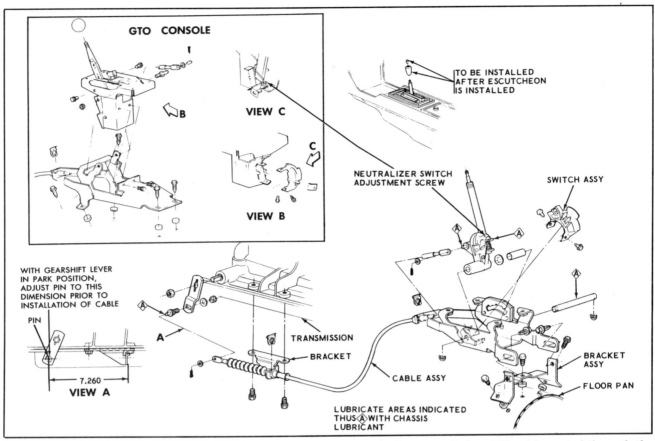

GTO CONSOLE

VIEW C

VIEW B

B

C

TO BE INSTALLED
AFTER ESCUTCHEON
IS INSTALLED

NEUTRALIZER SWITCH
ADJUSTMENT SCREW

SWITCH ASSY

WITH GEARSHIFT LEVER
IN PARK POSITION,
ADJUST PIN TO THIS
DIMENSION PRIOR TO
INSTALLATION OF CABLE

PIN

7.260

VIEW A

A

TRANSMISSION

BRACKET

CABLE ASSY

BRACKET
ASSY

FLOOR PAN

LUBRICATE AREAS INDICATED
THUS Ⓐ WITH CHASSIS
LUBRICANT

6. For automatic transmission-equipped cars, install the shifter assembly to the floor-mounted brackets and attach the transmission shift cable routed through the carpet.

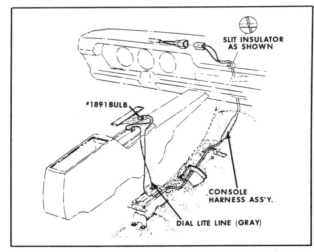

SLIT INSULATOR
AS SHOWN

#1891 BULB

CONSOLE
HARNESS ASS'Y.

DIAL LITE LINE (GRAY)

7. Carefully position the console over the shift lever, attach the harness to the gear selector lamp (on automatic transmission-equipped cars) and the courtesy lamp (if so equipped) and lower it onto the carpet. Attach the shifter cover plate and secure the console to the floor and mounting brackets with the correct screws. Thread on the shift ball or lever handle and the console is now installed.

Installing door panel watershields

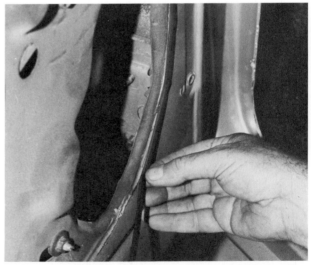

1. Before installing the door panel watershields, apply a bead of strip caulk to the door frame to prevent water leaks.

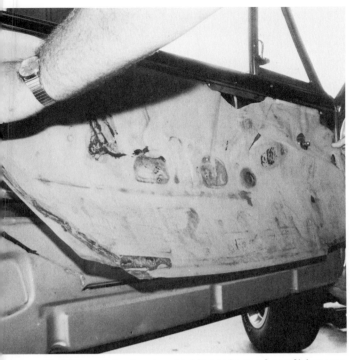

2. If the original watershields are in good condition, you can reinstall them. Position the watershield and press down to get a good seal against the strip caulk.

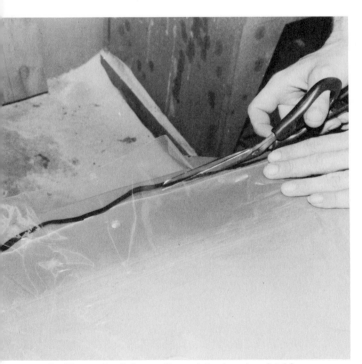

3. If you don't have the original watershields, you can use brown kraft paper or a sheet of plastic to make a new watershield. Lay the paper or plastic on the back of the door panel and cut it out about ½ in. narrower than the door panel.

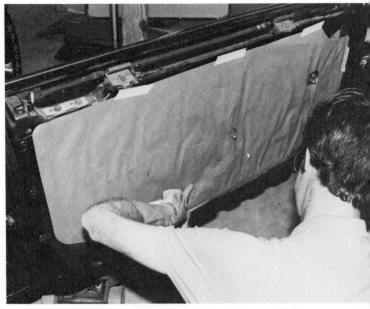

4. Tape the paper watershield in place and cut off the excess. Be sure to cut out for the armrest screws and window cranks. Use either glue or tape and secure the shield all the way around.

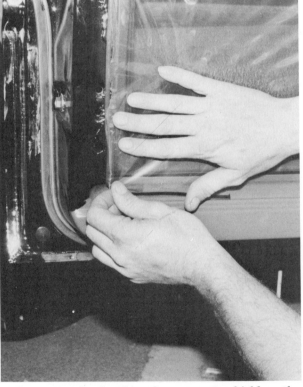

5. If you use plastic, place the new watershield on the door, stretch it gently and push it against the caulk strip to get a tight seal. Use a razor blade and make small slits in the shield to access the window and doorhandle studs.

313

6. Attach the upper and lower door panel retainer channel if so equipped. Now install the rear quarter watershields using the same procedures as outlined for the door watershields.

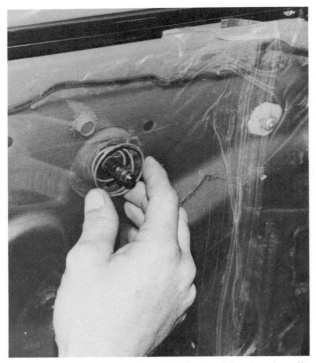

7. Finally, put strip caulk on the base of the doorhandle springs and push them into place.

Refinishing reproduction door panels

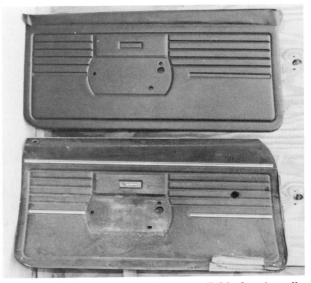

1. Reproduction door panels are available for virtually every musclecar make and model. Generally, these reproduction door panels are exact replicas of the original-equipment panels, however they are not finished with bright trim and emblems. That means you will have to transfer the ornamentation from the original door panel to the reproduction. To do that, you'll need the following tools: small hammer, door panel tool, straight- and Phillips-head screwdrivers, masking tape, drill, pop rivets and pop rivet gun, door panel installation clips, chrome trim screws, utility knife, double contact foam tape, trim adhesive and cleaning solvent.

2. Use a utility knife to cut moldings and emblems off the old panel. They will have to be reused on the new panels. After you have completely cut around the molding or emblem, use a wide-blade screwdriver to carefully pry the moldings and emblem off the door panel. Remove the old vinyl from the back of the moldings and emblems.

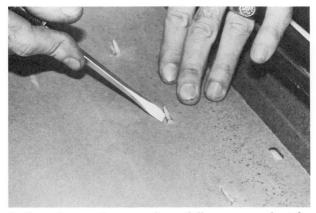

3. Turn the panel over and carefully pry open the tabs on the punch-through moldings. After the tabs are straight, turn the panel back over and carefully remove the molding.

4. Cut the vinyl at the seams between the door panel and covered metal garnish.

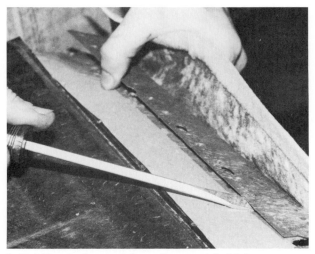

5. Fold back the vinyl from the garnish. Make sure you leave the garnish padding attached to the metal garnish. Carefully pry the metal garnish off the old door panel.

6. After the garnish is removed, straighten the punch-out tabs on the garnish molding so they can be repunched.

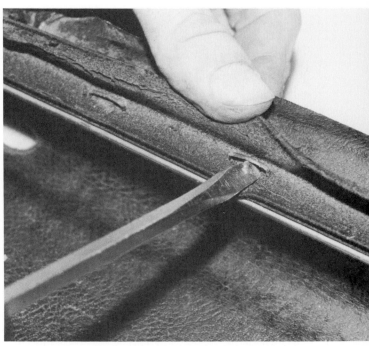

7. Remove the inner beltline weatherstripping by opening the staples and then carefully prying off the weatherstripping. You must be careful if this weatherstripping is to be reused.

8. With all the bright moldings removed from the door panel, now is a good time to polish the ones that will be reused. You want the moldings to look as good as the new panels.

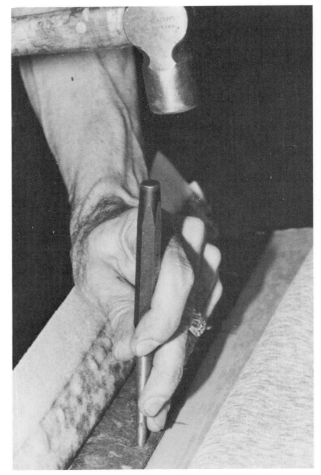

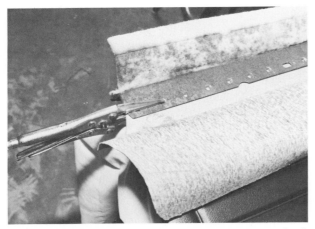

9. Use two vise grips to hold the garnish in place at both ends of the new door panels.

11. After you have pop-riveted the garnish in place, use a punch (the same size as the hole on the punch-out tabs on the garnish molding) to re-punch through the mounting tabs into the new panel. Now the garnish is secured by both the rivets and the tabs.

10. Drill through the panel and install pop rivets as per the manufacturer's instructions.

12. Spray adhesive on the garnish padding and glue into place. Then spray adhesive onto the vinyl flap of the door panel and glue that into place. (Use masking paper to cover the panel when you are spraying the adhesive.)

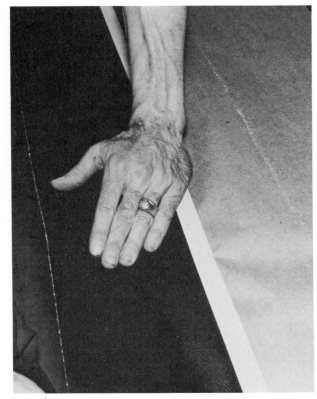

13. Work the vinyl from the bottom of the garnish up and over the edge. Work out all the wrinkles as you go.

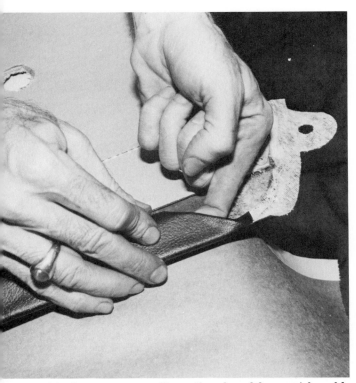

14. Cut any excess off over the edge of the garnish molding and glue the vinyl in place.

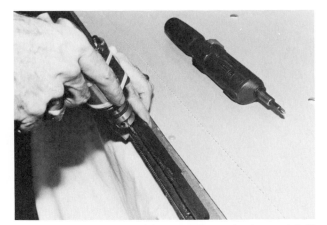

15. Line up the inner beltline weatherstripping and drill through it into the garnish molding. Use #8x⅜ in. Phillips pan-head screws to install the beltline. When the beltline is in place, use black paint and brush the screwheads. This way they are not noticeable after the installation.

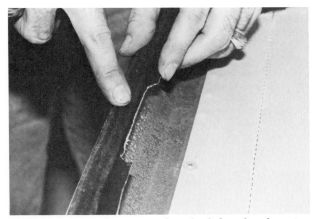

16. Remember to cut out the vinyl for the door-to-garnish installation clips.

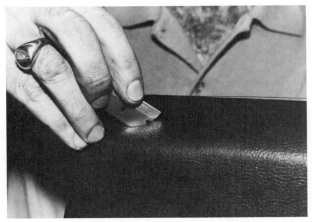

17. Cut out the door lock knob and install the door lock knob grommet. Bend the grommet tabs down under the panel to secure the grommet.

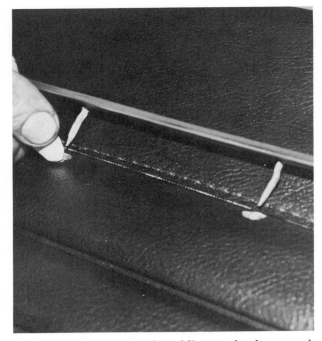

18. Line up the punch tab molding on the door panel. Mark the tabs with chalk and then drill through the door panel at each chalk mark. Install the molding. Turn the door panel over and bend the tabs over with a hammer to secure the molding to the panel. Clean the backs of all the moldings that have to be glued in place on the new panel. Use tar and wax remover, Prep-Sol or Pre-Kleano for this purpose. Also, clean the area on the door panel where the molding is to be placed.

20. Some ornaments use studs that go through the panel and are retained by clips.

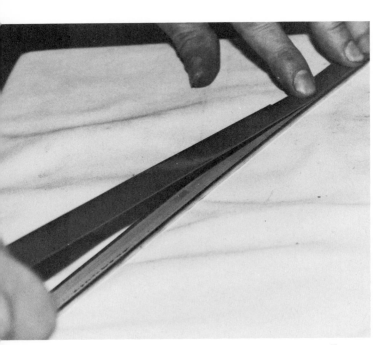

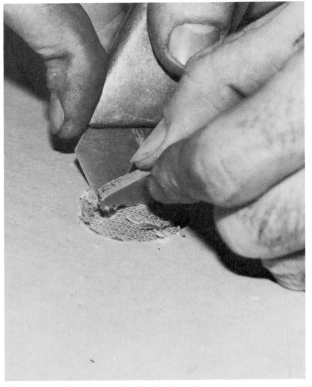

19. Use ½ in. 3M Super Automotive Attachment Tape to install the moldings to the door panel. Cut off any excess of the doublesided tape before installation.

21. Carefully cut out the holes for all window cranks and doorhandles. Use the old panel as a pattern if the reproduction panel doesn't have the holes prepunched.

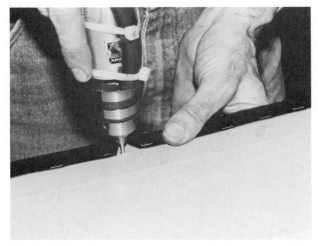

22. Prefit the door panel and mark the locations of the attaching screws and drill out the holes in the panel.

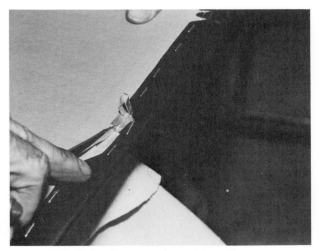

23. Install all the door panel retaining clips.

24. The completed reproduction door panel with garnish, clips and moldings installed looks exactly like the original panel and is ready to be installed. Follow the same procedures for reproduction quarter trim panels.

Door and quarter trim panel installation

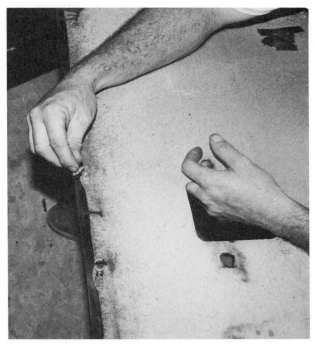

1. Whether you are installing new panels or reusing the originals, use new door panel retaining clips whenever possible. New clips will provide a snug fit.

2. Install any items onto the door panel that cannot be reinstalled when the panel is in place, such as the remote control outside mirror adjusting bracket and cable assembly or power window switch harness.

319

3. Some door panels cover the entire door frame. These fit over hooks at the top of the door frame and lock into place.

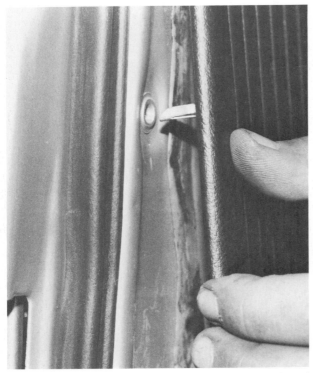

4. As you install the door panel, align the door panel retaining clips with the holes in the door and use your hand to gently tap the clips in place.

5. Check the alignment of the door panel by sighting the window crank and door release studs with the holes in the door panel.

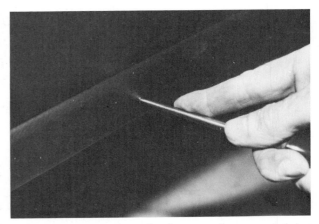

6. Use an awl to line up the door panel screw retaining holes with the holes in the door and attach with the correct mounting screws.

7. Repeat the process for the rear quarter trim panel. Once the panel is in place, slip on the windlace molding that trims the edge of the panel and the sheet metal. Install any upper garnish trim moldings and panels.

Package shelf and bulkhead restoration and installation

Some cars have a flat package shelf trim panel, which is usually the same color as the interior. This panel is constructed of Masonite or panel board material and may also be covered by fabric. If the car is equipped with a rear seat speaker, it may be mounted in the package shelf. While you're better off installing a reproduction package shelf, if the panel is not available as a reproduction, it can be easily duplicated.

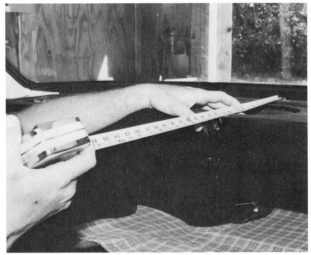

1. Measure the depth and width of the shelf. If you have the old panel, use it as a pattern.

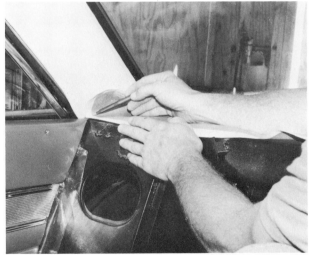

2. Cut a piece of paper the size of your measurements and lay it on the shelf. Take a pen or pencil and mark the contour of the corners and rear radius. Cut out the pattern to match your markings. Then fit it onto the package shelf, checking to make sure it fits correctly. Remember some package shelf trim panels have to fit under a lip below the rear window.

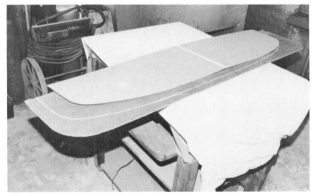

3. Now transfer your paper pattern onto a cardboard or panel board. If the car is equipped with a rear seat speaker, note the location of the grille. Cut out the cardboard pattern and fit it on the shelf.

4. Once you are satisfied it's correct, lay the cardboard pattern on the panel board or Masonite and transfer the pattern. Now cut out your pattern. If you are using Masonite board, cut the pattern out with a jigsaw.

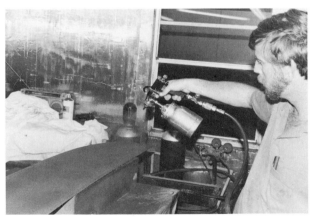

5. After the pattern is cut out, use the correct color spray vinyl dye. It will probably need five or six coats to cover completely. Spray medium-wet coats each time and allow approximately five minutes drying time between coats. Allow a longer time between coats if you're spraying in a colder temperature.

6. All package shelf trim panels had insulation under them. Use some type of ½ in. insulation under the panel before you install it.

7. Install the new package shelf trim panel on the top of the insulation and secure the leading edge with the retaining clips or glue it in place. If the car is equipped with rear seat speaker, install the speaker in the package shelf frame and position the speaker grill on the shelf and screw or clip it into place.

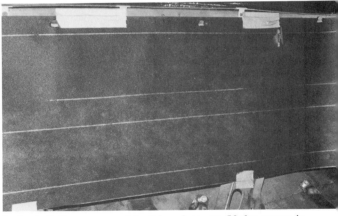

8. Install the rear seat bulkhead cover. If the cover is missing you can use either panel board (available from any interior shop or interior supply house) or 42 oz. roofing felt. If you have a pattern, lay the old bulkhead cover on the new material and trace out the pattern. Be sure to cut out all mounting holes. If you don't have a pattern, tape the new material in place and cut off any excess on the bottom and sides.

Upholstery work isn't for everyone. In fact, it's one of the most difficult jobs you can attempt during the course of a restoration. If you've never recovered seats, think twice before attempting it. Consider the costs: you'll probably spend anywhere from $400–$1,000 for a set of seat covers. If you make a mistake, you'll either ruin that particular piece of upholstery or have to take it to a professional to have it repaired. The only thing you'll have accomplished is raising the cost of your restoration.

Your best bet is to take your new seat covers to a competent, professional upholstery shop and have them install the covers for you. To help you get a correctly finished product, here's a checklist to go through before your seat restoration begins.

1. When you receive your new covers, compare them against your old upholstery, provided the old ones are original. Make sure they have the same grain and pattern.

2. If ornaments are installed in your old upholstery, take pictures and measurements of their placement. New seat covers don't come with any ornaments, and you'll have to reuse your old ones. Now is a good time to either replace or refinish them.

3. Check on the seat padding (or buns). Make sure you repad the seats before the new covers are installed. This will help eliminate wrinkles or low spots. Nothing looks worse than a worn, broken down seat frame covered with new upholstery.

4. Check all of the seat framework for damage or cracks and repair it now.

5. Check all of the mounting studs or mounting holes. If anything is damaged, repair it now. Your and your passenger's safety is riding on how well the seats and seat tracks are secured to the floor.

6. Check the seat track mechanism for operation. Clean and relube the mechanism and repair or replace any damaged springs or stops.

7. Repaint all of the seat frames and springs. Virtually every manufacturer painted these components gloss black.

8. When the padding is reinstalled, make sure burlap is placed against the springs *first*.

9. When the covers are installed, make sure all the edges are even and are on the edges of the seats. Make sure all of the pleats or seams line up between the seat cushion and the backrest. Make sure the covers are tight with no wrinkles. If the installed upholstery is wrinkled, the upholstery shop should repair it now because the wrinkles won't go away with use. Make sure the front seatbacks stand upright and that the seatback stops are in place.

10. Reinstall any side or backrest seat trim— you did replace or finish these items, didn't you?

If seat upholstery is not available for your car, you'll have to have it made. Most competent upholstery shops can provide this service. Make sure you use the original material and grain for your seat covers. This is sometimes hard to find, but in the long run it will make your finished project look factory correct instead of "just close." Use your old original seat cover patterns, and then follow all of the previously outlined steps to attain a finished product.

Dyeing upholstery

There are several reasons why redyeing interiors should be considered. Unless your original interior is absolutely pristine, redyeing can bring back the luster and depth of color the years have taken away. Second, reproduction interiors are now available for many musclecars, but there are still many makes and models for which no repro upholstery or door panels are available. That means you'll have to hunt the junkyards to replace any interior parts that you may not have or are damaged beyond repair.

Since you want all the numbers to match, that means the interior color must match the code on the trim tag. Let's assume your car's trim tag indicates a red interior, and the interior in your car is past saving. You find a perfect blue interior out of another car. Redyeing allows you to recolor the blue interior to red and achieve the correct appearance.

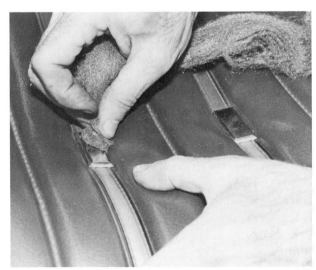

1. The first step in redyeing the interior is to thoroughly clean all upholstery, kick panels, armrests and door panels. Clean any bright seat trim that can't be removed. Using fine steel wool, gently scour the trim until all surface grime is removed.

2. The vinyl spray color can be mixed to match your interior. Take a sample of the upholstery to the paint shop so they can begin with the correct color from the trim book and then custom match the paint to your sample. You'll also need PPG Ditzler Vinyl Cleaner UK 403 and Vinyl Conditioner UK 405, along with a bristle brush, masking tape, a small paint gun and clean, soft towels.

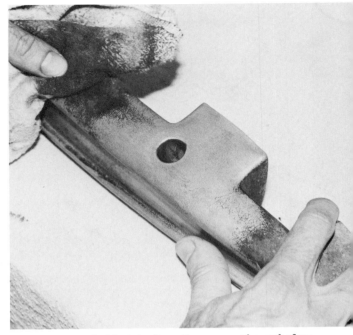

4. Remove any bright trim from the armrest bases before cleaning. If you can't remove the trim, cover it with tape. Dampen the bristle brush and clean again, scouring into the grain to lift out dirt and grime. Use a wet towel to wipe all the cleaner and dirt off. Keep turning the towel to ensure you're not spreading around the dirt you've just picked up. Work the towel thoroughly into all cracks and crevices.

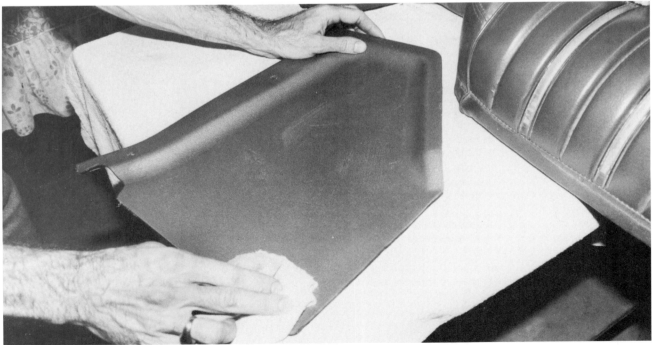

3. Wet a small, clean towel with the vinyl cleaner and thoroughly apply it to the vinyl surface. The cleaner works well if you want to simply clean a dirty interior, and you won't need to use the conditioner.

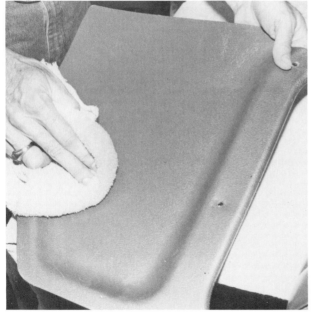

5. Once the upholstery surfaces are dry, apply the cleaner to remove any other grease. The conditioner also prepares the surface to accept the lacquer-based dye. Make sure your work area is well ventilated. Apply the conditioner to every interior surface that will be dyed. After application, allow the components to dry.

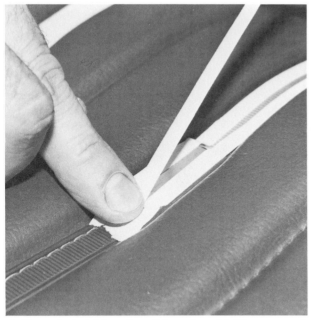

6. Since the brightwork on this seat couldn't be removed, we first cleaned the trim with fine steel wool and then applied masking tape over the trim prior to dyeing the seatback. Don't try to apply the tape perfectly—that's what razor blades are for. Using overlapping layers, make sure you've covered the edges and trim any excess with the blade. There's no need to apply lots of pressure. Just make a smooth, even cut that will give a clean edge.

7. With all the surface preparation completed, you're ready to apply the dye. The dye is premixed and requires no cutting. Pour it straight from the can into the spray cup. If you're redyeing the entire interior the same color, the job will require three quarts. Make sure you have more than enough to complete the job, because dye batches are never consistent, and buying more dye may result in two different shades. By purchasing more than enough of the same batch, you're guaranteed the color remains consistent. When spraying the dye, set the compressor between 35-40 psi and use thin, even strokes. Hold the spray nozzle about 10-12 in. away from the surface and move the gun around, spraying from different angles to get even coverage. Don't forget to spray the back side of the seat cushions.

8. Depending on the surface, you'll need to apply three to five coats. More coats will provide more depth and gloss to the finish. Don't lay on thick coats. Keep them thin or you'll fill the grain. Just like lacquer paint, in high humidity dye can blush. The term blush means the surface shine and luster are gone, replaced by a haze. It's caused by applying too much dye (or paint) too fast, and the top coat dries before the bottom coat. To cure the problem, let the component dry for at least half a day. Apply a thin coat and let dry. Then apply a second thin coat. Using thin coats eliminates blushing problems.

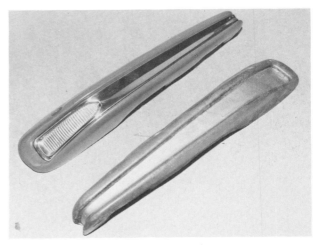

10. Any brightwork removed from the seats, armrests or panels should be polished. If there are any minor surface scratches, use a polishing and buffing wheel. Don't apply too much pressure or the trim can bend. Too much time on the wheel can also warp the trim. This comparison of a redyed armrest, top, shows how much better it looks next to an unrestored armrest, bottom.

9. While you are waiting between applications, use a safety lamp to check for even dye coverage. If you spot uneven coverage correct it immediately. The upholstery dye will dry in about an hour. You can install the redyed interior parts in two or three hours, however it's best if you allow 24 hours so the components can dry thoroughly, especially in humid weather. After the dye is dry, remove the tape from the seat brightwork. You can even redye the sun visors. After a good scrubbing with soap and water, allow the visors to dry and then apply the dye.

Rear and front seat installation

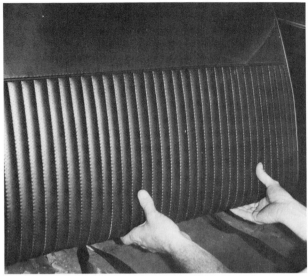

1. Install the rear seatback cushion. Remember to hook it at the top and screw it down at the bottom.

3. To remove box wrinkles and some assembly wrinkles, spray a fine mist of water on the seats and set them out in the sun. Wet the seat covers each time they dry. Do this about three or four times and most wrinkles will disappear.

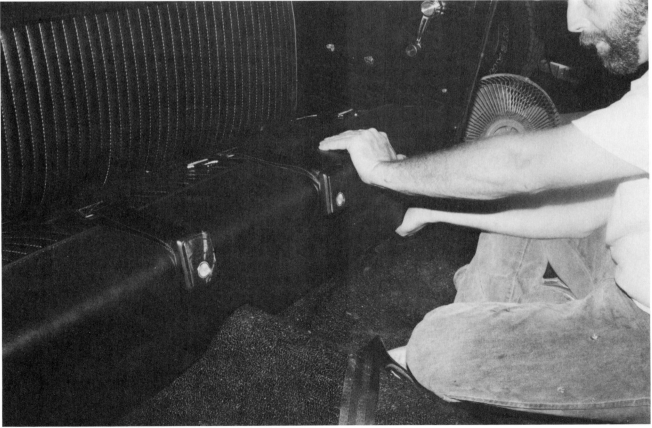

2. Lay the rear seat cushion in place. Put the seatbelts on top of the cushion, if so equipped. Push back and down at the same time to hook the lower cushion in place.

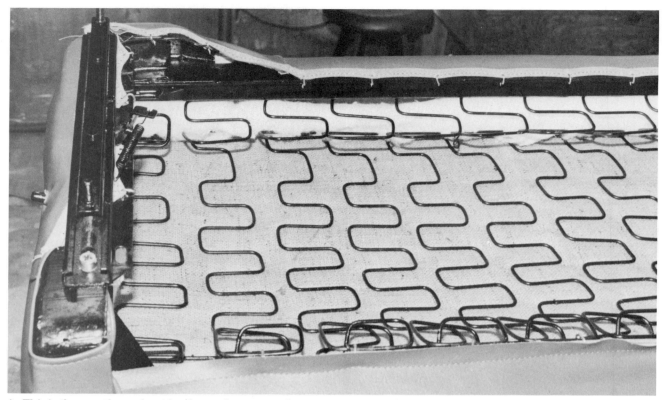

4. This is the way the underside of a newly recovered set of seats should look with the springs completely repainted and new burlap and cotton installed. Before placing the seats in the car, install the refinished seat tracks on the front seat frames. If equipped with power seats, check the operation of the motor prior to assembly.

Door trim installation

5. Put the front seats in the car. Align the mounting holes and screws and bolt into place.

1. Thread the door lock knob onto the lock rod. Push the knob down into the lock position and check the height. Make sure the left and right door lock knobs are at the same height.

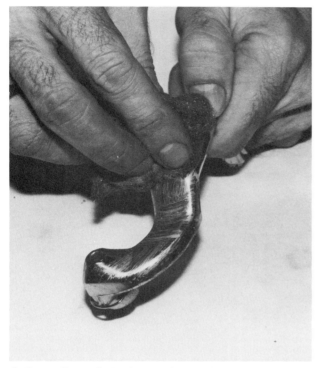

2. Regardless of whether you're reusing the old handles and cranks or installing new ones, clean them with chrome polish and fine steel wool before installation.

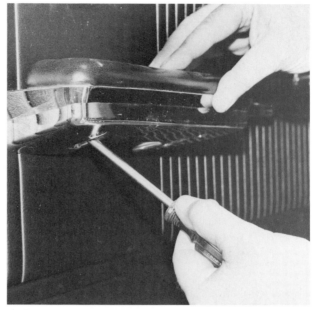

4. Remove and polish any trim or brightwork on the armrests before screwing the base to the door panel. If the padded armrest is attached to a base, secure the armrest to the base and use Phillips-head screws to install the assembly to the door panel.

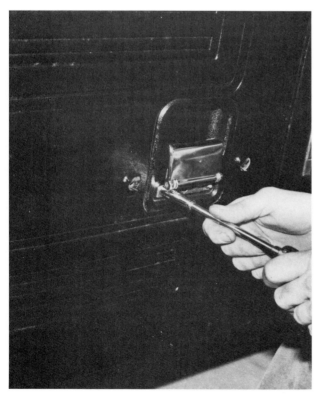

3. If the door release handle is recessed into the door panel, install it now.

5. Remember to use a washer behind all of the window crank handles to reduce wear and damage to the door and quarter trim panels.

6. Some makes use an Allen head screw to retain the window crank and door release handles to the regulator studs.

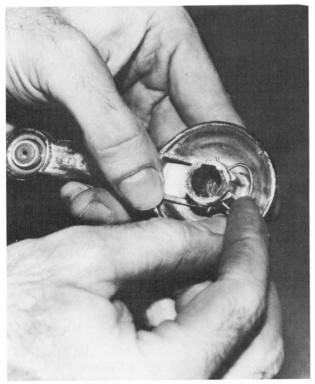

7. Other makes use a retaining clip to retain the handles.

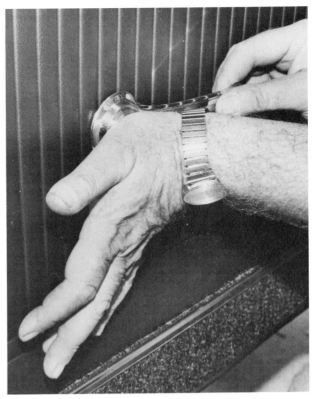

8. Slide the clip into the groove on the sleeve and press the handle onto the stud. It will click when it's seated. If you have trouble fitting the handles or they are misaligned, use the clip removal tool to take the handle off. Reinstall the clip and try again.

9. With the door panel and all handles, knobs and cranks installed, the interior is now completed.

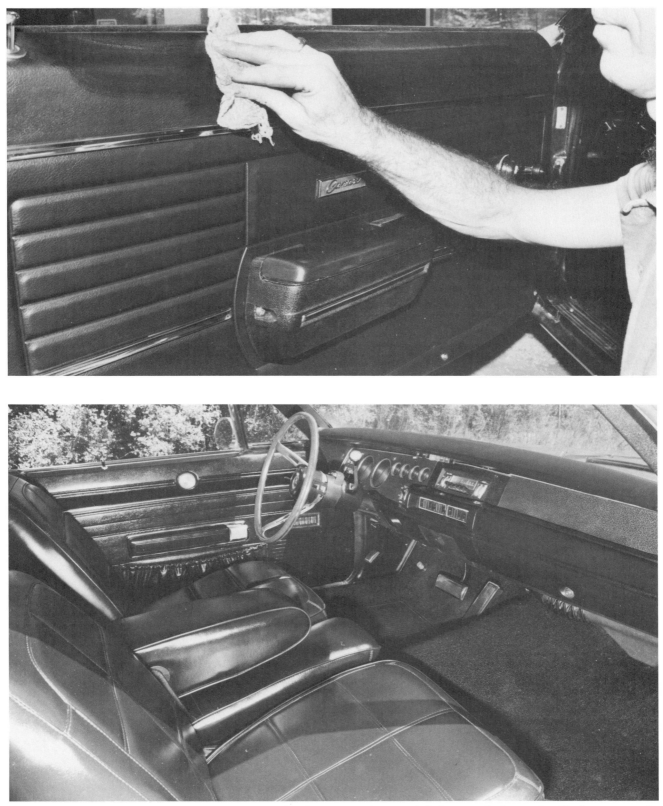

10. Use a top-quality vinyl dressing to put the final detail on your interior. Use it on the door panels, kick panels, dash, seats and any other vinyl or plastic surface. This will not only bring out the luster, it will also protect the interior and keep it pliable.

9

Completing the Restoration

After months of hard work, the restoration of your musclecar is now nearly finished. You've completed the interior, which was the last major hurdle. But the job isn't over yet. The final mechanical and cosmetic detailing still needs to be done.

Mechanically, you need to tune the engine, bleed the brakes and align the front end. The trunk has to be completed and the paint must be buffed to a mirror finish. The temptation to rush through these final steps is great, but to do so will only be rewarded with disappointment, especially when it comes to the paint. Work slowly and methodically through these last final steps. The payoff will be a superior-running car with million-dollar looks.

Starting the engine

1. Use a funnel to pour coolant into the radiator before you start the motor for the first time. Also fill the power steering reservoir, check the engine oil level and pour 5 gallons of premium gasoline into the fuel tank.

2. Always use the correct battery for your car. There are a variety of companies advertising in *Hemmings Motor News* that sell original-equipment batteries.

3. Never use clamp-on battery terminal ends on the positive post. These were never used by the factory. Always use the correct molded battery terminal clamps. Use felt washers under the battery terminal connectors to avoid corrosion.

4. Connect a battery tester and check the output of the battery after it's installed.

5. Connect a dwell meter and a remote starter. Check the point dwell before you start the engine.

6. Adjust the dwell to the specifications found in the factory service manual. On most GM cars, the distributor cap has a door that allows access to the points for adjustment without removing the cap.

7. Crank the engine slowly to pump oil through the passages. Now start the motor and set the timing to factory specifications. Remember to cap off the distributor vacuum advance hose if so equipped. Highlight the timing mark with chalk or soapstone so it will be easy to read with the timing light.

8. Adjust the timing as needed, then tighten down the distributor clamp and reconnect the distributor vacuum advance hose.

9. Now adjust the carburetor idle and mixture screws to the specifications found in the factory service manual.

Bleeding the brakes

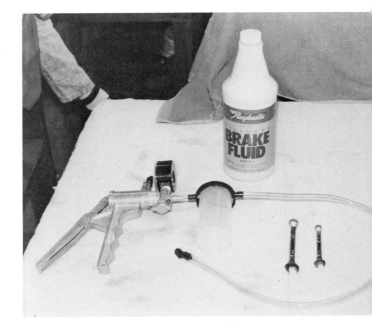

1. The Mightyvac system makes bleeding brakes easy. The only tools you'll need are a pair of line wrenches. The Mightyvac is available from The Eastwood Company. Also, since many musclecars are stored for long periods of time, we recommend using silicone DOT 5 brake fluid. It does not absorb moisture and, if accidentally spilled, won't harm the paint.

2. Begin the procedure by filling and bleeding the master cylinder.

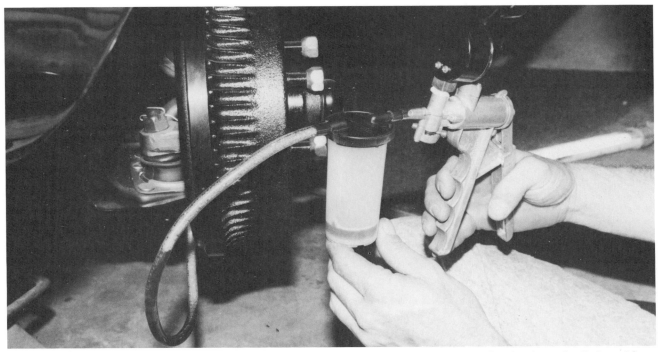

3. Once the master cylinder is bled, proceed to each brake as outlined in the Mightyvac instructions. By using this system, brake bleeding is a one-man operation. If you are bleeding the brakes manually, begin with the right rear brake. Have a helper sit in the car and pump the brakes at least four times and then hold the pedal to the floor. Loosen the bleeder and allow air and fluid to escape. Once the fluid is flowing from the fitting with no spurts or air bubbles, tighten the fitting and move to the left rear brake. Repeat the process at each brake until air has been completely purged from the brake system. Let the car sit undisturbed overnight, then bleed the brakes again. This will usually remove all of the remaining air in the system.

Front end alignment

You can either take your car to a professional alignment shop or do your own front end caster and camber alignment using the Hit Man Optical Alignment System (available from Hit Man Alignment Systems, 185 Pleasant Way, Penfield, NY 14526).

1. Set the tires on a doubled sheet of plastic and sight the scale as indicated in the instructions.

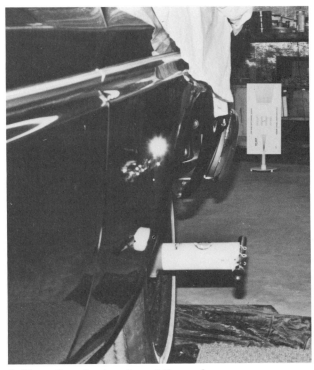

2. Turn the wheel and read the scale.

3. Return the wheel and read the scale again. Check the factory service manual for caster and camber measurements. Add shims as needed to achieve the correct factory specifications.

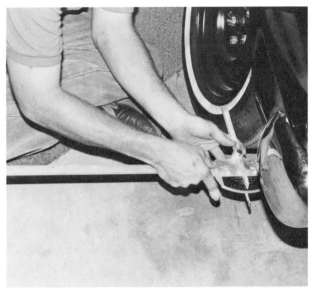

5. Check the toe-in and toe-out at the front and rear. Set the gauge at the rear of the front tires and take the measurements.

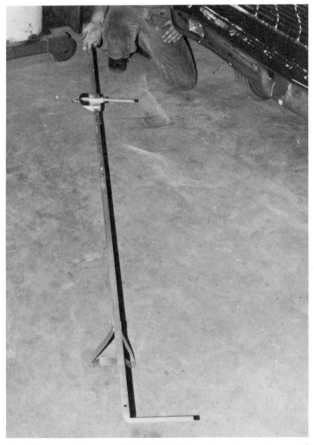

4. After you have dialed in the correct caster and camber, check the toe-in, using this wheel alignment tool available from The Eastwood Company.

6. Now go to the front and measure the difference to determine the amount of tie rod adjustment necessary. Refer to the factory service manual for the correct specifications. To adjust the tie rods, turn the adjusting sleeve to obtain the correct setting. Remember to set the gauge on the same ridge or surface of the tire for both the front and rear.

Headlamp adjustment

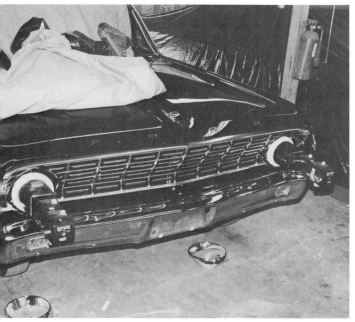

1. To begin the headlamp aiming process, remove the headlamp doors.

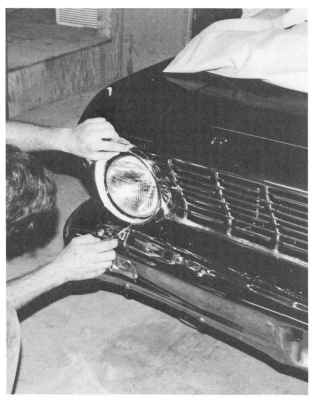

2. Install the headlamp aimers. Make sure the car is perfectly level and the tires are inflated to the correct factory specifications.

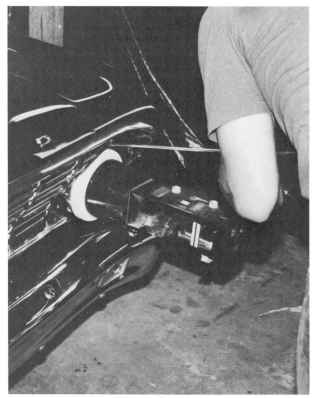

3. Level the headlamps first. Use the bubble balancer in the top of each adjuster to set the level.

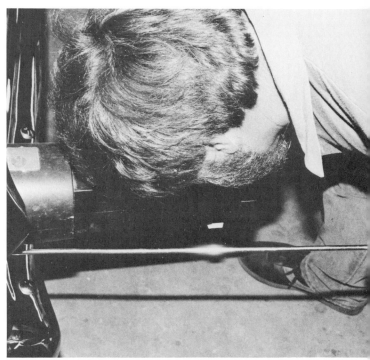

4. Now sight through the top of the adjuster and line up the vertical lines to achieve correct horizontal aim on both sides.

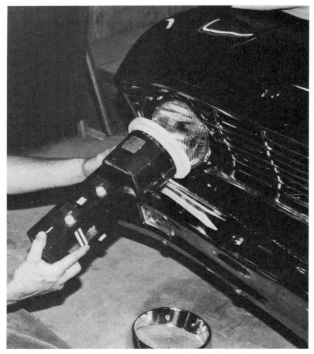

5. Remove the adjusters, reinstall the headlamp doors and you're done. There are also some inexpensive adjusters that can be purchased at your local auto parts store that can do an adequate job. Just remember the adjuster has to aim the lamps both vertically and horizontally. You can also adjust the aim of the headlamps using this equipment available from most tool rental companies.

Wheel touchup

1. Sometimes you'll have to touch up the wheels after they have been mounted. To do this easily, take contact paper and lay it completely across the wheel, covering it from bead to bead. Cut the contact paper right at the bead with a razor blade and remove the center, exposing the wheel.

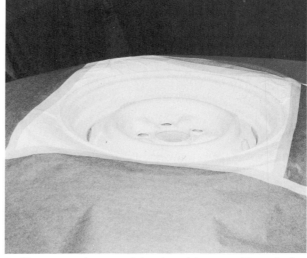

2. Now cover the rest of the tire with paper. Tape the lug and center holes with the tape from the rear, also covering any open wheel slots. Now scuff the wheel and you're ready to touch up the paint without dismounting the tire.

Finishing the trunk

1. Clean the spare tire thoroughly on both sides, using a nylon brush and dress the tire using a protectorant like Armor All.

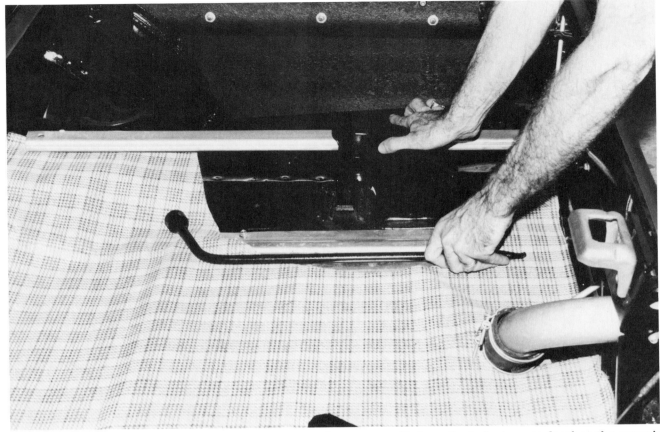

2. Install the trunk mat, smoothing it down so it fits the contours of the trunk. Recheck the routing and placement of all harnesses. Now arrange the jack and handle as specified on the jack stowage decal or the owner's manual.

3. Place the spare into the trunk with either the brand name up and legible or the valve stem indexed toward the bottom. Install the base and hold-down nut. Those cars equipped with a collapsible spare should have the inflator bottle detailed and installed with the spare.

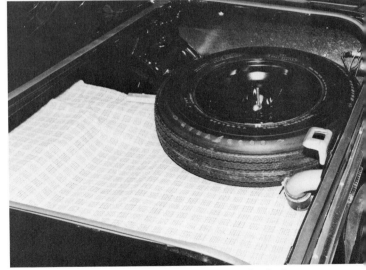

4. Remember that the trunk is the most overlooked area of the car. A quality restoration will always include a trunk that's as well detailed as the rest of the car. Sometimes a correctly detailed trunk can separate a first-place car from a second-place trophy.

Cleaning the cowl

1. The easiest product to clean buffing compound around the cowl grates is Pre-Kleano or tar and wax remover.

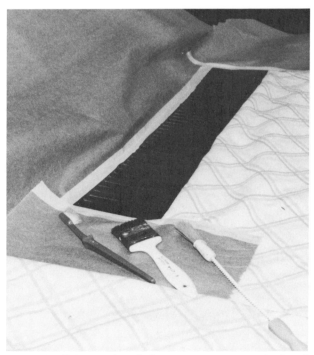

2. Mask off the cowl and also put a cover over the hood and fenders. You'll also need a kitchen basting brush, a detail brush and a toothbrush.

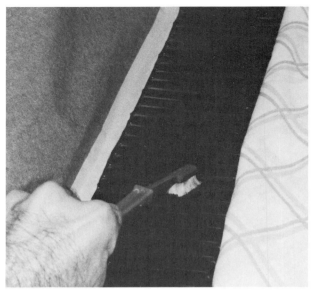

3. Dip the detail brush or a toothbrush into the Pre-Kleano and clean off each grate, moving the brush in one direction. After you have finished, go to the other side and do each of the grates on that side. Check the cowl grille after it's dried to see if you've removed all of the compound. If not, keep cleaning until you do. You can use the long-handled basting brush to clean down into the bottom of the cowl.

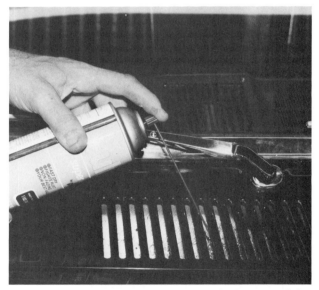

4. Sometimes you'll have to touch up the bottom of the cowl. To do this, use a spray can of paint in the correct color; many automotive paint stores can put exterior paint in aerosol cans for this purpose. There are also companies that advertise in *Hemmings Motor News* which offer this service. Attach a long nozzle (these are used in a lot of automotive aerosol products found in auto parts stores) to the spray head. Now slip the long nozzle down into the cowl and touch up the area requiring paint. After it's dried, rewax the area and the cowl is done.

Paint touchup and rubout

1. Before the final paint rub out, let the car stand out in the sun for four to six hours. This will actually help cure the paint, especially lacquer. The sun will cause any sanding scratches, draw marks and soft paint to show up. After it has set outside, bring the car indoors and you'll see all of the areas you'll now have to sand, buff or even repair. This work will have to be done before the final glaze wax and detail can be done. It's better to find these flaws now rather than at your first show.

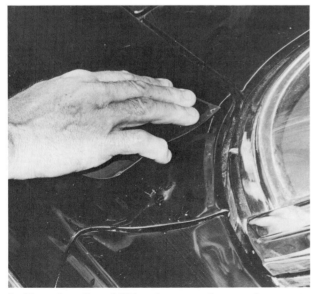

2. Use ultra-fine 1000 grit wet-n-dry sandpaper to remove scratches and draw marks. Wet the area and the sandpaper and just cut the surface of the paint.

3. All you want to do is remove the top layer. You can obtain the best results by using a sanding pad to keep the paper flat.

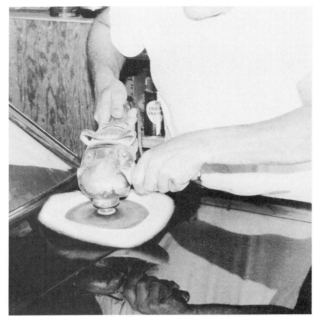

4. Now apply mild-grit compound with a brush or sponge and use a low-speed buffer (1500 to 2000 rpm) to cut and polish the area. Never put pressure on the buffer—let the weight of the buffer do the work. Don't stay in one spot too long. Move the buffer slowly over the area, and be careful of any edges.

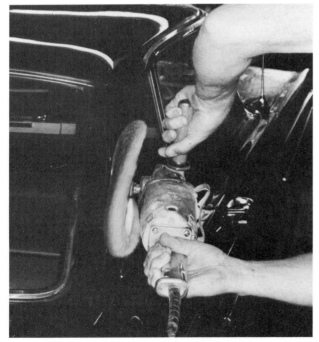

5. Move and tilt the buffer to get to different areas. Never lay the buffer down flat; always have a slight angle to it. This way you will maintain control of the buffer at all times. A 200 lb. man can be carried across the hood of a car if he lays the buffer flat and starts into a compound-covered area.

6. After you complete one section of the car, always clean the pad. Compound built up on the pad will scratch the finish instead of polishing it. Use a buffing spur to clean the pad.

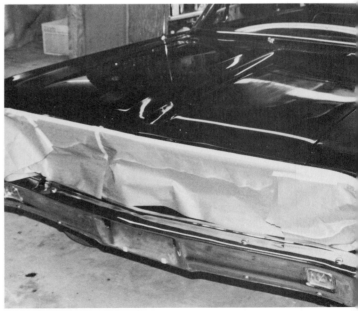

7. If you have to work on the hood area, paper and tape off the grille and all areas under the hood. Buffing compound is one of the hardest things to remove once it has dried.

8. After you have finished buffing the car, go around and touch up the nicks—don't worry, there will always be some! A pinstriping brush works well for touchup. It's easy to control and can be used on the smallest nick. Also check all of the edges; there will probably be some rub-through from the buffing.

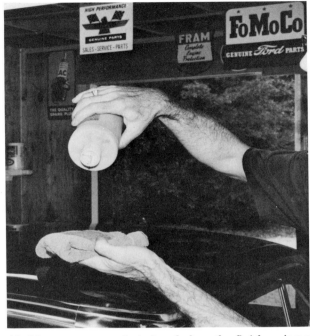

10. Now you are ready to hand-glaze the finish, using a product like 3M Imperial Hand Glaze. Apply the glaze to a small towel and rub it onto the finish. Use overlapping strokes and do a section no larger than 2x4 ft. at one time.

9. After you have finished buffing and completed the initial touch-up, wash the entire car thoroughly and then chamois it dry.

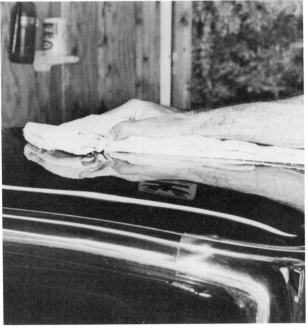

11. As soon as you have finished applying the glaze, take a soft Turkish towel and start to remove it. Use one side of the towel to remove it and the other side to buff the finish. The glaze is used to bring up the depth of shine and also to remove all the swirl marks produced by the buffer. Continue to do the entire car just as the roof was done.

12. After the car has been completely glazed, you are now ready to wax it. Use only a pure carnauba wax. Don't use any wax with a cleaner, detergent or silicone ingredient. Since this is a new finish, you won't need any type of cleaner or detergent and you don't want any kind of silicone on your new finish. Silicone waxes become embedded in the finish and make paint touchup impossible. Once you use silicone wax, it's too late! Use an orbital buffer for the first waxing.

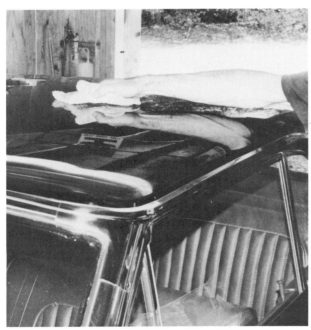

13. Wet a small towel and apply the wax to the towel. Now apply it to the car body, one small section at a time, using overlapping strokes. Allow the wax to form a haze on the paint.

14. Place the orbital with a soft bonnet onto the hazed waxed surface and start to move it slowly in the same direction that the wax was applied. If you used clockwise circles to apply the wax, move the buffer in clockwise circles.

15. After you have finished, take a soft towel and go over the whole area you just finished with the orbital sander. Proceed to do the entire car using the same steps and techniques. After every three sections, change the orbital bonnet. By using an orbital buffer after the glaze, you'll leave a perfect swirl-free finish. Then you can apply the final hand wax.

Waxing the paint

1. Once the glaze has been buffed, it's time to start the third step in the process—hand waxing. Apply a thin coat of wax, using overlapping strokes. Let it dry to a haze and then remove it with a soft towel, turning it frequently. Do the entire surface this way again.

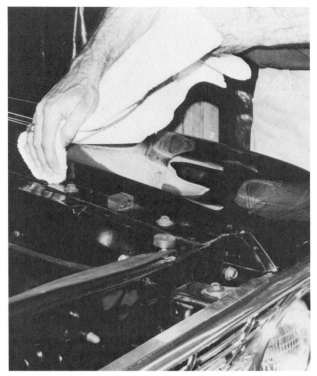

3. Don't miss waxing any painted surface. Wax each area by hand, then remove the wax just as you did on the body.

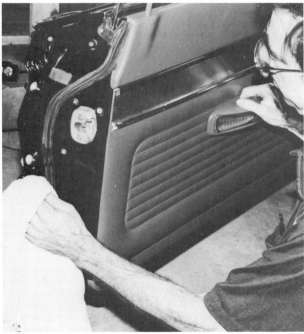

2. After you have finished waxing the body, do all the painted areas around the trunk, the doorjambs, pillars, hood lip.

4. Dried wax will accumulate in crevices and around emblems, letters and nameplates that your towel can't remove.

5. To get the wax out, use a detail brush or toothbrush and gently brush the wax out.

6. Once the car is completely waxed, polish all of the chrome using a top-quality chrome polish. Apply the polish liberally and let it dry to a haze. Use a soft towel to remove the polish and buff the chrome to a high luster.

7. Whenever you want to remove dust from your car, always use a high-quality natural-feather duster. This will remove dust easily without scratching the paint. Using a towel to wipe off dust will leave hundreds of scratches all across the paint, which will be highly visible on dark finishes. You can also use the feather duster under the hood.

346

Engine compartment detailing

1. Wipe the engine compartment down using clean water and a high-grade sponge, then towel dry. Now apply a pure carnauba wax to all underhood painted surfaces and let it dry to a haze. Remember to do the underside of the hood, unless it's painted semi-gloss black. If the car is equipped with an insulator pad, you'll install the pad after the wax has been removed.

2. Now hand buff off the wax. Use a detail brush or toothbrush to remove dried wax from areas your towel can't reach.

3. Using the chrome polish, cover all of the chrome items on the engine and let it dry to a haze.

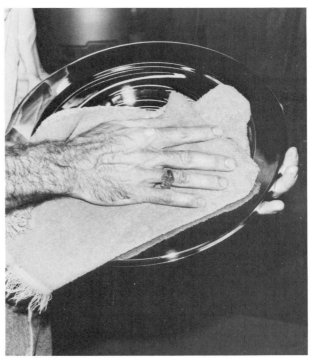

4. Buff the polish off. If the air cleaner cover is chrome, take it off and give it several coats of polish. Make sure you wipe all fingerprints off after you place it back on the engine.

5. Apply a rubber dressing to all the hoses in the engine compartment. Spray the dressing on the rag and then apply it to the rubber. If you spray it on the rubber, the dressing will mist onto paint and chrome surfaces.

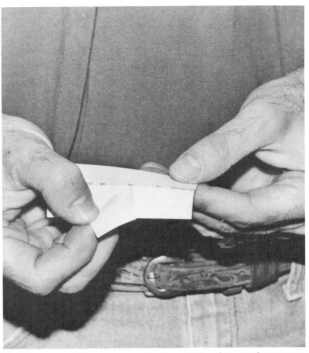

7. The manufacturer used decals in the engine compartment for maintenance instructions. Reproductions of these decals are readily available from a number of sources. Strip half of the backing. Be careful not to get your fingers on the sticky back side of the decal as they will leave oil and fingerprints.

6. After you're finished, touch up any nicks that you find. A lettering brush works well. Remember that doing this once may not be enough. Concours restorers have to repeat the process four or five times to achieve the show-winning results they're looking for.

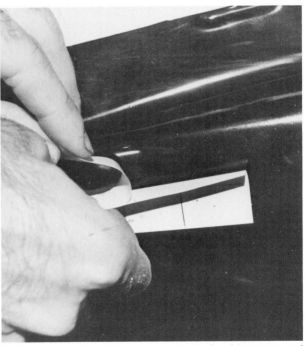

8. Place the side of the decal with the backing removed into place. Now press evenly across the decal, working out any air bubbles as you go.

348

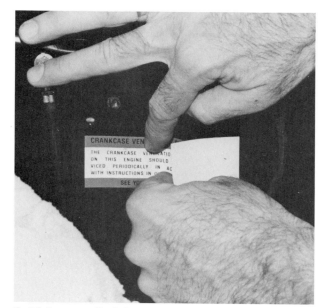

9. Make sure all of the edges are secure.

10. Use the smooth side of the decal backing paper to press around the decal after it is laid down so all air bubbles are gone and the decal is smooth.

The first drive

It's time to take your musclecar out for its maiden voyage. This shakedown cruise begins in your driveway. Slowly roll the car forward and gently apply the brakes. Do this several times and note how the brakes are operating. If the car pulls to one side, a brake may be dragging and you'll need to readjust it or the wheel alignment may need to be rechecked. Then set the parking brake and check its operation. If the car still rolls in gear with the brake set, adjust the cables so the parking brake holds the car.

After you're satisfied with the brakes' operation, it's time to take the car out for the initial road test. Prepare a road box in case of problems. Fill the box with a set of tools, dwell meter, timing light, some PVC tape, a can of brake and power steering fluid, some rags, and gallon jugs of water and anti-freeze.

Since you don't want the first drive to be in traffic, plan your initial excursion for a Sunday morning. Have someone follow you in another vehicle; if your car breaks down you won't be stranded. Since you want to concentrate on the car and not traffic, drive to the nearest school, office building, shopping center or other facility with a large, empty parking lot. Spend the next hour driving the car, first at low speed, and pay attention to the drivetrain and how the car steers, brakes and handles. Listen carefully to the engine and how the transmission shifts. Turn on all the lights, activate the horn, heater, defroster and all of the power or convenience options such as air conditioning, power windows, power antenna and so on. Check the function of each gauge for proper operation.

Make a checklist and write down any peculiarities that need to be corrected once you get the car back home.

After you've become familiar with the car's operation, increase your test speed. Don't try laying rubber or performing any 60-to-0 mph brake tests. This initial break-in should be done carefully and thoroughly to ensure there's no damage done to the drivetrain, brakes or suspension. This is simply a systems test, and you're the test driver. There will be plenty of time later to "see what she'll do."

Drive the car back home and correct any problems you noted on your checklist. Take the car back out again to the empty lot for the second test to make sure you've corrected the problems and that nothing else is wrong. Few restored cars are absolutely perfect the first few times out. How well the car operates during these first drives is directly proportionate to the quality of work you performed during the restoration. Regardless of how careful you were, expect a few problems, and correct them immediately.

After the first 100 miles of driving, pull out the factory service manual and torque *all* the bolts, screws and nuts to factory specifications. Drain the oil and change the filter. Check the fluid levels in the transmission, rear axle, master cylinder, power-steering reservoir and radiator. Check the air pressure in the tires.

Once you've straightened out any problems and performed the break-in maintenance, your restoration project is now complete. Whether you plan on driving or trailering it to shows, there's a special feeling you get when you win the first trophy because you restored your musclecar yourself.

Sources

Brakes
Stainless Steel Brakes
11470 Main Road
Clarence, NY 14031
  Disc brake systems and parts

Carburetors
Carbs Unlimited
19332 Briarwood
Mt. Clemens, MI 48043
  Carburetor rebuilding and refinishing
specialists

Decals
Jim Osborn Reproductions
101 Ridgecrest Drive Lawrenceville, GA
  30245

Electrics
Howard W. Sams
4300 West 62nd Street
Indianapolis, IN 46068
  Vintage car radio schematics

M&H Electric Fabricators
13537 Alondra Blvd.
Santa Fe Springs, CA 90670
  Reproduction wiring harnesses

Fasteners
Gardener-Wescott
30962 Industrial
Livonia, MI 48150

M&K Henderson Co.
P.O. Box 30266
Flagstaff, AZ 86003

S&R Fastener Co.
P.O. Box 4494
Clearwater, FL 34618

Miscellaneous restoration supplies
Gary's Plastic Chrome Plating
39312 Dillingham
Westland, MI 48135
  Plastic chrome plating specialists

Hit Man Alignment Systems
185 Pleasant Way
Penfield, NY 14526
  Hit Man Optical Alignment system

Metro Molded Rubber
11610 Jay Street
P.O. Box 33130
Minneapolis, MN 55433

OEM Glass
P.O. Box 362
Hwy. 9 East
Bloomington, IL 61702

Restoration Specialties and Supply
P.O. Box 328 RD #2
Windber, PA 15963

Sssnake Oyl
15775 North Hillcrest
Suite 508-541
Dallas, TX 75248

Year One
Box 2-23
Tucker, GA 30085
  Reproduction musclecar parts

Paint
Ames Performance Engineering
Bonney Road
Marlborough, NH 03455
  Rally wheel paint in spray cans

Mid-Country Mustang, Inc.
Route 100
P.O. Box 189
Eagle, PA 19480
  Rally wheel paint in spray cans

Publications
Classic Motorbooks
(Motorbooks International)
P.O. Box 1
Osceola, WI 54020
  Automotive books

Musclecar Review
P.O. Box 7157
Lakeland, FL 33807

Restoration services
Greg Donahue Collector Car Restorations,
  Inc.
12900 S. Betty Point
Floral City, Fl 32636

Tires
Coker Tire
1317 Chestnut Street
P.O. Box 72554
Chattanooga, TN 37407
  Reproduction red-line tires

Kelsey Tires Inc.
Box 564
Camdenton, MO 65020

Lucas Automotive
2141 West Main
Springfield, OH 45504

Universal Tire Co.
987 Stony Battery Road
Lancaster, PA 17601

Wade W. Wallace
4303-C Irving Blvd.
Dallas, TX 75356-0906
  Wholesale tires

Tools
The Eastwood Company
580 Lancaster Ave.
Malvern, PA 19355
  Wide selection of restoration tools,
supplies and paints

Pro Motorcar Products
713 US Hwy. 19 North
Clearwater, FL 34625
  Spot Rot and Pro Gauge tools

Transmission
Hurst Performance
Mr. Gasket Company
8700 Brookpark Road
Cleveland, OH 44129-6899
  Hurst shifter parts

Index